AQA French

Higher

GCSE

Marie-Thérèse Bougard

Jean-Claude Gilles

Oliver Gray

Steve Harrison

Ginny March

Nelson Thornes

Published in 2009 by:
Nelson Thornes Ltd
Delta Place
27 Bath Road
CHELTENHAM
GL53 7TH
United Kingdom

11 12 13 / 10 9 8 7 6 5 4

A catalogue record for this book is available from the British Library

ISBN 978 1 4085 0424 6

Cover photograph: Alamy/Hayden Richard Verry
Page make-up by eMC Design, www.emcdesign.org

Printed in China by 1010 Printing International Ltd

Contents

Nelson Thornes and AQA					7
How to use this book					8
Key Stage 3 Revision					9

Context 1 - Lifestyle — 15

Contents	Spread title	Main grammar point	Subsidiary grammar point	Strategy	Page
Key Stage 3 Revision: Food and drink; family members and pets. Ailments and solutions.					16
Topic 1 – Health	Mon régime alimentaire	Present tense of -er verbs	How to say 'some'	Tackling reading tasks	18
	Le bien-être	Adverbs of frequency	How to form -ir verbs and the verbs faire and dormir	Vocabulary learning	20
	On parle du tabac	Forming negatives	Using devoir + infinitive	Giving opinions	22
	L'alcool et la drogue	Asking questions	Expressions with avoir	Using questions in speaking	24
Reading and listening					26
Grammar practice					28
Vocabulary					30
Topic 2 – Relationships and Choices	La famille	How to say 'my', 'your', etc.	Position and agreement of adjectives	Working out the meaning of words	32
	Les rapports avec les autres	Reflexive verbs	Disjunctive pronouns and their use	Silent endings	34
	L'avenir	The future tense	Je voudrais, j'aimerais, j'ai l'intention de + infinitive	Predicting questions	36
	L'égalité des chances	Verbs which take the infinitive	Verbs that are followed by à or de before an infinitive	Agreeing and disagreeing	38
	Le racisme	Making comparisons	Masculine and feminine nouns	Verbs ending in -ger and -cer	40
	La pauvreté	Irregular future forms	More irregular future tense forms	Picking out key words	42
Reading and listening					44
Grammar practice					46
Vocabulary					48
Controlled Assessment – Speaking	Une vie saine				50
Controlled Assessment – Writing	Les rapports avec les autres				52
Context summary					54

Context 2 - Leisure   55

Contents	Spread title	Main grammar point	Subsidiary grammar point	Strategy	Page
Key Stage 3 Revision: Sport and leisure; clothes. Transport; places in town; simple directions.					56
Topic 1 – Free time and the media	Ce que j'ai fait chez moi	Perfect tense with *avoir*	Adverbial time expressions	Recognising time expressions	58
	Les loisirs	Perfect tense with *être*	Perfect tense with negatives and reflexives	Using more than one time frame	60
	L'argent et le shopping	Direct object pronouns	Demonstrative pronouns	Using all three time frames	62
	La mode	Indirect object pronouns	Verbs of liking/disliking followed by the infinitive	Working out the meaning of words	64
	Les nouvelles technologies	Superlative adjectives	Using the pronoun *on* with impersonal expressions	Justifying your opinions	66
Reading and listening					68
Grammar practice					70
Vocabulary					72
Topic 2 – Holidays	Vive les vacances!	The imperfect tense	How to say 'to' or 'in' a country, town or region	Saying what you know	74
	Des projets de vacances	Combining perfect and future tenses	Using *quand* with the future tense	Recognising prefixes	76
	Que faire en vacances?	The conditional	Singular imperatives	Structuring your answers	78
	Les excursions	The pronoun *y*	Plural or formal imperatives	Listening for gist	80
Reading and listening					82
Grammar practice					84
Vocabulary					86
Controlled Assessment – Speaking	**En vacances**				88
Controlled Assessment – Writing	**Mes loisirs**				90
Context summary					92

Context 3 – Home and environment | 93

Contents	Spread title	Main grammar point	Subsidiary grammar point	Strategy	Page
Key Stage 3 Revision: Compass points; house types and locations. Rooms in house; furniture and prepositions. Helping at home; daily routine. Home activities; perfect tense.					94
Topic 1 – Home and local area	On fait la fête	Combining perfect and imperfect tenses	Indefinite adjectives *chaque* and *quelque*	Including negative expressions	98
	Ma maison	Using *depuis* and *pendant*	Using *être situé(e)* and *se trouver* to indicate location	Qualifiers and intensifiers	100
	La où j'habite	Adjectives with special forms	*En* as an indirect object pronoun	Clues about size and quantity	102
	Des mondes différents	Passive voice and *on*	Prepositions of place	Percentages and fractions	104
Reading and listening					106
Grammar practice					108
Vocabulary					110
Topic 2 – Environment	La pollution	*Il faut* + infinitive or subjunctive	Revision of use of the definite article	Pronunciation of similar words	112
	Planète en danger	Common subjunctive expressions	Indefinite pronouns	Fluency techniques	114
	L'environnement et ma ville	Expressions of sequence	Emphatic pronouns *toi, vous*, etc.	Recognising words from ones already known	116
Reading and listening					118
Grammar practice					120
Vocabulary					122
Controlled Assessment – Speaking	Chez moi				124
Controlled Assessment – Writing	L'environnement				126
Context Summary					128

Context 4 – Work and education

129

Contents	Spread title	Main grammar point	Subsidiary grammar point	Strategy	Page
Key Stage 3 Revision: School buildings, rooms and equipment. School subjects; jobs.					130
Topic 1 – School / college and future plans	Comment est ton collège?	Position of object pronouns	Demonstrative adjectives	Working out answers	132
	Des écoles différentes	Relative pronouns	Recognise the relative pronoun *dont*	Making complex sentences	134
	Problèmes scolaires	The pluperfect tense	Using *il y a* meaning 'ago'	Covering all content	136
	Améliorer la vie scolaire	*On pourrait / on devrait*	Question words	Adding detail using different tenses	138
Reading and listening					140
Grammar practice					142
Vocabulary					144
Topic 2 – Current and future jobs	Stages et petits jobs	Present participle	Object pronouns with negatives	Distinguishing *-ant* and *-ement*	146
	Je cherche un emploi	Using *vous* (polite form)	Revise demonstrative pronouns	Masculine and feminine forms of jobs	148
	La vie commence	Interrogative forms	Comparative and superlative adverbs	Include a range of tenses	150
	Le monde du travail	*Venir de* and *après avoir / être*	Nouns without articles	Checking grammar	152
Reading and listening					154
Grammar practice					156
Vocabulary					158
Controlled Assessment – Speaking	Au travail				160
Controlled Assessment – Writing	Mon collège				162
Context summary					164
Frequently asked questions: Speaking					165
Frequently asked questions: Writing					167
Controlled Assessment (cross-context) – Speaking: *On fait du camping*					168
Controlled Assessment (cross-context) – Writing: *À propos de moi!*					169
Grammaire					170
Verb tables					192
Alphabet: French pronunciation; Using a dictionary					197
Glossaire					199

Nelson Thornes has worked in partnership with AQA to ensure this book and the accompanying online resources offer you the best support for your GCSE course.

All resources have been approved by senior AQA examiners so you can feel assured that they closely match the specification for this subject and provide you with everything you need to prepare successfully for your exams.

These print and online resources together **unlock blended learning**; this means that the links between the activities in the book and the activities online blend together to maximise your understanding of a topic and help you achieve your potential.

These online resources are available on which can be accessed via the internet at **www.kerboodle.com/live**, anytime, anywhere. If your school or college subscribes to you will be provided with your own personal login details. Once logged in, access your course and locate the required activity.

For more information and help on how to use visit **www.kerboodle.com**.

How to use this book

Objectifs

Look for the list of **Objectifs** based on the requirements of this course so you can ensure you are covering everything you need to know for the exam.

AQA Examiner's tip

Don't forget to read the **Examiner's Tips** which accompany the Controlled Assessment sample tasks, to help you prepare for the Speaking and Writing assessments. Listening and Reading **Examination-style questions** are available online so you can practise and prepare for the exam papers.

Visit **www.nelsonthornes.com/aqagcse** for more information.

AQA GCSE French – higher

How to use this book

This book is arranged in a sequence approved by AQA which matches precisely the structure of the GCSE specification.

- The book is split into four sections, one for each Context of the specification.
- Each Context is split into two Topics.
- The Topics are divided into sub-topics which fit the Purposes of the specification.

At the beginning of each Context you will find the sub-topics, grammar and communication strategies listed, so you can see precisely how the content you are learning matches the GCSE specifications and be sure you are covering everything you need to know.

The features in this book include:

Reading icon – you can listen to the reading texts in your book on *kerboodle!*, so you can hear the language spoken by native speakers as you read it. Interactive reading activities are also available.

Listening icon – audio material for listening and/or reading activities is online. Interactive listening activities are available on *kerboodle!*.

Video icon – videos can be found online to support listening activities, with further interactive activities also available on *kerboodle!*.

Speaking icon – an activity designed to practise speaking skills. Worksheets for further practice are also available on *kerboodle!*.

Writing icon – an activity designed to practise writing skills. Worksheets for further practice are available on *kerboodle!*.

Stratégie – outlines different strategies you can use to help you communicate effectively. The strategy box includes the icon of the activity it supports: Listening, Reading, Speaking or Writing.

Strategy icon – When this icon appears next to an activity, you should use the communication strategy introduced in the strategy box on that page to complete the task.

Astuce – provides handy hints which you can use to help you with your language learning.

Grammaire – provides a summary of the main grammar point. Further grammar points are also provided here. Go to the pages listed to find activities to practise them.

G Grammar icon – an activity designed to help you practise the grammar point introduced on the page. You will also find interactive grammar practice on *kerboodle!*.

V Vocabulary icon – a vocabulary learning activity. The essential vocabulary used within each Topic is listed on Vocabulary pages. Here you can learn key words for each Topic. You can also go to *kerboodle!* to hear how they sound. Some words are in light grey. This is to indicate that you do not need to learn them for your Listening and Reading exams, but you may still want to use them in your Speaking and Writing Controlled Assessments.

> **Language structure** – these boxes show you how to construct key sentences designed to help you carry out the Speaking and Writing tasks.

Controlled assessment – Controlled assessment tasks are designed to help you learn language which is relevant to the GCSE Topics and Purposes.

These tasks are not designed to test you and you cannot use them as your own Controlled Assessment tasks and submit them to AQA. Although the tasks you complete and submit to AQA may look similar to the tasks in this book, your teacher will not be able to give you as much help with them as we have given with the tasks in this book.

Go to *kerboodle!* to see sample answers. Look at them carefully and read the **AQA Examiner's Tips** to see how you can improve your answers.

AQA Examiner's tip

These provide hints from AQA examiners to help you with your study and prepare for your exams.

Résumé – a summary quiz at the end of each Context tests key language and grammar learnt in that Context. This is also available as a multiple-choice quiz, with feedback, on *kerboodle!*.

Le sais-tu? – an anecdotal insight into facts/figures relating to the Context.

Numbers 1–20, ages and days of the week

Tu as quel âge?

J'ai quinze ans.

Tu as des frères et sœurs?

J'ai deux frères et une sœur: Lucas a quatre ans, Léo a douze ans et Marie a dix-neuf ans.

A

14 ans – 2 sœurs (4 ans et 24 ans)

B

15 ans – 3 frères (2 ans, 14 ans et 19 ans)

C

15 ans – 2 frères (4 ans et 12 ans), 1 sœur (19 ans)

1a Read the bubbles and select the matching Post-it note: A, B or C?

1b ✐ Complete the text below to match the other two Post-it notes. Look at *Grammaire* to help you.

1 J'ai _____ ans. J'ai _____ sœurs. Nadia _____ _____ ans et Anissa _____ _____ ans.

2 J'_____ _____ ans. J'ai _____ frères. Mehdi _____ _____ ans, Karim _____ _____ _____ et Adel _____ _____ _____.

> **Grammaire**
>
> Remember you need to use *avoir* when saying how old you are.
>
> *Tu as quel âge?* How old are you?
> *J'ai quinze ans.* I am fifteen.
> *Elle a seize ans.* She is sixteen.
> *Il a dix-huit ans.* He is eighteen.
>
> page 184

1c ⬭ Work in pairs. Partner A calls five numbers between 1 and 20. Partner B notes them down, and uses them in sentences. Then swap parts.

Exemple: **A** Deux, sept, treize, dix-neuf, vingt.
B J'ai 2 frères: Tom a 7 ans et Sam a 13 ans. Ma sœur a 19 ans … ah non, 20 ans!

2 ✐ Solve the anagrams to find the correct days of the week.

1 dinlu
2 madichen
3 diuje
4 drinvede

Months, birthdays and time

1

Marion: Mon anniversaire, c'est au mois de décembre.

Pierre: Le vingt-cinq décembre?

Marion: Non, le quinze décembre. Et toi?

Pierre: Moi, c'est le dix janvier.

2

Charles: Mon anniversaire, c'est le quatorze avril. Et toi?

Chloé: Euh … Moi, c'est le premier octobre.

Charles: Le premier octobre? C'est aujourd'hui! Bon anniversaire!

1a Look at the two conversations above and write the remaining four dates digitally, for example 25/12, in the order they occur.

1b Read the conversations in pairs. Then have a similar conversation about your own birthdays.

2 Match each sentence to the corresponding clock.

1 Il est cinq heures.
2 Il est midi moins cinq.
3 Il est huit heures vingt.
4 Il est une heure et demie.
5 Il est trois heures et quart.
6 Il est onze heures moins le quart.

3a Reorganise the sentences below into chronological order, and write the times digitally (1–6).

Exemple: 6 07.15

1 Le soir, nous mangeons vers dix-neuf heures quarante-cinq.
2 Les cours finissent généralement à dix-sept heures.
3 Je prends mon petit déjeuner à sept heures vingt.
4 En général à vingt-deux heures trente, je dors.
5 J'arrive au collège à huit heures trente.
6 Je me lève à sept heures quinze.

3b Adapt the sentences above to describe your own typical school day.

Vocabulaire

janvier	January
février	February
mars	March
avril	April
mai	May
juin	June
juillet	July
août	August
septembre	September
octobre	October
novembre	November
décembre	December
bon anniversaire!	happy birthday!

Grammaire page 191

To say dates in French, use: *le* + number + month.

le six janvier (literally: the six January)

The only exception is for the first day of each month:

le premier avril (literally: the first April)

Vocabulaire

et quart	quarter past
et demi(e)	half past
heures	o'clock / hours
midi	midday
minuit	midnight
moins le quart	quarter to

Grammaire page 191

To ask the time, you can say:

Quelle heure est-il? (most formal)
Il est quelle heure?
Quelle heure il est?

A typical reply is:

Il est midi / deux heures et demie.

To say when something happens/ is happening, use *à* to introduce the time:

Je me lève à sept heures.

Weather and seasons

1 📖🎧 Read the weather report for today and forecast for tomorrow. Copy the grid and complete it.

La météo

Aujourd'hui, il y a du brouillard en montagne, mais il y a du soleil sur la côte et il fait assez chaud. Demain, il va continuer à faire beau avec beaucoup de soleil sur la côte, mais il va neiger en montagne. Dans la vallée, il ne pleut pas en ce moment, mais il y a des nuages. Il va probablement pleuvoir demain.

Region	Today	Tomorrow
in the mountains		
on the coast		
in the valley		

2a 📖🎧 Read the text and answer the questions.

Vous pouvez venir à Châtel en été si vous aimez le VTT. Si vous préférez le ski, venez en hiver. Il y a généralement assez de neige pour skier de décembre à avril. Les remontées mécaniques sont ouvertes pour les skieurs en hiver et pour les cyclistes en été. Évitez octobre et novembre, parce qu'il pleut beaucoup en automne. Il y a souvent du soleil au printemps, mais il fait assez froid. Si vous aimez les fleurs, venez en mai ou juin.

1 Which months have enough snow for skiing at Châtel?
2 Which season is best for mountain biking?
3 Are the ski lifts open in summer?
4 Which season is not recommended for a visit to Châtel?
5 What is the weather like in spring?
6 When would you go to look at flowers?

2b 🗨 Work in pairs. Partner A describes the weather. Partner B guesses the season in question.

> Il fait froid et il neige.   C'est en hiver.

2c 🖊 Adapt the text from 2a to describe the different seasons in your region.

Vocabulaire

il fait beau	the weather's nice
il fait mauvais	the weather's bad
il fait chaud	it's hot
il fait froid	it's cold
il pleut	it rains / it's raining
il neige	it snows / it's snowing
il y a …	it's …
du soleil	sunny
du brouillard	foggy
du vent	windy
des nuages	cloudy
le printemps	spring
l'été	summer
l'automne	autumn
l'hiver	winter

Describing weather

1 *il fait* + adjective: *Il fait beau.*
2 *il y a* + noun: *Il y a du vent.*
3 *il* + verb: *Il pleut.*

- Use *il va* + infinitive to talk about what the weather will be like:
  Il va pleuvoir.

- To say 'in summer / in autumn / in winter':
  en été, en automne, en hiver

- To say 'in spring':
  au printemps

Grammaire page 185

Classroom equipment and colours

description	prix	coloris
stylo GEL	2,50 € (les 2)	bleu, rouge, vert, violet, noir
crayon à papier	2 € (les 6)	noir
gomme	0,45 €	rose, orange, jaune
calculatrice SOLAIRE	15 €	gris, noir
règle plastique souple	1,20 €	rouge, jaune
cahier papier recyclé	3 €	blanc

SPÉCIAL RENTRÉE

Vocabulaire

blanc(he)	white
bleu(e)	blue
un cahier	notebook
une calculatrice	calculator
un crayon	pencil
un dictionnaire	dictionary
une gomme	eraser
gris(e)	grey
jaune	yellow
un livre	book
noir(e)	black
une règle	ruler
rose	pink
rouge	red
un stylo	pen
une trousse	pencil case
vert(e)	green
violet(te)	purple

1a 🎧 📖 Can these items be bought from the catalogue above?

 **1**
 2
 **3**
 4
 **5**
 **6**

1b 💬 Work in pairs. Partner A chooses from the items shown in 1a and describes what he/she is looking for. Partner B says the matching number. Then swap parts.

Exemple: **A** Je voudrais un crayon jaune et un stylo gris.
B C'est le numéro 3.

2a ✏️ Complete with *un*, *une* or *des*, and make the adjectives agree when necessary.

Je voudrais _____ calculatrice gris___ , _____ cahier et _____ dictionnaire. Je vais aussi commander _____ stylos (_____ stylo bleu___ et _____ stylo rouge___), _____ trousse jaune___, _____ règle vert___, _____ crayons et _____ gommes.

2b ✏️ Adapt the text in 2a to say what you would like to order.

Grammaire *pages 172, 173*

▪ How to say 'a(n)'/'some':

un stylo	a pen
une gomme	an eraser
des crayons	(some) pencils

Although you can leave out 'some' in English, you have to include *des* in French.

▪ When using adjectives, make them agree with the nouns when necessary.

un stylo vert	a green pen
une gomme verte	a green eraser

Parts of the body and useful words

A *'Portrait du père de l'artiste' par Paul Cézanne*

B *'Picasso et les pains' par Robert Doisneau*

Vocabulaire	
la bouche	mouth
le bras	arm
les cheveux (m)	hair
la jambe	leg
la main	hand
le nez	nose
l'œil (m) / les yeux	eye(s)
l'oreille (f)	ear
le pied	foot
la tête	head

1 📖🎧 Choose the correct word(s) to complete each sentence. In each case, say which of the two portraits is being described.

1 On voit   la   les   jambes.
2 On ne voit pas   le   les   mains.
3 Il porte un bonnet sur   la   le   tête.
4 Il tient un journal dans   la   les   mains.
5 On voit seulement   la   l'   oreille droite.
6 On voit   le   la   nez, mais pas   l'   les   pieds.

Grammaire *page 172*

How to say 'the':

▧ masculine: *le nez*

▧ feminine: *la tête*

▧ before a vowel: *l'oreille*

▧ plural: *les mains*

2 🗨 Work in pairs. Partner A says one thing about one of the portraits above. Partner B says which one it is.

> On voit les pieds.

> C'est le père de Cézanne.

3 📖🎧 Complete the description using words from the vocabulary list.

La photo en noir _____ blanc est un portrait de Picasso _____ Robert Doisneau. Sur la photo, Picasso a 60 _____ 61 ans, _____ il n'a pas _____ de cheveux! Il ne regarde pas le photographe, _____ on voit qu'il a les yeux _____ noirs. On ne voit pas les jambes, _____ il _____ assis à table. On voit la tête, les épaules et le haut des bras. Pour remplacer les mains, _____ des pains sur la table. C'est _____ amusant!

Vocabulaire	
alors	so
assez	quite
beaucoup	a lot
car	because
est	is
et	and
il y a	there is / there are
mais	but
ou	or
par	by
très	very

kerboodle!

Numbers and dates

1a  Replace the following digits with words from the vocabulary list.

> Mon père a 53 ans.
>
> J'ai économisé 99 euros …
>
> Ma grand-mère a 84 ans!
>
> Il y a 27 élèves dans ma classe.
>
> Mon nouveau jean a coûté 68 euros.
>
> Mon frère a regardé 75 matchs de foot.

1b ⬤ Work in pairs. Partner A reads one of the numbers from the chatroom posts above. Partner B reads the corresponding sentence. Then swap parts.

Exemple: **A** Vingt-sept.
             B Il y a 27 élèves dans ma classe.

2 📖🎧 Read the text in the bubble, then complete the quantities required for each ingredient – using digits.

> Pour ce gâteau, il faut cinq cents grammes de pommes, deux cent cinquante grammes de farine, cent vingt-cinq grammes de beurre et cent grammes de sucre.

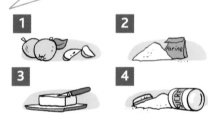

1   **2**
3   **4**

3a 🖊 Rewrite the following years using digits.

1   deux mille sept
2   mille neuf cent soixante-huit
3   mille neuf cent quarante-cinq
4   mille sept cent quatre-vingt-neuf
5   mille neuf cent quatre-vingt-seize

3b ⬤ Work out how to say the year you were born in French.

Vocabulaire

27	*vingt-sept*
30	*trente*
40	*quarante*
50	*cinquante*
53	*cinquante-trois*
60	*soixante*
68	*soixante-huit*
70	*soixante-dix*
71	*soixante et onze*
75	*soixante-quinze*
80	*quatre-vingts*
81	*quatre-vingt-un*
84	*quatre-vingt-quatre*
90	*quatre-vingt-dix*
91	*quatre-vingt-onze*
99	*quatre-vingt-dix-neuf*
100	*cent*
999	*neuf cent quatre-vingt-dix-neuf*
1000	*mille*
2000	*deux mille*

Grammaire *page190*

70 is literally 60, 10 *(soixante-dix)*

71 is literally 60 and 11 *(soixante et onze)*

72 is literally 60, 12 *(soixante-douze)*

And so on.

80 is literally 4, 20 *(quatre-vingts)*

81 is literally 4, 20, 1 *(quatre-vingt-un)*

And so on.

Use *mille* (the word for 1000) when saying years in French.

1995: *mille neuf cent quatre-vingt-quinze*

2010: *deux mille dix*

> Je suis né en _____.

> Je suis née en _____.

1 Lifestyle

Health

Healthy and unhealthy lifestyles and their consequences

1.1 Mon régime alimentaire
- Present tense of -er verbs
- Tackling reading tasks

1.2 Le bien-être
- Adverbs of frequency
- Vocabulary learning

1.3 On parle du tabac
- Forming negatives
- Giving opinions

1.4 L'alcool et la drogue
- Asking questions
- Using questions in speaking

Relationships and choices

Relationships with family and friends

1.5 La famille
- How to say 'my', 'your', etc.
- Working out the meaning of words

1.6 Les rapports avec les autres
- Reflexive verbs
- Silent endings

Future plans regarding marriage / partnership

1.7 L'avenir
- The future tense
- Predicting questions

Social issues and equality

1.8 L'égalité des chances
- Verbs which take the infinitive
- Agreeing and disagreeing

1.9 Le racisme
- Making comparisons
- Verbs ending in -ger and -cer

1.10 La pauvreté
- Irregular future forms
- Picking out key words

Food and drink; family members and pets

1 📖🎧 Find the correct label for each item.

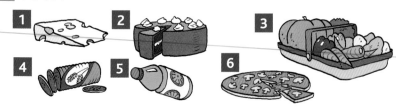

a beaucoup de légumes
b un paquet de biscuits
c un gâteau au chocolat
d une bouteille de jus d'orange
e un peu de fromage
f une pizza aux champignons

Vocabulaire

beaucoup de	a lot of
la boîte	box / tin
la bouteille	bottle
le champignon	mushroom
le citron	lemon
l'eau (f)	water
le fromage	cheese
le légume	vegetable
le paquet	packet
un peu de	a bit of

2 📖🎧 Use the words below to complete the Internet chat.

Clara Géniale, la photo de l'anniversaire de ta ❶ _____ avec le chat, le chien et le ❷ _____ rouge! Elle a quel âge?

Théo Elle a 80 ans!

Clara Ton ❸ _____ est où?

Théo Il est mort.

Clara Pardon ... Il y a aussi ta ❹ _____ et ton père?

Théo C'est mon beau-père. Mes ❺ _____ sont divorcés.

Clara Et ta sœur?

Théo Je n'ai pas de ❻ _____ . C'est Nadia, la petite amie de mon ❼ _____ avec Tintin, le ❽ _____ de ma grand-mère!

frère   mère   parents   grand-mère   grand-père

poisson   sœur   chat

Grammaire *page 187*

Words expressing contents and quantities are followed by *de* (*d'* before a vowel):

un litre d'eau
une boîte de tomates

Flavours and ingredients are introduced with *au, à la, à l'* or *aux*, and come at the end:

une tarte au citron	a lemon tart
une glace *à la fraise*	a strawberry ice cream

Vocabulaire

le beau-père	stepfather
la belle-mère	stepmother
le chat	cat
le chien	dog
divorcé(e)	divorced
la grand-mère	grandmother
le grand-père	grandfather
la mère	mother
mort(e)	dead
le père	father
le petit ami	boyfriend
la petite amie	girlfriend
le poisson rouge	goldfish

Ailments and solutions

1a 📖🎧 Match each complaint with the correct picture.

1 Ouille! J'ai mal aux oreilles.
2 Aïe, aïe, aïe! J'ai mal aux dents. Oh, là, là!
3 J'ai mal au ventre. J'ai mal au cœur. J'ai envie de vomir.
4 J'ai un gros rhume et j'ai mal à la gorge. Ça ne va pas très bien.
5 J'ai mal au genou et j'ai mal au bras. Je suis tombé de vélo hier.
6 J'ai mal à la tête et au dos. J'ai de la fièvre. J'ai la grippe.

a

b

c

d

e

f

1b 🗨 Work in pairs. Partner A says what's wrong. Partner B says which picture it relates to. Then swap parts.

> Aïe! J'ai mal aux oreilles.

> C'est "f".

2a 📖🎧 Use the words below to complete the advice.

1 Tu as mal aux dents? Va chez le _____.
2 Tu es tombé de vélo? _____ de l'arnica.
3 Tu as mal aux oreilles? _____ chez le médecin.
4 Vous avez mal à la tête? Prenez de _____ et allez au lit.
5 Vous avez un rhume et mal à la gorge? Prenez ces _____ et ce sirop.
6 Vous avez mal au ventre? _____ ces comprimés et buvez beaucoup d'eau.

> dentiste   l'aspirine   pastilles   prends   prenez   va

2b 📖✏ Reply to this message. Then compare your advice with your partner's.

> Je suis tombé de vélo. J'ai mal au dos et à la jambe.
> Qu'est-ce que je fais? Merci d'avance.

Grammaire page 187

J'ai mal is followed with *au, à la, à l'* or *aux* + part of the body.

J'ai mal au pied.	My foot hurts.
J'ai mal à la tête.	I have a headache.
J'ai mal à l'œil.	I have a pain in my eye.
J'ai mal aux oreilles.	I have earache.

Vocabulaire

le cœur	heart
les dents (f)	teeth
le dos	back
le genou	knee
la gorge	throat
la grippe	flu
l'oreille (f)	ear
le rhume	cold
le ventre	stomach

Vocabulaire

bois / buvez	drink
le comprimé	tablet
mets / mettez	put
la pastille	pastille / lozenge
prends / prenez	take
le sirop	(cough) syrup
va / allez	go

Grammaire page 183

Use the imperative to give advice:

Informal singular (the *tu* form):
Va chez le dentiste.
Prends de l'aspirine.

Formal or plural (the *vous* form):
Allez chez le médecin.
Prenez un comprimé.

1.1   Mon régime alimentaire

Objectifs

Discussing your diet

Present tense of -er verbs

Tackling reading tasks

1   **V** Put these foods into three groups: *bon pour la santé, mauvais pour la santé, bon pour la santé mais avec modération.*

les haricots verts	un gigot d'agneau	les abricots	du saumon
des crevettes	des pâtisseries	des côtelettes de porc	le gratin dauphinois
le concombre	le fromage	des crêpes au chocolat	des œufs

Trois jeunes nous parlent de leur régime alimentaire

Je suis végétarienne depuis deux ans parce que je pense que manger de la viande est cruel et barbare. Je mange beaucoup de fruits et de salades, mais en général je n'aime pas tellement les légumes. Mes copines aiment manger des hamburgers, mais moi, je refuse de les accompagner quand elles vont au McDo. Je déteste boire des boissons sucrées. Je mange de temps en temps du chocolat et des bonbons, mais je sais que c'est mauvais pour la santé.

Floriane, 15 ans

Je fais attention à ce que je mange parce que je suis allergique aux noix. J'évite les biscuits, le chocolat et les gâteaux parce qu'ils peuvent me rendre très malade. En général je préfère la cuisine étrangère, surtout les pâtes et les pizzas. Je bois beaucoup d'eau. Le steak-frites est mon plat préféré. Je mange du fast-food mais avec modération. Les légumes sont bons pour la santé mais j'en mange rarement. Je n'aime pas le goût.

Patrice, 16 ans

Je ne mange jamais de porc parce que c'est interdit aux musulmans. Hier, j'ai mangé de l'agneau et j'ai bu de l'eau. J'adore les légumes, surtout les haricots verts et les petits pois. J'ai horreur du fast-food parce qu'il y a trop de graisse et de sucre dedans. En revanche, je prends souvent des desserts. Je ne peux pas résister aux petits gâteaux que ma mère prépare. J'en mange presque tous les jours. J'aime boire du thé à la menthe.

Halima, 14 ans

2a 📖🎧 Match the people to the pictures (A–C).

   1   Floriane   2   Patrice   3   Halima

2b 📖🎧 Who says the following? Is it Floriane, Patrice or Halima?

1   I have a food allergy.
2   I can't eat certain things because of my religion.
3   I never eat meat.
4   I never eat sweet things.
5   I like eating vegetables.
6   I like Italian food.
7   I eat fast-food occasionally.
8   I eat sweet things quite often.

📖 **Stratégie** When approaching a reading text, look out for clues to help you understand the main messages, such as the layout, the title, the typeface and any photos or drawings. Start by picking out the words you know already, and then look at words whose meaning you can easily work out, such as words which are the same or similar in English (e.g. *végétarienne, pizzas*).

3a 🎧 Listen to Section A and find the sentence that is true according to Hamidou's description.

1 Au Sénégal, on ne mange pas beaucoup de poisson.
2 On mange assez rarement de la viande.
3 Il n'y a pas beaucoup d'épices dans les sauces.

Astuce

Remember that verbs beginning with a vowel or silent 'h' take *j'* rather than *je – j'aime, j'adore*. Note too the *nous* form of *manger – nous mangeons*.

3b 🎧 Listen to Section B and find the four sentences that are true according to Hamidou's description.

1 Le plat préféré d'Hamidou contient du poisson.
2 Il mange du doussa presque tous les jours.
3 On mange régulièrement du riz.
4 Chez Hamidou, on ne mange pas à l'intérieur de la maison.
5 La famille ne mange pas à table.
6 On ne mange pas toujours avec des couteaux et des fourchettes.
7 Beaucoup de Sénégalais n'ont pas assez de nourriture.

4 Ⓖ Fill in the correct form of the verb.

1 Au petit déjeuner, je _____ du thé. (boire)
2 Elle ne boit jamais de thé, elle _____ mieux le café. (aimer)
3 Je bois souvent du jus d'orange, mais mes parents _____ de l'eau minérale. (boire)
4 J'aime manger du fast-food, mais mes copines _____ les frites. (détester)
5 Tous les soirs, nous _____ le dîner. (préparer)
6 Est-ce que vous _____ beaucoup de fruits? (acheter)

Grammaire *page 180*

Present tense of -*er* verbs

Most verbs in French are -*er* verbs and follow the same pattern:

préparer = to prepare

singular	plural
je prépare	nous préparons
tu prépares	vous préparez
il / elle / on prépare	ils / elles préparent

However, the verb *boire* is irregular. Look it up in the verb tables on pages 192–196 and draw a table similar to the one above to learn how to conjugate it correctly.

Also revise how to say 'some' in French.
See page 28 ➡

5 💬 Work with a partner and answer these questions.

- Est-ce que tu aimes le fast-food? Pourquoi?
- Tu aimes manger des fruits et des légumes?
- Tu manges souvent des choses sucrées?
- Tu es végétarien(ne)? Pourquoi (pas)?
- Quel est ton plat préféré?
- Est-ce que tu prends toujours un petit déjeuner?
- Qu'est-ce que tu as mangé et bu hier soir?

Est-ce que tu aimes le fast-food? Pourquoi?

Oui, je pense que le fast-food est pratique, délicieux et ce n'est pas cher.

Non, je n'aime pas le fast-food parce que c'est mauvais pour la santé.

J'aime / Je n'aime pas manger les fruits / les légumes	parce que	c'est bon pour la santé.
		le goût est horrible.
J'aime beaucoup le chocolat et les bonbons	mais c'est mauvais pour les dents.	
Je suis végétarien(ne)		j'adore les animaux.
Je ne suis pas végétarien(ne)		j'adore manger de la viande.
Je préfère le poisson-frites / le rosbif / les pizzas	parce que	c'est délicieux / pratique / équilibré.
Je prends toujours le petit déjeuner		c'est un repas important.
Je ne prends jamais de petit déjeuner		je n'ai pas le temps.
Hier soir, j'ai mangé et j'ai bu	une grosse pizza / de la salade	
	un verre d'eau / un verre de coca.	

1.2 Le bien-être

Objectifs

Discussing well-being

Adverbs of frequency

Vocabulary learning

Les jeunes: comment gardent-ils la forme?

Carole, 14 ans, est en bonne forme parce qu'elle mène une vie active. Par exemple, elle s'entraîne au gymnase deux fois par semaine pour faire de la musculation. Le week-end, elle fait souvent des randonnées à la campagne. Ça lui fait du bien de respirer l'air pur.

Henri, 15 ans, trouve qu'il est essentiel de se détendre parce que le lycée est très stressant, et il n'aime pas trop travailler, les devoirs l'épuisent. Après ses devoirs, il passe toujours une heure à écouter de la musique ou à jouer de la guitare ou de la flûte. De temps en temps, il lit un bon livre. Le samedi, il fait toujours la grasse matinée.

Audrey, 16 ans, n'a pas envie d'être en mauvaise santé. Elle mange équilibré et elle évite de manger des matières grasses et des sucreries. Elle nous avertit qu'il faut dormir huit heures par nuit, sinon on risque de se sentir fatigué au lycée. Tous les jours, elle se lève à la même heure et elle prépare le petit déjeuner pour tout le monde. La routine est importante pour elle.

Christian, 15 ans, est rarement en bonne forme. Il dit que le sport lui cause des douleurs dans les jambes. Il a beaucoup de devoirs et il se couche très tard parce qu'il veut réviser pour ses examens. Ses parents insistent pour qu'il travaille dur et il veut les rendre heureux.

1a 📖 🎧 Read the article and write down the name of the person best described by each of these adjectives.

1 stressé(e)   2 sportif(-ve)   3 paresseux(-se)   4 organisé(e)

1b 📖 🎧 Write down the name of the person best summed up by each of the following titles.

1 Comment se relaxer
2 L'activité physique est indispensable
3 Le sommeil est important
4 Il faut réussir les examens

1c 📖 🎧 Note the following information in English.

1 Give two examples of how Carole leads an active life.
2 Give two examples of how Henri unwinds.
3 Give two examples of Audrey's daily routine.
4 Give two reasons why Christian does not do any sport.

2 Ⓥ Decide whether each of the statements below fits better with cartoon A or B.

1 Il mange beaucoup de frites.
2 Il évite le sucre et la graisse.
3 Il est trop passif.
4 Il ne dort pas bien.
5 Il se sent bien dans sa peau.
6 Il passe trop de temps devant la télé.
7 Il veut prévenir les crises cardiaques.
8 Il aime le repos.
9 Il veut garder la forme.

3 🎧 🌐 Listen to Sections A and B and fill in the blank spaces with a word chosen from the list.

🎧 See the *Stratégie* box on page 30 for ideas on how to learn new vocabulary.

Stratégie

A 1 Pour le docteur Bernard, le plus important, c'est de faire du _____.

2 Le sport peut prévenir les maladies du _____.

3 Le sport est une bonne manière de se faire des _____.

4 Pour elle, les jeunes passent trop de temps devant _____.

B 5 Le docteur Bernard considère qu'il faut bien _____.

6 On est moins stressé si on _____ bien.

7 La _____ empêche de dormir.

8 Il ne faut pas se coucher trop _____.

amis	l'ordinateur	dort	sport	lycée
manger	tôt	tard	chaleur	cœur

4 🄶 Ask and answer these questions with a partner and add an appropriate adverb of frequency.

1 Tu manges de la viande?

2 Tu dors bien?

3 Tu vas souvent au centre sportif?

4 Tu manges souvent des frites?

5 Tu manges souvent du poisson?

6 Tu fais de la natation?

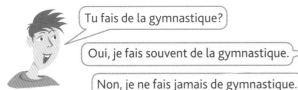

Tu fais de la gymnastique?

Oui, je fais souvent de la gymnastique.

Non, je ne fais jamais de gymnastique.

Grammaire (page 176)

Adverbs of frequency

Use these adverbs to say how often you do something. Look up these adverbs in the vocabulary section on page 30 and learn them: *quelquefois*, *une fois par semaine*, *parfois*, *souvent*, *jamais*, *toujours*, *tous les jours*, *rarement*, *encore*, *de temps en temps*, *régulièrement*, *généralement*.

Also learn how to form *-ir* verbs and the verbs *faire* and *dormir*.

See page 28 ➡

Astuce

Remember when using *jamais* that you need *ne* in front of the verb and *de* instead of *un*, *une*, *du*, *de la* or *des* after it. *Je ne fume jamais. Je ne mange jamais de viande.*

5 ✏️ Write a few paragraphs about your own lifestyle.

■ What do you drink and how often?

■ How often do you do physical exercise?

■ How many hours do you sleep?

■ How much time do you spend on homework?

■ How do you relax?

■ What did you do last weekend to avoid stress?

■ What do you eat and how often?

Je mange / bois / prends	souvent / rarement / quelquefois	des frites / boissons sucrées / de la viande rouge.
Je fais Je joue	régulièrement / de temps en temps	des randonnées / de la natation / du sport. au foot / au basket / au rugby.
Je dors Je me couche	toujours / normalement	huit heures par nuit. de bonne heure / tôt / tard / à la même heure.
Je travaille		dur / trop / deux heures tous les soirs.
Pour me détendre, je		lis / fais du sport / regarde la télé.
Le week-end dernier, j'ai		lu un bon livre / écouté de la musique.

Les multinationales encouragent les jeunes Africains à fumer

Aujourd'hui, les jeunes sont arrivés dans le village, habillés de leurs plus beaux vêtements. Devant un écran géant, un présentateur montre un film. Dans la foule enthousiaste, de jolies filles distribuent gratuitement des cigarettes.

Cette scène est quotidienne en Afrique subsaharienne, offerte par les multinationales du tabac qui essaient de persuader les Africains, en particulier les jeunes, que «fumer, c'est cool». En dix ans, le nombre de fumeurs a progressé de 33% en Afrique, c'est un triste record! Au Niger, une enquête sur le tabagisme des jeunes est alarmante: «22% des élèves de 13 à 15 ans fument des cigarettes et commencent à fumer à un âge de plus en plus jeune».

Il n'y a pratiquement pas de programmes anti-tabac en Afrique francophone. Beaucoup d'enfants ne vont pas à l'école et donc ils ne reçoivent pas d'éducation sur la santé.

Les compagnies de tabac mènent une politique agressive de sponsoring d'activités culturelles et sportives. Dans les cafés au Niger, il y a souvent des posters qui invitent les jeunes à des soirées-spectacles où on distribue des cigarettes gratuites. Autre innovation: dans les paquets, les jeunes trouvent parfois des billets de loterie. Pas assez d'argent pour acheter un paquet de cigarettes? Pas de problème: il est aussi possible pour les enfants d'acheter une seule cigarette.

Le gouvernement du Niger ferme les yeux sur ce problème parce que les cigarettes donnent du travail à beaucoup de monde: cultivateurs, employés d'usines, vendeurs, etc.

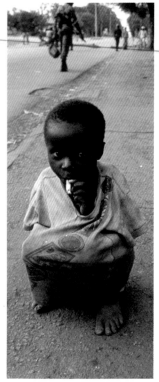

1a 📖 🎧 According to the article, which two sentences are true?

1 Tobacco companies provide free film screenings for young people in Africa.
2 Large tobacco companies are trying to stop young Africans from smoking.
3 In Niger, half of 13 to 15 years olds smoke.
4 Most African children receive health education.
5 The tobacco industry creates a lot of jobs in Niger.

1b 📖 🎧 According to the article, each one of the sentences below contains a mistake. Find the mistakes and correct them.

1 De jolies filles vendent des cigarettes aux jeunes.
2 En Afrique, le nombre de jeunes fumeurs a diminué en dix ans.
3 Des programmes anti-tabac sont très fréquents en Afrique francophone.
4 Dans certains paquets, on trouve des billets pour des concerts.
5 Quand on n'a pas beaucoup d'argent, il est impossible d'acheter du tabac.

2 🎥🎧 Choose the correct sentence for each speaker. Watch or listen to Section A for 1–2 and Section B for 3–4.

1 Coralie

a Je ne fume pas.
b Les cigarettes me calment les nerfs.
c Mes parents ne savent pas que je fume.

2 Félix

a Je fume toujours des cigarettes.
b Mes amis fument pour faire plus adulte.
c Les cigarettes coûtent beaucoup d'argent.

3 Maika

a Je suis accro aux cigarettes.
b Le tabagisme passif m'inquiète.
c Ma mère est en bonne santé.

4 Olivier

a Certains jeunes fument pour faire comme leurs amis.
b Il est facile pour les jeunes d'arrêter de fumer.
c Personne ne fume dans mon école.

3 **G** With a partner, make these sentences negative, using as many negative expressions as you can.
Partner A reads out the sentence and Partner B says a negative version of the same sentence.

1 Je fume.
2 Les cigarettes sont chères.
3 Il va arrêter de fumer.
4 Les cigarettes aident à combattre le stress.
5 Le cancer des poumons inquiète les jeunes fumeurs.
6 Les jeunes sont touchés par les campagnes anti-tabac.

4 🖊 🌐 What do you think? Write about your views on smoking and on encouraging others to smoke.

■ Why do young people smoke?
■ What are the consequences of smoking?
■ Have you ever smoked? Why or why not?
■ How do tobacco companies encourage young people to buy cigarettes?
■ What is your own opinion of these methods?

> ## Forming negatives
> *Je **ne** fume **plus**.*
> *Les fumeurs **ne** respectent **personne**.*
> *Je **ne** fume **jamais**.*
> *Ça **ne** me dit **rien**.*
> *Je **ne** fume **que** dix cigarettes par semaine.*
> *Elle **n'**écoute **ni** ses parents **ni** ses amis.*
>
> To make a verb negative put *ne* in front of the verb (*n'* if it starts with a vowel or a silent 'h') and the negative expressive after the verb.
>
> Also learn about using *devoir +* infinitive. *See page 29* ➡
>
> **Grammaire** *page 186*

> 🖊 Use a variety of phrases to give your opinions, e.g. *Je pense que …*(I think that…), *À mon avis* (In my opinion…). A list of different ones is given in the vocabulary section on page 31.
>
> **Stratégie**

> Include some information about what you don't do, think or believe in, to demonstrate that you know how to use the negative.
>
> **Astuce**

À mon avis, les jeunes fument pour	être sociables / faire comme les autres / se relaxer.
Le tabac cause	des maladies graves / le cancer des poumons / des crises cardiaques.
J'ai fumé une fois	mais je n'ai pas aimé ça.
Je n'ai jamais fumé	parce que je ne veux pas devenir accro.
Les fabricants encouragent les jeunes à fumer en	distribuant des cigarettes gratuites / faisant de la publicité / sponsorisant des événements sportifs.
Je trouve ces méthodes	dégoûtantes / affreuses / injustes / acceptables / justes / normales.

L'ivresse du samedi soir

Voici le témoignage de Patrick, 15 ans:

A «J'ai besoin de boire. Je suis réservé, et l'alcool m'aide à être sociable. Mais je sais que boire est dangereux, surtout quand on boit pour essayer d'oublier quelque chose, pour cacher les réalités difficiles. Par exemple, pour moi, l'alcool m'aide à oublier mes problèmes avec ma famille et avec mon travail scolaire. J'ai peur de ne pas réussir. L'alcool du samedi soir ne m'a pas rendu dépendant, mais j'ai quelquefois peur de boire trop d'alcool. Je pense que je peux arrêter si je veux. Mais se passer d'alcool, est-ce que ça va être aussi facile que ça? Je n'en sais rien.»

B La consommation excessive d'alcool le samedi soir par les adolescents (ce que les Anglais appellent le «binge-drinking», c'est-à-dire la cuite du samedi soir) est maintenant habituelle. Les jeunes sont exposés à des risques importants: accidents de voiture, violences et maladies (vomissements, perte de

Est-ce que tu t'es vu quand tu es ivre?

connaissance, coma). Les risques à long terme sont bien connus: l'alcoolisme, les maladies sérieuses du foie et les crises cardiaques. On risque de gâcher sa vie. Lors d'une fête, l'alcool aide à mettre une bonne ambiance et renforce le sentiment de faire partie d'un groupe. Les jeunes consomment de plus en plus de bière au taux d'alcool élevé (11%) et des cocktails d'alcool fort très sucrés, vendus à bas prix dans les supermarchés. Est-ce qu'on va voir de plus en plus d'alcooliques dans l'avenir?

1a 📖 🎧 Read the first paragraph (Section A) and complete the sentences with words chosen from the list.

avec　　sans　　timidité

arrogance　　réalité

parents　　école

maison

1　Patrick boit pour combattre sa _____.
2　Selon lui, certains boivent pour échapper à la _____.
3　Il dit qu'il a des difficultés chez lui et à l'_____.
4　Il croit qu'il peut vivre _____ alcool.

1b 📖 🎧 Read Section B and complete the sentences with words chosen from the list.

rare　　commune

s'amuser　　chers

accident　　agression

graves　　alcoolisés

1　La consommation excessive d'alcool chez les jeunes est _____.
2　On risque de devenir victime d'une _____ quand on boit trop.
3　L'alcool peut provoquer des maladies _____.
4　Beaucoup de jeunes boivent pour _____.
5　Les cocktails sucrés ne sont pas _____.

2a 🎧 Listen to the information in Section A and correct the mistakes in the sentences below.

1　Paul has been an addict for five years.
2　He started taking drugs at home.
3　It's a habit he finds easy to kick.
4　He will have rehabilitation next year.
5　He wants to quit the habit by the end of the month.

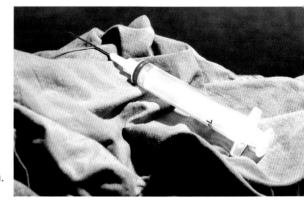

2b 🎧 Correct the mistakes in the sentences below, according to the interview with Stéphanie (Section B).

1 Stéphanie started taking drugs at school.
2 She stole money from her friends.
3 She was involved in a car accident.
4 She has completed her rehab.
5 She wants to leave school next year.

3 Ⓖ Match the questions to the correct answers.

1 Combien de verres vas-tu boire?
2 Où vas-tu ce soir?
3 Qu'est-ce que tu vas boire?
4 Comment est-ce que tu rentres chez toi?
5 Qui va acheter de la bière?
6 Pourquoi bois-tu de l'alcool?

a Pour combattre le stress.
b En taxi.
c Chez Michèle.
d Deux ou trois.
e De la vodka.
f Mon frère.

4 💬 🔊 With a partner, work out the questions you would ask to get these answers. Then change the answers to make up your own interview.

■ J'ai commencé il y a deux ans, à l'âge de 15 ans.
■ Je bois pour être sociable et parce que mes amis boivent.
■ Je bois dans les bars et dans les boîtes de nuit.
■ Je bois uniquement le week-end.
■ Généralement, je bois de la bière.
■ Je bois avec mes amis.

> À quel age est-ce que tu as commencé à boire de l'alcool?
>
> J'ai commencé il y a deux ans, à l'âge de 15 ans.
>
> Je bois pour être sociable et parce que mes amis boivent.

Qu'		Je bois beaucoup / un peu de vin.
Où		Je bois chez moi / des amis.
Pourquoi	est-ce que tu bois (de l'alcool)?	Je bois parce que ça me relaxe / me rend moins timide.
Quand		Je bois à des fêtes / les week-ends.
Avec qui		Je bois avec ma famille / mes amis.

Asking questions   Ⓖ **Grammaire** *page 186*

You can start a question by inverting the subject and the verb, e.g. *Avez-vous arrêté?* (Have you stopped?) but often you need a question word instead or as well, e.g. *Quand avez-vous commencé à vous droguer?* (When did you start taking drugs?).

For a list of question words see the vocabulary section on page 31.

Also learn how to form the verb *avoir*, and the expressions that take *avoir,* e.g. *avoir peur*.

See page 29 ➡️

💬 **Using questions**   🔊 **Stratégie**

Be ready to ask questions as well as to answer them. The easiest way to make a question is to put *est-ce que* at the start of the question: *Est-ce que tu bois de la bière?*

For more specific information, use a question word followed by *est-ce que?* e.g. *Quand est-ce que tu as commencé à boire?*

Astuce

If someone asks you a question and you want to ask it back, there is no need to repeat the question. Simply say *et toi* or *et vous?*

Health

Bien se préparer aux examens

Comment ne pas paniquer?

Tu peux être bien préparé pour les examens si …

La veille de l'examen:

Tu ne révises pas à la dernière minute, mais …

a) Tu continues à faire des activités que tu aimes (sport, loisirs).

b) Tu limites les visites chez les copains: le stress se communique et les copains vont parler de l'examen!

c) Le soir, tu manges léger, par exemple: salade, steak, yaourt, fruit.

d) Tu prépares ton sac et tu penses à emporter le matériel nécessaire (stylos, calculatrice) et les documents importants.

e) Tu diminues les excitants (thé, café, tabac).

Le jour de l'examen:

f) Tu prends le temps de déjeuner: sucres lents (pain, biscottes, céréales …), fruit, produit laitier (lait, yaourt, fromage blanc …) et boisson (thé, café, chocolat …).

g) Tu ne quittes pas la maison au dernier moment. Comme ça tu vas arriver calme.

h) Tu bois assez d'eau. Tu peux apporter une bouteille d'eau dans la salle.

i) Tu manges quelque chose pendant la matinée (barre de céréales, carrés de chocolat, biscuits …).

j) Tu ne paniques pas pendant l'examen: tu vas avoir le temps de lire ta copie avant la fin de l'examen. À l'oral: parle calmement, articule bien.

1a Read the advice a–j for the day before, and the day of, an exam. Decide which piece of advice fits with each of the titles below.

1 Preparing equipment
2 Having a good breakfast
3 Preventing friends from making you worry more
4 Cutting down on stimulants (e.g. caffeine)
5 Allowing enough time to get to school
6 Staying calm during the exam
7 Making time for leisure
8 Keeping hydrated
9 Eating sensibly the night before
10 Eating an energy-boosting snack during the morning

1b Voilà un petit quiz pour voir si tu t'es bien préparé(e) pour les examens. Si tu peux répondre «oui» aux questions suivantes, tu as bien commencé!

OUI   NON

A Est-ce que tu travailles dans un environnement calme?

B Fais-tu des pauses pendant que tu travailles?

C Te fixes-tu un horaire de révision tous les jours?

D Manges-tu des plats qui sont bons pour ton cerveau, avec de la vitamine B par exemple?

E Dors-tu bien?

F Est-ce que tu trouves du temps pour faire une activité physique?

G Est-ce que tu évites les jeux vidéo ou les sorties tardives le soir?

H Est-ce que tu évites le tabac et l'alcool?

1c 📖 Match the answers below with the questions in the quiz in activity 1b. Decide which questions and answers go together, and whether the answers should start with *Oui* or *Non.* Put a cross next to the ones that are not in the quiz.

Exemple: **1 D Non.**

1 _____ je mange trop de gâteaux et de frites.

2 _____ ce n'est pas un problème parce que j'ai ma propre chambre.

3 _____ je dîne avec ma famille à 19 heures.

4 _____ je trouve le sommeil difficile avant une heure du matin.

5 _____ je fais un arrêt pendant 15 minutes toutes les deux heures.

6 _____ si je sors, je rentre avant 22 heures.

7 _____ le soir, je ne travaille plus après 20 heures.

8 _____ je fais une liste d'objectifs chaque matin.

9 _____ je dois dire que je fume de temps en temps, et j'aime prendre une bière avec mes copains.

10 _____ je prends le bus seulement quand il pleut, autrement j'utilise toujours mon vélo.

2a 🎧 Listen to Thomas describing a typical training day. In what order does he mention the things shown in the pictures?

AQA **Examiner's tip**

Before listening to the recording, consider what words you are likely to hear linked to each picture. Remember, it may not be the word for the actual item shown, but something connected, e.g. for picture 1 he may refer to breakfast in general, rather than cereal.

Vocabulaire

le but	goal
le cerveau	brain
s'entraîner	to train
la musculation	weight training
le sommeil	sleep
tardif(-ve)	late

Éloïse uses *ne … pas* several times when talking about things she cannot do. She also uses two other forms of negatives that you have met recently. Which ones?

For more information on negatives see page 23.

Grammaire *page 186*

2b 🎧 Éloïse, another young athlete, is asked about the more negative aspects of fitting her training into her life. List, in English, at least six things that she says she is unable to do, or has to avoid.

(G) Health

How to say 'some'; some present tense verbs

1 For each of the items pictured, write a sentence starting with *Je voudrais* followed by *du, de la, de l'* or *des* plus the name of the item.

Exemple: Je voudrais de la soupe.

> **How to say 'some'**
>
> The French words for 'some' or 'any' are *du* (masculine), *de la* (feminine), *de l'* (before vowels) and *des* (plural). Note that most food nouns ending in -e are feminine, and that the French for 'pasta' is always plural.
>
> **Grammaire** *page 172*

2a Copy the *finir* table from the grammar box and learn it. Make five more for *remplir, choisir, réussir, dormir* and *faire*.

2b Replace the infinitives in italics with the correct form of the present tense each time.

- Qu'est-ce que vous **1** *faire* pour être en forme?
- Je **2** *faire* de la musculation et l'été, avec ma copine, nous **3** *faire* beaucoup de randonnées en montagne.
- Vous **4** *dormir* bien?
- Oui, je **5** *dormir* environ huit heures par nuit. Par contre, mes copains ne **6** *dormir* pas assez parce qu'ils **7** *finir* souvent leurs soirées dans un bar, et ils ne **8** *faire* jamais la grasse matinée.
- Au restaurant, vous **9** *finir* toujours le repas avec un bon dessert?
- Non! Mon copain Arthur **10** *choisir* souvent un énorme dessert au chocolat. Mais pas moi!
- Quand vous **11** *faire* vos courses, comment **12** *remplir* -vous votre panier?
- On voit beaucoup de gens qui **13** *remplir* leurs paniers de nourriture très grasse, mais nous **14** *choisir* surtout des fruits, des légumes et des céréales. Bien sûr!

> **Some present tense verbs**
>
> *Finir* and a few other -*ir* verbs such as *remplir* (to fill), *choisir* (to choose) and *réussir* (to succeed) follow a regular pattern in the present tense. Remove the -*ir* and then add the endings (underlined) below.
>
> **finir = to finish**
>
> | singular | plural |
> |---|---|
> | je fin<u>is</u> | nous fin<u>issons</u> |
> | tu fin<u>is</u> | vous fin<u>issez</u> |
> | il / elle / on fin<u>it</u> | ils / elles fin<u>issent</u> |
>
> Some -*ir* verbs, such as *dormir* (to sleep) are irregular. You can look these up in the verb tables on pages 192–196. Another one to check is *faire* (to make or do). Many of these verbs follow the pattern of endings -*s*, -*s*, -*t* in the singular.
>
> **Grammaire** *page 180*

Devoir + infinitive; expressions with *avoir*; question words and inversion

3a Make a table for the present tense of *devoir*, similar to the ones you made for activity 2a.

3b In each sentence, replace the English in brackets with the correct French.

1 Je (mustn't eat) trop de frites.
2 Ils (mustn't) se coucher trop tard.
3 Il (must learn) à aimer les légumes.
4 On (mustn't smoke) dans les lieux publics.
5 Elle (mustn't buy) de boissons alcoolisées.
6 Nous (must) faire attention à notre poids.
7 Tu (must stop) de fumer.
8 Vous (must say) «non» à la drogue.

4a Complete the sentences with the correct form of *avoir* in the present tense, then translate them into English.

1 Elles _____ tort de fumer.
2 Qui _____ un cancer du poumon?
3 Vous _____ peur d'être allergique?
4 Pourquoi _____ -nous envie de nous droguer?
5 Tu _____ raison: ils n'_____ pas d'alcool chez eux.

4b Complete each sentence with the correct form of *avoir* or *être* in the present tense, then translate them into English.

1 Ils _____ envie de drogues qui _____ très dangereuses.
2 Je n'_____ pas d'énergie parce que je _____ fatigué.
3 Nous _____ trop de travail et nous _____ stressés.
4 Il n'_____ pas envie de sortir car il _____ malade.
5 Vous n'_____ pas en bonne santé et vous _____ mal au cœur.

5 Use the words in brackets to change the following statements into questions. Do not forget the inversion.

Exemple: Tu bois trop d'alcool. (Pourquoi?)
Pourquoi bois-tu trop d'alcool?

1 Elle part à l'hôpital. (Quand?)
2 Tu fêtes ton anniversaire. (Où?)
3 Il court sur la plage. (Avec qui?)
4 Elles rentrent chez elles. (Comment?)
5 Nous sortons ce soir. (À quelle heure?)
6 Vous mangez beaucoup de légumes. (Pourquoi?)

Grammaire *page 185*

Devoir + infinitive

Use *devoir* to say what you must and must not do. Remember it is followed by an infinitive. To check how to conjugate *devoir* in the present tense, go to the verb table on page 193.

Grammaire *page 184*

Expressions with *avoir*

Avoir normally means 'to have', e.g. *J'ai beaucoup d'énergie* – 'I have lots of energy', but in certain cases the English equivalent is 'to be', e.g. *J'ai faim* – 'I am hungry'. This literally means 'I have hunger'. Make sure you know the expressions below.

Look up *avoir* and *être* in the verb tables (pages 192–196) and make your own tables to help you learn them.

Vocabulaire

avoir … ans	to be … years old
avoir froid / chaud	to be cold / hot
avoir faim / soif	to be hungry / thirsty
avoir peur	to be afraid
avoir mal au cœur	to feel sick
avoir raison	to be right
avoir tort	to be wrong
avoir envie de	to want to / to feel like

Grammaire *page 186*

Question words and inversion

A formal way of asking questions is to change the word order so the verb comes before the subject. This also works after question words like *pourquoi? quand? où?* etc.

Statement	Question
Tu bois.	*Pourquoi bois-tu?*
You drink.	Why do you drink?
Il part.	*Quand part-il?*
He's leaving.	When is he leaving?

(V) Health

Mon régime alimentaire ➡ pages 18–19

l'	abricot (m)	apricot
	accompagner	to accompany
l'	alimentation (f)	diet
	assis(e)	sitting down / seated
la	boisson	drink
la	côtelette	chop / cutlet
le	concombre	cucumber
la	crêpe	pancake
la	crevette	prawn
	dehors	outside
	épicé(e)	spicy
	étranger(-ère)	foreign / strange
le	gigot d'agneau	leg of lamb
le	goût	taste
la	graisse	fat
les	haricots verts (m)	green beans
	interdit(e)	forbidden
le / la	musulman(e)	Muslim
la	noix	nut
	par terre	on the ground
les	pâtes (f)	pasta
la	pêche	fishing
le	saumon	salmon
le	thé à la menthe	mint tea
	végétarien(ne)	vegetarian
la	viande	meat

Le bien-être ➡ pages 20–21

l'	activité physique (f)	physical activity
le	cœur	heart
le	conseil	advice
la	crise cardiaque	heart attack
la	douleur	pain
	en bonne forme	in good shape
	se détendre (détendu)	to relax / to calm down
	empêcher	to prevent
	encore	again
s'	entraîner	to train
	éviter	to avoid
	faire la grasse matinée	to have a lie in
	garder la forme	to keep in shape
	généralement	usually
	jamais	never
la	maladie	illness
	manger équilibré	to eat a well-balanced diet
la	musculation	weight training
l'	obésité (f)	obesity
	parfois	sometimes
	prévenir (prévenu)	to prevent
	quelquefois	sometimes
la	randonnée	hiking
	rarement	rarely
	régulièrement	regularly
le	sel	salt
le	sommeil	sleep
	souvent	often
	stressant(e)	stressful
les	sucreries (f)	sweets
de	temps en temps	from time to time
	toujours	always
	tous les jours	every day
	une fois par semaine	once a week

On parle du tabac ➡ *pages 22–23*

	à mon avis …	in my opinion …
	arrêter	to stop
	augmenter	to increase
	choquant(e)	shocking
	difficile à croire	hard to believe
	être accro	to have a habit (addiction)
	être hors d'haleine	to be out of breath
	fumer	to smoke
le / la	*fumeur / fumeuse*	smoker
	gratuitement	free
	il me semble que …	it seems to me that …
s'	*inquiéter*	to worry
	je crois que …	I believe that …
	je pense que …	I think that …
	je trouve cela …	I find that …
	je trouve que …	I find that …
	offrir	to give (e.g. a present)
le	*paquet*	packet
	passif(-ve)	passive
le	*poumon*	lung
	ridicule	ridiculous
le	*tabac*	tobacco
le	*tabagisme*	addiction to smoking

L'alcool et la drogue ➡ *pages 24–25*

l'	*alcool (m)*	alcohol
	alcoolisé(e)	alcoholic (e.g. drinks)
	avoir peur	to be afraid
	avoir tort	to be wrong
une	*bonne ambiance*	a good atmosphere
	cacher	to hide
	combien?	how much / many?
	comment?	how?
le	*comprimé*	tablet
la	*connaissance*	knowledge / consciousness
la	*consommation*	consumption
	consommer	to consume
la	*crise cardiaque*	heart attack
se	*droguer*	to take drugs
les	*drogues douces (f)*	soft drugs
les	*drogues dures (f)*	hard drugs
	excessif(-ve)	excessive
	faire une cure	to take a course of treatment
le	*foie*	liver
la	*guerre*	war
l'	*habitude (f)*	habit
	mentir	to lie
	oú?	where?
	oublier	to forget
se	*passer de*	to do without
	quand?	when?
	que?	what?
	quel / quelle?	which / what?
	qui?	who?
le	*risque*	risk
le	*vomissement*	vomiting

---

1 ❤ Read the slogans and summarise what each message is in English.

1
Le tabac tue.

2
Le tabagisme passif nous concerne tous.

3
Les cigarettes sont dangereuses pour les poumons.

4
C'est cool? Ça fait adulte? Je ne sais pas mais ça tue 40 000 Français par an.

5
Tu achètes des cigarettes? Ton argent part en fumée!

6
Tu veux une mauvaise haleine et les dents jaunes? Commence à fumer!

La famille

Une famille nombreuse

Aminata habite au Cameroun en Afrique. Elle nous parle de sa famille.

A Depuis l'âge de quatre ans, moi, ma mère et mes deux frères habitons avec une belle-mère, c'est-à-dire la deuxième femme de mon papa. Quand j'avais huit ans, mon père s'est marié pour la troisième fois: j'ai donc une seconde belle-mère. Et maintenant, j'ai aussi cinq demi-frères et quatre demi-sœurs. Au total, douze enfants, trois femmes et un mari vivent ensemble dans une petite maison au nord de Yaoundé, la capitale.

B Les mères préparent les repas à tour de rôle. Pendant les repas, nous mangeons tous ensemble. Mon père ne veut pas de division dans la famille. Quand j'étais petite, je me disputais beaucoup avec mes demi-frères et sœurs. Mais avec le temps, nous avons appris à être plus tolérants.

C Vous savez, pour un Africain, le fait de vivre en concubinage, comme ça arrive en France, c'est choquant. La règle pour habiter ensemble au Cameroun, c'est le mariage. Il ne faut pas oublier que la communauté est très importante dans mon pays, plus importante que l'individu.

Et puis en **D** France la monogamie ne semble pas toujours être un bon modèle. Les séparations sont devenues très fréquentes. Combien de femmes, par exemple, se retrouvent seules et sans argent après un divorce? Combien d'enfants sont déprimés à cause de la séparation de leurs deux parents? Et combien de pères ne voient pas leurs enfants qu'ils aiment? Je crois que la famille au Cameroun est plus stable que la famille en France.

Aminata

1 **V** Choose a word from the list below to go with each of these definitions.

a une personne qui n'est pas mariée

b une femme dont le mari est mort

c un homme dont la femme est morte

d le fils de mon frère

e la fille de ma sœur

f le fils de ma belle-mère

g le nouveau mari de ma mère

neveu nièce célibataire veuf veuve beau-père demi-frère

2a Read the article and choose a suitable title for each paragraph.

1 The distress caused by divorce and separation

2 Arrangements for meal times

3 Living together is frowned upon

4 A very large family

2b Answer the questions in English.

1 How many people are there in Aminata's family? (Give details.)

2 What does she say about meal times?

3 How has her relationship with her half brothers and sisters changed?

4 What does she think about couples living together outside marriage?

5 How does she explain the importance of marriage in Cameroon?

6 What three consequences of divorce does she mention?

Stratégie

📖 Use your knowledge of English to work out the meaning of French words. It is clear what *le cousin* means, but note the feminine *la cousine* – it is still understandable even with the extra letter. You can work out terms such as *le caractère*, *de mauvaise humeur* and *fiancé(e)* quite easily. What about *le petit-fils* and *la petite-fille*?

3 🎧 Listen to Sections A and B and correct the mistakes in these sentences.

A
1 Florence does not get on with her brother.
2 Her parents are strict.
3 Her father is serious.
4 Abdul gets on well with his father.
5 He is getting good marks at school.

B
6 Liliane's mother has remarried.
7 She finds her step-brother amusing.
8 Her mother thinks Liliane is hard-working.
9 Maxime's uncle and aunt are too strict.
10 His sister is married.

4a Ⓖ Fill in the gaps in the table.

	masculine	feminine	plural
my	*mon père*	_____ *mère*	*mes parents*
your	*ton* _____	*ta tante*	*tes neveux*
his / her	*son frère*	*sa sœur*	_____ *ami(e)s*
our	*notre grand-père*	*notre* _____	*nos grands-parents*
your	*votre ami*	_____ *amie*	*vos ami(e)s*
their	_____ *cousin*	*leur cousine*	*leurs cousin(e)s*

How to say 'my', 'your', etc.

To say 'my', 'your', 'his', 'her', 'our' and 'their' in French, you need to remember that the word changes according to the person and also the gender and number of the item owned.

For example: *mon père, ma mère, mes sœurs*. These words are called possessive adjectives.

Also revise the position and agreement of adjectives.

See page 46 ➡

Grammaire pages 174–175

4b Ⓖ Follow the English prompts to complete these sentences with the correct words.

1 Je m'entends bien avec _____ parents. (my)
2 _____ amis se disputent tout le temps. (our)
3 Comment vous entendez-vous avec _____ parents? (your)
4 _____ mère et _____ père vont divorcer. (her)
5 Il ne se dispute jamais avec _____ parents. (his)
6 _____ enfants ne sont pas très aimables. (their)

5 ✏ You work in a scriptwriting team developing a new family for a TV soap. In a group, decide who is in the family, then each person describes one member of the family.

- What are the family members like?
- How do they get on with each other and why?
- What do they argue about?
- Describe a recent event to illustrate their relationship.
- What will happen in next week's episode?

Dans la famille, il y a	une mère célibataire et trois enfants.
Le père / La mère est	sportif(-ve) / amusant(e) / généreux(-euse).
xxxxx aime / a de bons rapports avec son frère / sa sœur parce qu'	il / elle est (très / assez) gentil(le) / aimable / sympa / compréhensif(-ve).
xxxxx n'aime pas / a des rapports difficiles avec sa sœur / son frère parce qu'	il / elle est méchant(e) / désagréable / casse-pieds / sérieux(-se).
Ils / Elles se disputent au sujet	du travail à l'école / du travail à la maison.
La semaine dernière,	ils se sont battus.
Dans le prochain épisode,	xxxxx va avoir un accident de voiture.

Astuce

Always try to include adjectives in your writing, in order to make it more individual and interesting. Remember that most adjectives in French follow the noun and you need to check you have put on the correct ending. Ask yourself: Is it masculine or feminine? Is it singular or plural?

Les rapports avec les autres

L'amitié

Pierre

Je n'ai pas de meilleur ami, mais je sors souvent avec le même groupe de garçons. On trouve toujours des choses à faire parce qu'on s'intéresse aux mêmes choses: le football, jouer de la guitare, voir des films d'horreur.

Aurélie

J'ai beaucoup de copines, mais ma meilleure amie s'appelle Sandrine. On s'amuse ensemble. Le week-end, nous allons dans les magasins et nous achetons plein de vêtements. Sandrine est toujours très calme, elle ne se met jamais en colère avec moi. Elle est souriante et pleine de vie, elle me fait rire. Mon père se fâche parce que je parle souvent avec elle au téléphone même quand nous avons passé la journée ensemble. Il me dit que je n'arrête pas de parler quand je suis avec Sandrine.

Bernard

Je n'ai pas beaucoup d'amis, car je suis assez timide. J'ai des problèmes en ce moment parce que mon meilleur ami, Philippe, est déprimé. Il est toujours de mauvaise humeur. Il a des difficultés chez lui et il se dispute avec ses parents. Ce qui est pire, c'est qu'il a aussi des ennuis au lycée. Les profs ne sont pas très compréhensifs, mais moi, je ne sais pas comment l'aider. Je ne sais pas quoi faire.

Hortense

Je viens de me disputer avec ma meilleure amie, Claire. J'ai décidé de me confier à elle. Je lui ai dit que j'aimais un garçon de ma classe mais que j'étais trop timide et que je ne pouvais pas lui parler. Claire a annoncé mon secret à toute la classe. J'étais terriblement gênée. En plus, elle s'achète toujours les mêmes vêtements que moi et elle me prend des choses qu'elle ne me rend pas. J'en ai marre!

---

1 ⓥ Match each word or phrase with a suitable cartoon.

1 gêné   4 souriant

2 timide   5 il en a marre!

3 déprimé   6 en colère

2 📖🎧 Read the blog entries above and find the correct sentence endings.

1 Pierre et ses amis font …   a triste.

2 Sandrine et Aurélie font …   b du shopping ensemble.

3 Selon Aurélie, Sandrine n'est jamais …   c très bavardes.

4 Les deux filles sont …   d assez sportif.

5 Selon Bernard, Philippe est …   e les mêmes activités de loisirs.

6 Bernard voudrait …   f indiscrète.

7 Hortense dit que Claire a été …   g un garçon malheureux.

8 Claire s'habille …   h de la même façon que sa copine.

                                        i de bonne humeur.

                                        j des conseils.

3a 🎧 Listen to the descriptions of five people and pick an adjective to describe each one (1–5).

sincère   dynamique   intelligent   sportif   amusante

égoïste   travailleur   calme

3b 🎧 Listen again and correct these sentences.

1 Les filles détestent Thomas.
2 François est un garçon réservé.
3 Georges est gentil.
4 Delphine aime raconter des histoires tristes.
5 Caroline s'intéresse aux films.

4 Ⓖ Work with a partner. Partner A says the sentence with the missing reflexive pronoun, and Partner B translates the sentence into English. Swap over for each sentence.

1 Elle _____ habille comme moi.
2 Je ne _____ entends pas bien avec mon frère.
3 Nous _____ disputons tout le temps.
4 Elles _____ parlent souvent au téléphone.
5 Ils _____ confient souvent.
6 Tu veux _____ reposer avant de sortir?

Reflexive verbs

These are used:

▪ when you carry out an action that involves yourself, e.g. *je me lave* (but *je lave la voiture*).
▪ to talk about interactions between people, e.g. *elle se dispute avec son frère*.

Don't forget to shorten the reflexive pronouns *me, te* and *se* before a vowel, e.g. *s'appelle*.

See the verb table on page 192 for more information.

Also learn about disjunctive pronouns and their use.

See page 46 ➡

Grammaire page 181

5 🗨🔊 Work with a partner (not your best friend) and interview them about their own and their friends' qualities.

▪ Quelles sont tes qualités?
▪ Comment s'appelle ton meilleur ami / ta meilleure amie?
▪ Tu t'entends bien avec lui / elle tout le temps?
▪ Quelles sont les qualités importantes d'un bon ami / d'une bonne amie?
▪ Qu'est-ce que tu as fait le week-end dernier avec tes copains / copines?
▪ Tu as un petit ami / une petite amie?

🗨 When speaking in French, remember that many endings are silent. The following consonants are usually silent at the end of a word:

d (froid), g (long), m (parfum), n (balcon), p (beaucoup), s (trois), t (vert), x (deux), z (riz).

These consonants are usually sounded:

b (club), c (avec), f (sportif), k (anorak), l (avril), q (cinq), r (hiver).

Stratégie

Quelles sont tes qualités?

On dit que je suis assez amusante, mais de temps en temps je suis un peu timide.

On dit que je suis	(très / un peu) sympa / amusant(e).	
Je m'entends bien avec lui / elle parce que / qu'	nous nous intéressons aux mêmes choses.	
	il / elle est amusant(e) / fidèle.	
Un(e) bon(ne) ami(e) doit être	loyal(e) / compréhensif(-ve).	
Le week-end dernier, nous avons / on a	joué au foot / fait du shopping ensemble.	
Nous sommes / On est	allé(e)s en ville, sorti(e)s ensemble.	
J'ai un petit ami / une petite amie	et il / elle est vraiment sympa.	
Je n'ai pas de petit(e) ami(e)	parce que	je suis trop jeune / je veux passer mes examens avant de sortir avec quelqu'un.

To talk about your own qualities, you might like to mention what others say about you. You can use the expression *On dit que je suis …* (People say that I am …).

Astuce

L'avenir

1 Maintenant: Mes parents sont divorcés, comme beaucoup d'autres. Je vis avec ma mère et mes sœurs. Ma mère trouve que le mariage n'est pas nécessaire, et moi aussi. Vivre en concubinage, c'est moins cher que de se marier. À mon avis, il n'est pas important de se marier pour avoir une famille.

2 Maintenant: J'apprécie la solitude. Je n'ai pas beaucoup d'amis de mon âge, mais je fais du babysitting quelquefois et ça me plaît.

3 Maintenant: Pour moi la religion est importante. Je suis chrétien. J'ai une petite amie, et on est ensemble depuis un an. Elle habite chez ses parents. Je ne veux pas vivre avec elle sans être marié.

a À l'avenir: Je trouverai un partenaire très sympa et loyal, et on vivra ensemble. On aura tous les deux un bon travail. Je ne resterai pas à la maison pour m'occuper des enfants, je payerai quelqu'un pour les garder.

b À l'avenir: Je me marierai à l'église, peut-être dans trois ou quatre ans. Je trouve que la cérémonie de mariage est très romantique. Ça sera un bon souvenir pour toute la vie. Mais nous n'aurons pas d'enfants. Ils m'énervent.

c À l'avenir: J'achèterai un appartement en ville. Je ne me marierai pas, mais j'aurai peut-être un enfant. À mon avis, une famille monoparentale n'est pas une mauvaise idée.

1a 📖🎧 Match up each picture (A–C) with one of the paragraphs about life at the moment (1–3) and one of the paragraphs about life in the future (a–c).

1b 📖🎧 Who says the following? Write the letter of the picture (A–C) in each case.

1 J'ai l'intention de vivre avec un partenaire sans me marier avec lui.
2 J'aime vivre seule.
3 Je voudrais me marier quand je serai assez jeune.
4 Je ne vais pas avoir d'enfants.
5 Le mariage coûte cher.
6 Pour moi, avoir un bon emploi est important.
7 Je vais avoir un bon souvenir du jour de mon mariage.

2a 🎧 Listen to the three speakers and choose three qualities that each person would like in his / her ideal partner.

1 Chloé   2 Vincent   3 Patricia

a musical   d clever   g quiet   j rich
b self-confident   e good-looking   h average height   k fond of children
c shy   f funny   i generous

2b 🎧 Listen again and answer the questions in English.

1 How would Chloé's partner show his generosity?
2 What is the most important quality in a partner for Vincent?
3 How does he see the future? Give three details.
4 What qualities does Patricia not like?
5 How does she envisage her partner's marriage proposal?

3a **G** Fill in the gaps in the table.

travailler	to work	attendre	to wait
je travaillerai	I shall work	j'_____	I shall wait
tu _____	you will work	tu attendras	you will wait
il / elle travaillera	he / she will work	il / elle _____	he / she will wait
nous _____	we shall work	nous attendrons	we shall wait
vous travaillerez	you will work	vous _____	you will wait
ils / elles _____	they will work	ils / elles attendront	they will wait

The future tense

To form the future tense for *-er* and *-ir* verbs, use the infinitive as the stem and add the following endings: *-ai, -as, -a, -ons, -ez, -ont*.

If the infinitive ends in *-re*, remove the *-e* before adding the endings, e.g. *elle attendra*.

Revise phrases such as *je voudrais, j'aimerais, j'ai l'intention de* + infinitive to express future intentions.

See page 46 ➡️

Grammaire page 183

3b **G** Transform the following sentences so they are in the future tense.

1 Ils vont fêter leurs fiançailles.
2 Je vais sortir avec ma petite amie ce soir.
3 Elle va répondre à ma demande en mariage.
4 Je vais tomber amoureuse à l'âge de 25 ans.
5 Vous allez vivre ensemble?
6 Nous allons nous marier à l'église.

4 🗨️ 🌐 Conduct a survey on the qualities people would like in their future ideal partner. Here are some possible questions but you could invent more of your own. Ask the questions to each person in your group.

- Comment sera-t-il / elle?
- Qu'est-ce qu'il / elle aimera faire de son temps libre?
- Est-ce qu'il / elle aimera les enfants?
- Qu'est-ce qu'il / elle fera dans la vie comme métier?
- Tu te marieras avec lui / elle?
- Si tu réponds oui à cette question, où et quand?
- Si tu réponds non à cette question, pourquoi pas?

🗨️ Part of your examination will involve answering questions for which you have not prepared. If, for example, you are talking about your future plans, you may be asked if you want to get married. Also think of the likely follow-up questions, such as: How old will you be? Describe your ideal partner. Do you want children?

Stratégie

It is better to use the future tense when talking about future plans, e.g. *sera* (will be) rather than *va être* (is going to be). Verbs that are irregular in the future tense (*être, avoir*, etc.) are covered on pages 42–43.

Astuce

Mon / Ma partenaire idéal(e) sera	gentil(le) / sympa / généreux(-euse).
Il / elle aimera	faire du sport / aller au ciné / écouter de la musique / danser / faire du cyclisme.
Il / elle va avoir des enfants / ne vas pas avoir d'enfants	parce qu'ils sont (souvent) adorables / mignons / casse-pieds / méchants.
On se mariera	à l'âge de … ans / à l'église / dans un château.
Je vivrai avec mon / ma partenaire sans me marier	parce que (pour moi) le mariage n'est pas important / essentiel.

1.8 L'égalité des chances

Discussing gender issues
Verbs which take the infinitive
Agreeing and disagreeing

1 **V** Match each phrase with its English translation.

1 l'égalité des chances
2 un métier traditionnellement masculin
3 un métier traditionnellement féminin
4 un métier d'homme
5 un métier de femme
6 lutter contre la discrimination

a a man's job
b equality of opportunity
c a job usually done by women
d a job usually done by men
e to fight discrimination
f a woman's job

Des livres scolaires sexistes?

A Aujourd'hui, l'école est présentée comme le lieu où on doit lutter contre toute forme de discrimination et pour l'égalité des chances. Mais malheureusement, selon une enquête récente, ce n'est pas le cas. Le sexisme existe toujours dans les livres scolaires.

B Dans beaucoup de livres, les filles font des activités traditionnellement féminines, comme le ménage ou le shopping. On les voit souvent dans la cuisine, tandis que les garçons font du sport au terrain de foot.

C Voici un exemple des exercices de maths dans un livre publié récemment: «À 13 ans, Julie pesait 50 kg. Depuis, son poids a augmenté de 10 % chaque année. À 16 ans, elle décide de faire un régime. Elle perd 5 kilos. Combien pèse-t-elle?» «Pierre a placé 20 000 euros à un taux d'intérêts de 4 % chaque année. Calculez la somme dont Pierre disposera dans trois ans». Aux garçons donc la performance financière et professionnelle, aux filles la tâche de s'occuper de leur corps pour plaire.

D Certains livres vont plus loin encore: dans un livre d'anglais, un dessin représente «une femme qui ne sait pas utiliser

son sèche-cheveux: elle n'a pas compris que les prises électriques n'étaient pas les mêmes en France et en Angleterre!» Ici, c'est le stéréotype de la femme stupide! Voilà comment on perpétue le sexisme de la société dans nos écoles, tandis que dans la vraie vie les femmes sont capables de faire la plupart des métiers traditionnellement masculins – et de les faire aussi bien (ou mieux) que les hommes.

2a Read the article and choose a suitable title for each paragraph.

1 Sexist sums!
2 The conclusion of a recent study
3 Women trapped in the home
4 Women are every bit as competent as men

2b According to the article, decide whether the sentences are true (T), false (F) or not mentioned (?).

1 Les livres scolaires ne sont plus sexistes.
2 Dans certains livres, les filles font des activités dangereuses.
3 Dans certains livres, les garçons font souvent des activités physiques.
4 Dans le livre de maths, Julie était préoccupée par son apparence physique.
5 Dans le même livre, Pierre voulait travailler dans une banque.
6 Dans le livre d'anglais, on donnait une mauvaise image de la femme.

3 🎧 Listen to the three speakers and answer the questions in English.

1 What does **Emma** particularly like about her job?

2 What are her plans for the future?

3 What does she need to do to achieve her plans? (2)

4 In what way have mentalities changed, according to **Margot**?

5 What was her father's reaction to her choice of career and what does he think now? (2)

6 What is the only drawback of her job?

7 What problem did **Océane** find after she had started her new business?

8 Why was this problem soon overcome?

9 For what other reason does she not have difficulty finding customers?

Astuce

Watch out for *faux amis* (false friends) in listening and reading texts. These words look like English words but have different meanings in French. Some common ones are: *un car* (a coach), *sensible* (sensitive), *une journée* (a day) and *la déception* (disappointment).

4 Ⓖ Complete each sentence with the correct infinitive from the list.

1 Elle veut _____ mécanicienne.

2 Je ne peux pas _____ de nuit.

3 Est-ce que tu sais _____ un camion?

4 Elles doivent _____ des études pendant deux ans.

5 Pouvez-vous me _____ des conseils?

6 On doit _____ les clients avec le sourire.

conduire	devenir	donner	faire
	servir	travailler	

Grammaire page 179

Verbs which take the infinitive

All verbs of liking, disliking and preferring (such as *aimer, adorer, préférer, détester*) are followed by the infinitive. The same applies to *savoir* and to modal verbs: *vouloir*, *pouvoir* and *devoir*.

J'aime danser. – I like dancing.
Je dois travailler. – I have to work.

Also revise the verbs which are followed by *à* or *de* before an infinitive.   *See page 47* ➡

5 🗨 🔊 Work with a partner and say if you agree or disagree with these statements.

■ Il y a certains métiers qui sont réservés aux hommes.

■ Les filles ne font pas d'activité physique.

■ Les garçons ne s'intéressent pas à leur apparence.

■ Les femmes avec des enfants doivent rester à la maison.

■ Les garçons ne font pas assez de tâches ménagères.

■ Les femmes reçoivent toujours le même salaire que les hommes pour le même travail.

Stratégie

🗨 When discussing a subject with someone, you will need to know phrases for expressing your agreement or disagreement with their point of view.

To agree: *c'est vrai / tu as raison / je suis d'accord / exactement / justement*

To disagree: *c'est faux / tu as tort / je ne suis pas du tout d'accord / certainement pas / ce n'est pas exact*

Il y a certains métiers qui sont réservés aux hommes.

C'est faux. Les femmes sont capables de faire exactement les mêmes métiers que les hommes. Par exemple, ma sœur travaille comme mécanicienne.

Tu as tort! Les filles sont souvent très actives …	Elles font du sport, elles font de la danse …
Ce n'est pas vrai. Les garçons s'occupent de plus en plus de leur apparence …	Ils s'intéressent à la mode, ils achètent des vêtements …
C'est ridicule! Les femmes ont le droit de travailler …	Elles sont plus travailleuses que les hommes … Les hommes doivent garder les enfants eux aussi.
C'est peut-être vrai. Les garçons sont paresseux …	Ils ne savent pas cuisiner, ils n'aiment pas faire la lessive / la vaisselle …
Malheureusement, ce n'est pas exact …	Les femmes sont souvent mal payées et c'est un scandale.

1.9 Le racisme

Objectifs

Discussing race issues

Making comparisons

Verbs ending in *-ger* and *-cer*

1 ⓥ Find the correct definition for the following words.

1	un musulman	a	un vêtement qui couvre la tête
2	la fête de l'Aïd el Kebir	b	un lieu où l'on met les morts dans les tombeaux
3	la mosquée	c	une personne de la religion islamique
4	un réfugié	d	un lieu de prière pour les musulmans
5	la discrimination	e	une personne de la communauté israélite
6	un cimetière	f	le traitement inégal d'un groupe de personnes
7	le foulard	g	une personne de la religion catholique ou protestante
8	un juif	h	une personne qui a quitté son pays pour éviter un danger
9	un chrétien	i	on la célèbre pendant le dernier mois du calendrier islamique

Les immigrés en France

A Il y a cinq millions d'immigrés en France. La plupart de ces immigrés viennent de l'Afrique du Nord (la Tunisie, le Maroc ou l'Algérie). Ils habitent surtout dans les grandes villes industrielles. Ils sont venus en France principalement pour des raisons économiques, pour trouver du travail. Les immigrés ont influencé la musique, la cuisine et la culture françaises.

B Halima, 15 ans, parle de son expérience …

«Mes parents sont arrivés de Tunisie il y a trente ans parce qu'ils voulaient trouver du travail et une meilleure vie. Nous habitons dans la banlieue parisienne dans un appartement au sixième étage d'un grand immeuble. Je suis née en France et je suis Française mais je suis fière de la culture tunisienne. J'aime la cuisine tunisienne et j'écoute de la musique populaire d'Afrique du Nord. Mes parents m'ont dit qu'ils ont rencontré des gens racistes surtout quand ils cherchaient du travail. Mais moi, je crois que les gens sont plus tolérants maintenant. Tout le monde s'entend bien dans mon école. En revanche, je ne peux pas porter le foulard islamique quand je vais au collège. Je trouve cela inacceptable. Beaucoup de mes profs sont d'accord avec moi.»

2 📖🎧 Decide whether the statements are true (T), false (F) or not mentioned (?) in the article. Read Section A for statements 1–3 and Section B for statements 4–9.

1 La Tunisie est un pays nord-africain.
2 Beaucoup d'immigrés sont venus en France pour retrouver leur famille.
3 Les immigrés ont influencé ce qu'on mange en France.
4 La famille d'Halima habite au centre de Paris.
5 Halima est née en Tunisie.
6 Les parents d'Halima travaillent dans une usine parisienne.
7 Ils ont été victimes de discrimination raciale.
8 Halima veut porter le foulard islamique au collège.
9 Elle veut devenir professeur.

3a 🎧 Listen to the five news reports (a–e) and match these headlines with the correct news items.

1 Vandalism of graves
2 Racist incident in school
3 A racist mugging
4 Campsite owner guilty of racism
5 Racism in a stadium

40 quarante

3b 🎧 Listen again and correct the mistakes in these statements.

1 L'élève musulmane était absente parce qu'on ne lui permettait pas de porter le foulard islamique.
2 On a agressé l'homme parce qu'il était riche.
3 Un incident raciste a eu lieu pendant un match de basketball.
4 On a trouvé des graffitis sur des tombeaux chrétiens.
5 La propriétaire du camping a refusé un emplacement aux deux sœurs parce qu'elles étaient en retard.

4 🅖 Give your opinion of the following statements, using *plus*, *moins* or *aussi* plus an appropriate adjective.

Exemple: L'éducation est <u>plus efficace</u> que les campagnes publicitaires.

Use these adjectives or choose your own.

efficace	intelligent	travailleur
sérieux	actif	joli	pratique

1 Les femmes sont _____ que les hommes.
2 Les jeunes sont _____ que les personnes plus âgées.
3 La France est _____ que la Grande-Bretagne.
4 Les campings sont _____ que les hôtels.
5 Le foot est _____ que le rugby.
6 Le racisme est _____ que le sexisme.

5 ✏️ 🔍 Write an account for a newspaper about a racist incident you have witnessed or read about, giving your views on the subject.

- ▪ Where and when did the incident take place?
- ▪ What happened?
- ▪ How did it make you feel?
- ▪ What do you think should happen as a result?

L'incident a eu lieu	samedi / il y a un mois / la semaine dernière	dans la rue / dans un bus / au stade.
Un homme a	agressé … / insulté … / refusé de …	
Un groupe de jeunes ont		
Cet incident m'a	attristé(e) / déprimé(e) / fâché(e) / enragé(e).	
À mon avis, il faut	punir les coupables / supprimer … / interdire …	
On devrait		

Grammaire   *page 174*

Making comparisons

To make a comparison you use the words *plus* (more), *moins* (less) or *aussi* (as), then an adjective followed by *que* and whatever it is you are comparing.

Note that *meilleur* means 'better' and *pire* means 'worse'.

Les agressions racistes sont plus inquiétantes que les slogans.

Ces gens-là sont pires que des animaux.

Also examine gender patterns in nouns.   *See page 47* ➡️

Stratégie

✏️ A *c* or *g* followed by *e* or *i* is soft.

To soften a *c* before *a*, *o* or *u* you need a cedilla. For example, in verbs ending in *-cer: je commence* ➡️ *nous commençons*.

To soften a *g* before *a*, *o* or *u* you need to add an *e*. For example, in verbs ending in *-ger: je mange* ➡️ *nous mangeons*.

Astuce

When writing French, you can often start with a phrase such as: *Ce que j'aime, c'est …*, *Ce que je n'aime pas, c'est …*, *Ce qui me plaît, c'est …*, *Ce qui ne me plaît pas, c'est …*, *Ce qui me choque, c'est …*, *Ce qui me surprend, c'est …* etc.

Objectifs

Discussing poverty

Irregular future forms

Picking out key words

Le travail bénévole

A

1 Léon habite à Paris, où il y a environ 5 000 hommes et femmes sans domicile fixe dans les rues. Il travaille pour une organisation qui s'occupe des personnes défavorisées. Presque toujours, ces personnes sont sans travail, elles ont faim et elles n'ont pas de logement. «Ma responsabilité, c'est d'offrir de la soupe et une tranche de pain à chaque personne malheureuse qui arrive au centre», dit Léon.

2 Thomas travaille comme bénévole pour une association caritative. Il remplit des cartons de toutes sortes de choses pour les SDF, par exemple des sacs de couchage, du shampooing et du savon. Comme ils sont au chômage, ils n'ont pas assez d'argent pour s'acheter les choses indispensables. «Ces pauvres gens attendent avec impatience notre arrivée. À l'avenir, je ferai de mon mieux pour aider les sans-abri», déclare Thomas.

B

C

3 Jules est bénévole pour un groupe sportif qui aide les jeunes des quartiers défavorisés. Il passe cinq heures par semaine à faire du sport dans les centres de loisirs d'un quartier de Paris où il y a beaucoup de familles pauvres. Jules dit que «la première fois, il n'y avait que cinq garçons et trois filles, mais ils ont parlé à leurs voisins et maintenant on a trente jeunes personnes dans notre groupe! Il y aura bientôt un deuxième groupe et on aura besoin de plus de volontaires.»

1a 📖🎧🌐 Read the article and write the name of the appropriate person for each picture (A–C).

1b 📖🎧🌐 Which four of the following sentences are true according to the article?

1 La plupart des sans-abri sont au chômage.
2 L'organisation de Léon donne des vêtements aux sans-abri.
3 Les sans-abri sont toujours contents de voir les travailleurs bénévoles.
4 Jules gagne de l'argent en travaillant pour son association.
5 Le sport donne de l'espoir aux jeunes défavorisés.
6 Jules vient d'une famille pauvre.
7 Le groupe de Jules a réussi à encourager plus de jeunes à faire du sport.

📖 **Stratégie** Searching for key words can save time and lead you to the answer more quickly. For example, if you are asked the question 'when?' you would look for a time, a date, a month, a day, etc. If you are asked about the advantages of something, you would look for positive words, such as *utile* or *intéressant*.

2 🎧 Listen to Sections A and B and correct the following sentences.

A 1 The new programme has been launched to help adults suffering from hunger.

    2 The vast majority of children in Rwanda are homeless.

    3 Vitamins are being given to all children under the age of five.

B 4 There is a lack of food due to the cold.

    5 Many farms were damaged during the earthquake.

    6 Many children have no parents due to malaria.

    7 The charity would like to build new schools.

    8 They want children to have more information about careers.

> **Le sais-tu?**
>
>
>
> Médecins Sans Frontières est une association humanitaire fondée en 1971 par un groupe de médecins français. L'association aide les victimes de la guerre et des catastrophes naturelles un peu partout dans le monde. Les médecins et les infirmiers qui travaillent pour l'association sont des volontaires.

3 Ⓖ Complete each sentence by choosing the correct verb you need from the list, then write it in the future tense, using the correct stem and ending.

    1 Je _____ du travail bénévole quand je serai plus âgé.

    2 Les enfants _____ contents de recevoir le nouveau matériel scolaire.

    3 Le gouvernement _____ à combattre le problème.

    4 Elle _____ en Afrique pour aider les enfants malades.

    5 Est-ce que les sans-abri _____ leur soupe ce soir?

    6 Il _____ pour *Médecins Sans Frontières*.

aller	travailler	être
avoir	faire	commencer

> **Grammaire** — *page 183*
>
> **Irregular future forms**
>
> Most verbs use the infinitive to form the future tense, but some irregular verbs use a different stem:
>
> *être* ➡ *ser-: je serai* – I shall be
>
> *avoir* ➡ *aur-: il aura* – he will have
>
> *aller* ➡ *ir-: nous irons* – we shall go
>
> *faire* ➡ *fer-: ils feront* – they will do
>
> See further examples of irregular future tense verbs.   *See page 47* ➡

4 ✏ Imagine that you do some voluntary work for a charity on a regular basis. Give some information about your work.

- What kind of organisation do you work for?
- What hours do you work each week?
- What do you do?
- What do you think of the work?
- Who will benefit from your work?
- What are the plans of the organisation for the future?

> **Astuce**
>
> Try to make your sentences longer by using connectives wherever possible. *Parce que, car, alors* and *donc* are all useful words for lengthening your sentences.

Je travaille pour une organisation qui	aide les enfants / s'occupe des animaux / combat la pauvreté / collecte de l'argent pour les SDF.
Chaque semaine je consacre Chaque semaine je passe	deux heures à ce travail / une partie du week-end à l'organisation. une soirée à travailler pour cette organisation.
Je vends J'organise Je collecte Je passe du temps avec	des magazines / des vêtements. des jeux / des événements spéciaux. pas mal d'argent. des enfants / des personnes âgées / des animaux.
Je trouve le travail J'aime le contact avec	satisfaisant / enrichissant. les personnes défavorisées.
Notre travail est / sera utile aux enfants Notre organisation est / sera utile aux gens	parce qu'ils comprendront qu'ils ne sont pas seuls. parce qu'ils recevront des conseils / de l'aide / de l'argent / de quoi manger.
À l'avenir, on fera construire On aidera	un nouveau centre d'accueil. encore plus de gens.

Relationships and choices

Pavel – bon fils, bon frère

A Je m'appelle Pavel. J'habite avec mon père et ma sœur, Sonia. Elle a six ans et elle est handicapée. Mon père est veuf depuis trois ans. Sa vie est difficile car il travaille dans un hôpital, mais il doit aussi s'occuper de ma sœur. Moi, je m'entends bien avec mon père et ma sœur.

B Comme mon père travaille, je passe beaucoup de temps avec Sonia. Le matin, je l'aide à se laver et à s'habiller. Normalement, elle passe la journée à l'école primaire et moi, je vais au collège. À trois heures et demie, je vais chercher Sonia et je m'occupe d'elle avant la rentrée de papa.

C S'il fait beau, nous allons au parc. Elle adore donner du pain aux oiseaux sur le lac et en été, si j'ai de l'argent, j'achète des glaces au kiosque. Le trajet du parc à la maison peut être difficile car les trottoirs de notre ville ne sont pas bien adaptés aux fauteuils roulants et souvent les automobilistes ne sont pas très patients quand nous traversons la rue.

D Hier, nous avons parlé des vacances d'été. Nous allons passer une semaine dans un hôtel à la campagne. Ce sera la première fois depuis la mort de ma mère que nous allons partir en vacances car papa ne gagne pas beaucoup d'argent. C'est ma grand-mère qui a réservé les chambres et elle va nous accompagner.

E Pour moi, c'est difficile de sortir avec mes copains ou de faire du sport en semaine, à cause de ma sœur, mais le samedi, ma grand-mère passe la journée chez nous. Elle reste avec ma sœur et range un peu la maison. Ça permet à mon père de faire du shopping et je peux aller au centre sportif. Je joue au basket et j'aime nager. J'adore ma sœur, mais j'aime aussi beaucoup le samedi car je suis avec mes copains.

F Je passe la plupart des dimanches à la maison, mais dimanche dernier, j'ai joué dans un tournoi de basket, et l'après-midi, papa et Sonia sont venus voir le dernier match. C'était bien parce que notre équipe a gagné.

> **Grammaire** page 181
>
> There are several reflexive verbs in the article. Can you find three examples when Pavel is talking about himself, and three when he is talking about his sister or father?
>
> To remind yourself how to use reflexive verbs, see page 35.

1a 📖 🎧 Read the article and choose a suitable title for each paragraph.

1 Du travail au collège et à la maison
2 Des projets pour un séjour en famille
3 La famille va au centre sportif
4 Une petite famille avec de grandes responsabilités
5 Les promenades – un moment important malgré les efforts
6 Un samedi sportif

1b 📖🎧 Read the article in detail and answer the questions in English.

1 When did Pavel's mother die?

2 What does Pavel do at 3.30pm?

3 What does Sonia especially like to do at the park?

4 What two difficulties does Pavel mention about the walk home from the park?

5 Why has Pavel not had a holiday recently?

6 Why is Saturday important to Pavel?

AQA *Examiner's tip*

The type of task in activity 1b refers to the whole article, but usually the questions roughly follow the order of the text. It is unlikely that you will need to read the whole passage six times to find the answers.

2a 🎧 Listen to five participants speaking on a radio phone-in programme about discrimination related to work. From the choices below, identify what each person is complaining about.

1 **Élodie**

  a The attitude of the men she works with

  b The quality of refreshments in the office

  c The rude manners of her boss

2 **Dolorès**

  a Her colleagues at work

  b Her working hours

  c Conditions in the nursery

3 **Thierry**

  a The type of work he had to do

  b The behaviour of colleagues towards him

  c The behaviour of colleagues towards another employee

4 **Graziella**

  a The number of people she has to supervise

  b The amount she earns in comparison to others

  c The amount of work she has to do

5 **Jean-François**

  a The conditions where he works

  b Having to give up playing rugby when he starts his new job

  c The attitude of his friends towards his job

Vocabulaire

le fauteuil roulant	wheelchair
gagner	to win / earn
se moquer de	to make fun of
le niveau	level
s'occuper de	to be busy with / to look after
ranger	to tidy
le veuf	widower

Grammaire pages 182, 183

Two of the speakers are talking about something that they are going to do. They could have said, e.g. *j'en parlerai* … or *je commencerai* … but they use a different form of the future tense. Can you pick out exactly what they say?

For more information on talking about the future, see page 37.

2b 🎧 Listen again to all the speakers. Who is being referred to in each of the sentences below? Write E (Élodie), D (Dolorès), T (Thierry), G (Graziella) or JF (Jean-François).

1 xxxxx is talking about a new job he/she is about to start.

2 xxxxx works for a construction company.

3 xxxxx witnessed racism at work.

4 xxxxx is in charge of a number of employees.

5 xxxxx has difficulties with childcare arrangements.

6 xxxxx has recently worked in a car repair business.

7 xxxxx earns less than a man who does the same work.

AQA *Examiner's tip*

Activity 2b is an example of a task where you need to think about what clues there are in the questions that might help you. For example, question 1 is about the future, while question 6 refers to the past, so you need to listen for people using the appropriate tense.

G Relationships and choices

Adjective agreement; disjunctive pronouns; *je voudrais* and *j'ai l'intention de*

1 Complete each sentence with the correct form of the adjective(s) given.

1 Il a des parents riche et célèbre .
2 Ses petit sœurs sont très mignon .
3 Elle vient d'une famille monoparental .
4 J'ai une copine très gentil mais timide .
5 Ma grand sœur est très jaloux .
6 Ta grand-mère est déprimé parce qu'elle est seul .

2 Follow the English prompts to complete these sentences, then translate them into English.

1 Tu te disputes souvent _____? (with her)
2 Tu ne peux pas vivre _____! (without me)
3 Je ne m'entends pas bien _____. (with them – F)
4 Le chat est _____. (for you – singular informal)
5 J'ai l'intention de loger _____. (at their house – M & F)
6 Tu voudrais être _____? (like him)

3 Complete the sentences with words chosen from the list.

1 Je _____ remercier mes parents.
2 J' _____ avoir beaucoup d'enfants.
3 Je ne _____ pas _____ sans voisins.
4 Ils n' _____ pas l'intention de _____!
5 Elle _____ _____ un gâteau.
6 J' _____ l'intention de me marier.

ai   aimerais   divorcer   être

manger   ont   voudrais

voudrais   voudrait

Adjective agreement

Adjectives have different endings depending on whether they describe masculine, feminine, singular or plural nouns. You usually add -e for feminine and -s for plural nouns.

un grand frère et deux petites sœurs

When you look up a word in the vocabulary section, feminine forms of adjectives are given in brackets, e.g. *mignon(ne), gentil(le), jaloux(-se)*.

Adjectives usually go after the noun. However, *petit, grand* and *joli* go before the noun, e.g. *une jolie maison*.

Grammaire page 173

Disjunctive pronouns

Use these pronouns after prepositions (e.g. *avec, sans, chez, pour, comme*).

moi	me
toi	you (singular informal)
lui	him
elle	her
nous	us
vous	you (plural or singular formal)
eux	them (masculine)
elles	them (feminine)

Il s'entend bien avec moi.   He gets on well with me.

Tu es triste sans lui.   You are sad without him.

These pronouns are also known as emphatic pronouns.

Grammaire page 178

Je voudrais and *j'ai l'intention de*

When *je voudrais, j'aimerais* or *j'ai l'intention de* are followed by another verb, that verb is in the infinitive.

J'aimerais avoir un chien.   I would like to have a dog.

Elle voudrait avoir deux enfants.   She would like to have two children.

Il a l'intention d'écrire à son père.   He intends to write to his father.

Grammaire page 179

Verbs that take *à* or *de*; masculine and feminine nouns; irregular future tense

4 Choose between *à* and *de / d'* to complete each gap in the text below.

Le mois dernier, mon cousin Théo a décidé ❶ _____ arrêter ❷ _____ fumer. Il a réussi ❸ _____ ne pas allumer une seule cigarette! Comme ça, il a commencé ❹ _____ mettre de l'argent de côté. Il essaie aussi ❺ _____ faire du sport et il apprend ❻ _____ jouer au tennis. J'espère qu'il va aider sa copine Mona ❼ _____ faire la même chose. Pour l'instant, elle continue ❽ _____ acheter des cigarettes et elle refuse ❾ _____ arrêter.

5 Masculine or feminine? Find the odd one out in each box.

alimentation   citron   obésité   pomme

activité   alcoolisme   tabagisme   tabac

désintoxication   cancer   relaxation   spécialité

6a Same verb – different tense. Match up the verbs to make pairs.

1 faudra   a je sais
2 verras   b tu veux
3 sauront   c nous pouvons
4 viendra   d elles viennent
5 pourra   e vous voyez
6 voudrez   f il faut

6b Use the six future tense verbs from activity 6a to complete the sentences.

1 On _____ fêter ton anniversaire.
2 Il _____ en vacances avec nous.
3 Est-ce que vous _____ loger chez moi?
4 Il _____ que tu remercies ta grand-mère.
5 Ils ne _____ pas se débrouiller seuls.
6 Tu _____ mieux avec des lunettes.

Grammaire page 179

Verbs that take *à* or *de*

These verbs need *à* to introduce the infinitive that follows:

aider *à*   to help
apprendre *à*   to learn
arriver *à*   to manage
commencer *à*   to start
continuer *à*   to continue
réussir *à*   to succeed
J'apprends à nager.   I am learning to swim.

These verbs need *de* (or *d'*) before the infinitive that follows:

arrêter *de*   to stop
décider *de*   to decide
essayer *de*   to try
oublier *de*   to forget
refuser *de*   to refuse
Il a arrêté de fumer.   He stopped smoking.

Grammaire page 171

Masculine and feminine nouns

When learning a new noun, always learn whether it is masculine or feminine. There are patterns to help you remember the correct gender.

All words ending in *-isme* are masculine:
l'alcoolisme, le tabagisme.

Most fruit items ending in *-e* are feminine:
la banane, la cerise, la fraise, la poire, la pomme.

Words ending in *-tion* are usually feminine:
l'alimentation, la dégustation.

Words ending in *-ité* are usually feminine:
l'activité, l'obésité, la spécialité.

Grammaire page 183

Irregular future tense

Here are some common irregular future tense forms that are worth learning by heart.

il faut   ➡ *il faudra*   It will be necessary to
pouvoir   ➡ *je pourrai*   I'll be able to
vouloir   ➡ *je voudrai*   I'll want to
savoir   ➡ *je saurai*   I'll know
voir   ➡ *je verrai*   I'll see
venir   ➡ *je viendrai*   I'll come

Relationships and choices

La famille ➡ pages 32–33

le	beau-père	stepfather (also means father-in-law)
la	belle-mère	stepmother (also means mother-in-law)
	casse-pieds	infuriating / a pain
	compréhensif(-ve)	understanding / tolerant
le	concubinage	living together (without being married)
le	demi-frère	half brother
	déprimé(e)	depressed
	se disputer	to argue
	s'entendre (avec quelqu'un) (entendu)	to get on (with someone)
l'	épouse (f)	wife (spouse)
l'	époux (m)	husband (spouse)
la	femme	woman / wife
	fier / fière	proud
	jaloux(-se)	jealous / possessive
le	mari	husband
le	mariage	marriage / wedding
	méchant(e)	nasty / naughty
	mignon(ne)	cute
	naître (né)	to be born
	pénible	annoying / a nuisance
le	sens de l'humour	sense of humour
	vivre (vécu)	to live

Les rapports avec les autres ➡ pages 34–35

j'en	ai marre!	I'm fed up!
s'	amuser	to have fun / to enjoy oneself
	calme	quiet / placid
se	confier à	to confide in
l'	ennui (m)	worry / problem / boredom
	ensemble	together
se	fâcher	to get cross

	gêné(e)	embarrassed
de	mauvaise humeur	in a bad mood
se	mettre en colère	to get angry
	plein(e) de vie	lively
	rendre (rendu)	to give back
	rire	to laugh
	souriant(e)	cheerful

L'avenir ➡ pages 36–37

	divorcé(e)	divorced
l'	église (f)	church
	épouser	to marry (someone)
	fêter	to celebrate
les	fiançailles (f)	engagement (to be married)
la	mairie	town hall
	se marier	to get married
	monoparental(e)	single-parent
	rencontrer	to meet
	vivre en concubinage	to live together (without being married)

1 **V** Match each term with its English translation.

1	des parents divorcés	a	parents who have separated
2	se marier à l'église	b	the joy of having children
3	vivre en concubinage	c	to get married at the town hall
4	des parents qui se sont séparés	d	divorced parents
5	une famille monoparentale	e	to get married in church
6	le bonheur d'avoir des enfants	f	a married couple
7	tomber amoureux de	g	to live with a partner
8	un couple marié	h	a single-parent family
9	se marier à la mairie	i	to fall in love with

L'égalité des chances ➡ *pages 38–39*

l'	avis (m)	opinion
	augmenter	to increase
le	camion	lorry
le / la	client(e)	customer
l'	égalité (f)	equality
l'	enquête (f)	enquiry / investigation
l'	entreprise (f)	business
	garder	to look after
le	lieu	place
	lutter	to struggle
le	métier	job / profession
	passer un examen	to take an exam
le	plombier	plumber
la	prise électrique	electric socket
le	régime	diet
le	sèche-cheveux	hair-dryer
la	tâche	task

Le racisme ➡ *pages 40–41*

	agresser	to attack / to assault
le	cimetière	cemetery
l'	emplacement (m)	place / site
la	fête de l'Aïd el Kebir	Id Ul Fitr festival
le	foulard	scarf
l'	immigré(e) (m / f)	immigrant
l'	immeuble (m)	building
	juif(-ve)	Jewish
la	manifestation	(public) demonstration
le	racisme	racism
	raciste	racist

La pauvreté ➡ *pages 42–43*

	améliorer	to improve
l'	argent (m)	money
le / la	bénévole	volunteer
la	chaleur	warmth / heat
le	chômage	unemployment
	consacrer	to devote (time)

	collecter (de l'argent)	to collect / to raise (money)
	défavorisé(e)	disadvantaged
	désespéré(e)	desperate
l'	espoir (m)	hope
la	guerre	war
le	manque	lack
	manquer	to miss / to be lacking
la	nourriture	food
	pauvre	poor
la	pauvreté	poverty
la	pluie	rain
l'	organisation caritative (f)	charity / charitable organisation
	sans domicile fixe	homeless
le / la	sans-abri	homeless person
le / la	SDF (sans domicile fixe)	homeless person
le	sida	AIDS
	souffrir (souffert)	to suffer
le	travail bénévole	voluntary work

2 Ⓥ Find the correct definition for each term.

1 un sans-abri
2 le chômage
3 une organisation caritative
4 un quartier défavorisé
5 le travail bénévole
6 la guerre
7 la faim

a le combat entre deux armées
b être sans travail
c un endroit où il y a beaucoup de pauvreté
d une personne qui n'a pas de maison
e quand on n'a pas assez à manger
f une association qui essaie d'aider les autres
g quand on aide les autres sans être payé

1 🗩 Une vie saine

You are talking to your French friend Anne-Marie about your lifestyle. She wants to know:

1 if you are in good health
2 if you eat healthily
3 if you exercise regularly
4 if you have a stressful lifestyle
5 if you smoke
6 if you drink alcohol
7 !

! Remember you will have to respond to something that you have not yet prepared.

1 **If you are in good health**
- Say that you are usually in good health and in good shape.
- Mention the last time you weren't well. Say what was wrong and how long it lasted.
- Say what you and others did about it.
- Say what you will do to avoid a recurrence of the problem.

2 **If you eat healthily**
- Say what you like to eat and drink and whether it is good for your health.
- Say whether you follow a particular diet and say why / why not.
- Say what you think people should do to avoid obesity.
- Say what you think is an ideal diet, mentioning all three meals.

3 **If you exercise regularly**
- Say which sports you play, when, where and who with.
- Explain the benefits of playing a sport, e.g. stay in good shape, sleep better, a way of meeting people, etc.
- Say how much walking and cycling you do (how far, how long for, how frequently).
- Say how fit you are and say what you intend to do to get fitter.

AQA Examiner's tips

Start off with *Oui, je suis en bonne santé.*
Use the imperfect tense to describe your symptoms, e.g. *J'avais de la fièvre,* but the perfect tense to say how long it lasted and what was done about it, e.g. *ça a duré ...*
Use the immediate future or the future tense to say what you will do, e.g. *Je vais porter .../ Je porterai ...*

AQA Examiner's tips

Now, start your plan. Write a maximum of six words for each of the seven sections that make up the task, remembering that the maximum altogether is 40, so two sections will need to have only five. Here are some suggested words for the first section: *bonne santé, rhume, symptômes, solution, s'habiller.*
Choose a complaint that you know the French for to write in your plan. You do not have to tell the truth. It is the quality of your French that is being assessed, not your ability to tell the truth in French.

AQA Examiner's tips

Use *Je fais un régime ...* to say that you follow a particular diet.
Use *Pour éviter l'obésité, il faut / il ne faut pas ...*
Start the last bullet point with *Pour un régime idéal, il faut / il ne faut pas* + verb in the infinitive.
Use key words like *régime* and *obésité* in your plan. They are good indicators that will remind you of what you intend to talk about.

AQA Examiner's tips

To explain the benefits of playing a sport, start with *Quand on fait du sport, on ...*
Start the last bullet point with *Pour être plus en forme, je vais / j'ai l'intention de ...* + infinitive.
As one word in your plan often represents more than one sentence, e.g. *sports* for the first bullet point, make sure you remember that you should talk about which sports you play, when, where and who with, i.e. four pieces of information. Associating sports with four pieces of information may well be enough for you to be able to recall what the pieces of information are.

4 If you have a stressful lifestyle

- Say whether you work too hard. Mention school work, homework and your part-time job.
- Say whether you sleep well. Mention the reasons for that.
- Say what makes you feel stressed, and what you do to avoid being stressed.
- Say what you think are the best ways of relieving stress.

> To say what makes you feel stressed, start with *Ce que je trouve stressant, c'est …*
> Use *Pour me relaxer, je …* to introduce the last point.
> If, when you take the task, you don't remember what a particular word is supposed to suggest to you, think back to the day when you were preparing for the task. If this process does not remind you, be creative and use other details.
>
> AQA Examiner's tips

5 If you smoke

- Say whether you have tried smoking and what you think of it.
- Say whether your friends / members of your family smoke and whether it is a problem.
- Say why you think young people start smoking. Explain why many continue to smoke later on.
- Explain the consequences of smoking in terms of health.

> Use *commencer à, continuer à, s'arrêter de* when 'start', 'continue' and 'stop' are followed by a verb, e.g. *Ils commencent à fumer …*
> To explain the consequences of smoking, use *le cancer du poumon / de la gorge.*
> Whenever possible, use words that are immediately understandable in your plan, e.g. *problème, conséquences.*
>
> AQA Examiner's tips

6 If you drink alcohol

- Say how often you drink alcohol and what you think of it.
- Say whether you think alcohol should be more expensive than it is.
- Say what you think the minimum legal age for drinking alcohol should be and say why.
- Explain what problems arise from people abusing alcohol.

> Use *devrait être* for 'should be', but with age use *avoir*, e.g. *On devrait avoir seize ans …*
> Use *Quand les gens boivent trop d'alcool …* to introduce the final point.
> Don't use the word *alcool* in your plan. As the question is 'Do you drink alcohol?', it is clear that everything you will talk about will refer to alcohol. Every word in your plan must be a help.
>
> AQA Examiner's tips

7 **!** At this point you may be asked:

- if you take drugs
- what you have done recently to improve your fitness
- how you intend to change your lifestyle in order to improve your health
- about the importance of peer group pressure in trying to have a healthy lifestyle.

> Choose the two options which you think are the most likely, and for each of these, note down three different ideas. In your plan, write three words that illustrate each of the two most likely options. For the first option you might choose: *opinion, prix, conséquences.* Remember to check the total number of words you have used. It should be 40 or fewer.
>
> AQA Examiner's tips

You should now have completed your plan and prepared your answers. Give your plan to your teacher for feedback. Compare your answers with the online sample version – you might find some useful hints to make yours even better.

kerboodle!

1 ✏ Les rapports avec les autres

You are writing to your French friend about relationships with family and friends and also about your choices for the future. You could include:

1 how you get on with your family
2 details of the person you get on with best
3 what you like to do with that person
4 what happened last time you went out as a family
5 details about your friends
6 where you intend to live in the future
7 what you plan to do when you leave home.

1 **How you get on with your family**
- Introduce the members of your family and say something different about each person.
- Mention the people you get on well with and say why.
- Mention who you have arguments with and say why.
- Give a short account of an argument.

2 **Details of the person you get on with best**
- Mention how he / she is related to you. Give his / her name, age and a physical description.
- Describe his / her personality and say which features of his / her personality you like.
- Say what you have in common and how you are different.
- Say how he / she gets on with the rest of the family.

3 **What you like to do with that person**
- Write about the activities that you do together and what you think of them.
- Mention your favourite activity (what, when, where, frequency).
- Write about what you like but he / she doesn't like and vice versa. Mention his / her favourite activity.
- Mention how often you go out together and if you would like to go out more frequently.

AQA Examiner's tips

Use *je ne m'entends pas bien avec …* to say that you don't get on with someone.
Use *se disputer* for 'to have an argument', e.g. *je me suis disputé(e) avec …* (I had an argument with …). If you are unsure of the perfect tense of reflexive verbs with *nous* or *on*, check the grammar section on page 181.

AQA Examiner's tips

Now, start your plan. Write a maximum of six words for each of the seven sections that make up the task. Remember that the total maximum is 40 words, so two sections will need to have only five. Here are some suggested words for the first section: *famille, membres, s'entendre, disputes, exemple.*
Your plan is very personal. Every word acts as a trigger that allows you to deliver several French sentences. Such connections in the brain would not be made by someone else using your plan.

AQA Examiner's tips

'Best' is a difficult word. *Le meilleur* is used with a noun, *le mieux* is used with a verb. In this case, use *le mieux* e.g. *Je m'entends le mieux avec …*
Use *pourtant, cependant, par contre, d'une part … d'autre part …* to introduce something that contrasts with what you have just said.
In order for you to know if the six words on your plan are the most useful ones, hide the four bullet points and see if you can remember everything you intended to say about them by looking only at your plan.

AQA Examiner's tips

Use a variety of verbs to describe activities, e.g. *faire, jouer, aller, écouter, regarder,* etc.
Remember that when one verb follows another, the second one should be in the infinitive, e.g. *j'aime jouer, il n'aime pas faire.*
Remember that you can only write verbs as the infinitive or the past participle on your plan.

4 What happened last time you went out as a family

- Mention when you went out, how you travelled and how long it took to get there.
- Mention where you went and why that particular place was chosen.
- Describe what you and other members of the family did together and separately.
- Include what was good about the day and what wasn't so good.

> **AQA Examiner's tips**
>
> Use expressions such as *d'abord, après, ensuite, finalement* to sequence the events you are describing in the perfect tense. When you are talking about you and someone else, you can use *nous* or *on*.
>
> Use the imperfect tense to give your opinion and say what things were like, e.g. *c'était ... , il y avait ...*
>
> Add up to six words to your plan.

5 Details about your friends

- Introduce them: who they are and why you are friends with them.
- Include what you like doing with them and when and where it takes place.
- Give details about your best friend and say how long you have been best friends for.
- Give details of an outing with your best friend and say what you thought of it.

> **AQA Examiner's tips**
>
> Use object pronouns (*le, la, l', les*) in order to avoid repetition of friends' names. Remember that the place of these pronouns is before the verb in French, e.g. *Je l'aime bien ...* See grammar section page 177.
>
> Use present tense + *depuis* to say how long you have been friends, e.g. *Nous sommes copains depuis ...* See grammar section page 188.
>
> The name of a place on your plan might be enough to account for a whole bullet point, e.g. Bournemouth might remind you of where you went, what you did there, when it was, how you got there, what the weather was like and whether you had a good time.

6 Where you intend to live in the future

- Write about when you intend to leave home and why.
- Write about where you intend to live and why that particular place.
- Mention how you will keep in touch with your family and how frequently.
- Mention how often you will visit them and why.

> **AQA Examiner's tips**
>
> Use various ways of referring to a future event, e.g. the future tense, *aller* + infinitive, *j'aimerais, je voudrais, j'espère, j'ai l'intention de ...*
>
> Use *garder le contact avec* for 'to keep in touch with'.
>
> Remember only to use words you know the meaning of on your plan. If you decide to add any new words, learn them well!

7 What you plan to do when you leave home

- Mention whether you would like to take a gap year and what you would do.
- Include whether you intend to get married and when.
- Include whether you would like to have children and why (not).
- Conclude by saying how important family and friends are to you and why.

> **AQA Examiner's tips**
>
> Use *une année sabbatique* for 'a gap year', then use the conditional, e.g. *J'irais ...* See grammar section page 183.
>
> Use *se marier* for 'to get married'. As you will use *je*, make sure you also use *me*. See grammar section on reflexive verbs page 181.
>
> Remember to check the total number of words you have used in your plan. It must be 40 or fewer.

You should now have completed your plan and prepared your answers. Give your plan to your teacher for feedback. Compare your answers with the online sample version – you might find some useful hints to make yours even better.

kerboodle!

1

Résumé

1 Choose the correct expression to complete this sentence:

Pour rester en forme, il faut boire beaucoup …

  a d'eau   c de bière

  b de coca   d de café

2 Choose the correct form of the verb to complete this sentence:

Les jeunes ne … pas assez de sport.

  a faire   c font

  b fait   d fais

3 Which of the following sentences is negative?

  a J'adore manger des fruits.

  b Je mange souvent des bananes.

  c Je ne mange plus de viande.

  d J'aime mieux manger au restaurant.

4 Which of the following contains a reflexive verb?

  a Je peux compter sur mes parents.

  b Je ne m'entends pas bien avec ma sœur.

  c J'ai souvent des disputes avec mes parents.

  d Mes parents sont trop stricts avec moi.

5 Find the correct French translation for this sentence:

I'm going to get married at the age of 25.

  a Je vais me marier à l'âge de vingt-cinq ans.

  b Il va se marier à l'âge de vingt-cinq ans.

  c Je vais me marier à l'âge de vingt-sept ans.

  d Je vais me reposer à l'âge de vingt-cinq ans.

6 Find the correct English translation for this sentence:

Beaucoup de sans-abri n'ont pas de travail.

  a Many homeless people have no means of transport.

  b Many unemployed people have no money.

  c Many disadvantaged people have no homes.

  d Many homeless people do not have jobs.

2 Leisure

Free time and the media

Free-time activities

2.1 Ce que j'ai fait chez moi
- Perfect tense with *avoir*
- Recognising time expressions

2.2 Les loisirs
- Perfect tense with *être*
- Using more than one time frame

Shopping, money, fashion and trends

2.3 L'argent et le shopping
- Direct object pronouns
- Using all three time frames

2.4 La mode
- Indirect object pronouns
- Working out the meaning of words

Advantages and disadvantages of new technology

2.5 Les nouvelles technologies
- Superlative adjectives
- Justifying your opinions

Holidays

Plans, preferences, experiences

2.6 Vive les vacances!
- The imperfect tense
- Saying what you know

2.7 Des projets de vacances
- Combining perfect and future tenses
- Recognising prefixes

What to see and getting around

2.8 Que faire en vacances?
- The conditional
- Structuring your answers

2.9 Les excursions
- The pronoun *y*
- Listening for gist

Sport and leisure; clothes

Je ne fais pas de musique, mais je fais de l'athlétisme et je joue au foot.

Je fais de la natation, mais ma passion, c'est la musique. Je joue du piano et de la flûte.

Nadia | **Théo** | **Alice** | **Mehdi**

Je joue au basket le samedi. L'été, je fais de la voile et du surf. Autrement, je joue de la guitare.

Je ne joue pas d'un instrument. Comme sport, je fais du judo et du skate.

Grammaire page 185

- When talking about games, use *jouer + au / à la / à l' / aux*.
Je joue au tennis / à la pétanque / aux cartes.

- For other sports and pastimes, use *faire + du / de la / de l' / des*:
Je fais du karaté / de la natation / de l'équitation.

- For musical instruments, use *jouer + du / de la / de l' / des*:
Je joue du violon / de la batterie.

a   b   c   d

e   f   g   h

1a 📖🎧 Read about each person's activities, and find the correct symbols for each one.

1b 🗨 Work in pairs. Partner B chooses one of the symbols from activity 1a. Partner A asks questions to find out which one it is. Then swap over.

Exemple: **A** Tu joues du piano?   **B** Non.
           A Tu fais du judo?

2a 📖🎧 Choose the correct picture to match the bubble.

Quand je joue dans mon orchestre, je porte une robe violette et des chaussures marron.

a    b    c

2b 📖✏ Complete these two speech bubbles to match the other two pictures from activity 2a.

1   Quand je _____,
     je porte un _____.

2   Quand je _____.

2c ✏ Describe what you normally wear for your two favourite activities.

Vocabulaire	
l'alto (m)	viola
l'athlétisme (m)	athletics
la batterie	drums
l'équitation (f)	horse riding
la flûte	flute
la natation	swimming
le skate	skateboarding
le violon	violin
la voile	sailing
les baskets (f)	trainers
la capuche	hood
le chapeau	hat
les chaussures (f)	shoes
la chemise	shirt
le jean	jeans
la jupe	skirt
le maillot de bain	swimming costume
le pantalon	trousers
la robe	dress
le short	shorts
le sweat	sweatshirt
For colours, see page 12.	

Transport; places in town; simple directions

1a 📖🎧 Read the report on how people get to school in Théo's class and find the matching pie chart.

> On a demandé aux élèves de ma classe «Comment est-ce que tu vas au collège?» Voici les réponses: 10% des élèves vont au collège en voiture, 20% y vont à vélo, 30% à pied et 40% en bus.

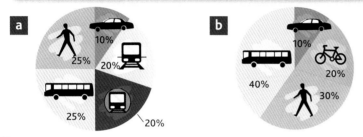

a

25%   10%   20%

25%   20%

b

10%   20%   30%

40%

1b ✏️ Write a report to go with the other pie chart from activity 1a.

1c 💬✏️ Interview at least ten of your school friends about how they travel to their holiday destinations and write a similar report.

2a 📖🎧 Find the correct sketch map for each dialogue.

1
– Pour aller à l'hôtel de ville, s'il vous plaît?
– Allez jusqu'au rond-point, puis continuez tout droit. Ce n'est pas loin.
– D'accord. Merci.

2
– Excusez-moi. Où est le marché, s'il vous plaît?
– Prenez la première rue à gauche. C'est à deux minutes.
– Je vous remercie.

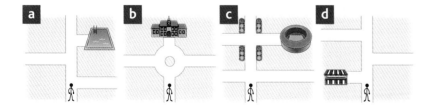

a   **b**   **c**   **d**

2b 💬 With a partner, read out the dialogues from activity 2a. Then make up two more dialogues to fit the other two maps.

Grammaire *page 187*

Use *au, à l', à la* or *aux* to introduce the names of places you are going to:
Je vais au cinéma. (m: à + le = au)
Tu vas à la patinoire. (f: à + la)
Elle va aux halles. (pl: à + les = aux)

Ce que j'ai fait chez moi

1 **V** Put these activities into groups – leisure activity, chore or both. Give an opinion about each activity.

promener le chien	faire les devoirs	lire un roman	faire la cuisine
ranger la chambre	faire du jardinage	jouer aux cartes	faire la lessive
jouer de la clarinette	faire des mots croisés	jouer aux fléchettes	surfer sur le net

Trois jeunes nous parlent de leur samedi

Charlotte

Samedi, j'ai rangé ma chambre et j'ai fait la lessive puis j'ai fait du jardinage pour mes parents. Samedi soir, j'ai joué aux cartes avec ma sœur et j'ai gagné cinq parties. Elle a pleuré parce qu'elle a perdu. Dimanche, j'ai regardé mon feuilleton favori et les actualités. J'ai fait mes devoirs de maths, quelle barbe! Et enfin, ma meilleure copine et moi avons bavardé au téléphone.

Alexis

J'ai dû rester à la maison parce que mes parents m'ont dit que je ne pouvais pas sortir avec mes copains. Il y a deux semaines, j'ai reçu de mauvaises notes au lycée, donc mon père m'a demandé de faire du travail dans ma chambre. En réalité, ma sœur et moi avons passé des heures à surfer sur le net. On a chatté avec des amis et plus tard, on a regardé des DVD.

Marine

Samedi dernier, j'ai fini mes devoirs puis j'ai promené le chien, comme d'habitude. Ensuite, j'ai écouté de la musique sur mon lecteur mp3 et j'ai joué de la clarinette. Plus tard, j'ai aidé mes parents et nous avons préparé le déjeuner ensemble. Le soir, j'ai lu un bon roman comique qui s'appelle *Miss la gaffe*. Je l'ai trouvé très amusant. J'aime aussi feuilleter les bandes dessinées. La télé ne me dit rien. Il y a beaucoup de chaînes mais généralement la télé-réalité est idiote. Avant de me coucher, j'ai aidé ma sœur à faire ses devoirs. Elle n'a pas compris ses devoirs de maths. Je l'aide souvent en ce moment.

2a 📖📖🎧 🌐 Read the article. Who says the following? Write C, A or M.

1 Je n'ai pas fait de travail scolaire.
2 J'ai fait le ménage.
3 J'ai fait la cuisine.
4 Je ne regarde pas la télé.
5 Je m'intéresse à l'informatique.
6 J'adore la lecture.

> 📖📖 You can often work out whether a sentence is in the past or present tense by looking at the time expressions used. *Aujourd'hui* (today), *en ce moment* (at the moment) and *d'habitude* (usually) generally indicate present tense. Expressions such as *l'année dernière* (last year), *hier* (yesterday) and *il y a quatre jours* (four days ago) indicate past tense.
>
> **Stratégie**

2b 📖🎧 🌐 Answer the following questions in English.

1 Why do you think Charlotte's sister is unhappy with her?

2 Name two things that Charlotte did after watching TV.

3 Why was Alexis not allowed out?

4 What was he supposed to do and what did he really do?

5 How do you think Marine gets on with her sister? Give a reason for your answer.

3a 🎧 Listen to Section A. What does Valentin think of the following? Is his attitude positive (P), negative (N) or mixed (P / N)?

1   **2**  **3**   **4**

3b 🎧 Listen to Section B. What does Lucie think of the following (P, N or P / N)?

1 TV
2 the newspaper
3 the soup
4 the sandwich
5 chess
6 chatting online

> **Perfect tense with *avoir***
>
> This is used to describe finished actions in the past. To form it, use *avoir* + the past participle.
>
> For -*er* verbs, remove the -*er* and add -*é*, e.g. *J'ai rangé ma chambre.* For -*ir* verbs, simply remove the -*r*, e.g. *Il a fini.* Regular -*re* verbs end in -*u*, e.g. *Elle a vendu.* Irregular past participles are given in the vocabulary lists.
>
> Also learn about adverbial time expressions.   *See page 70* ➡
>
> **Grammaire** *page 181*

4 🄖 Convert these sentences into the perfect tense.

Exemple: Je mange des fraises. ➡ J'ai mangé des fraises.

1 Je finis le travail.

2 Est-ce que tu fais du jardinage?

3 Elle lit le magazine.

4 Nous jouons aux cartes.

5 Est-ce que vous gagnez le jeu?

6 Ils écoutent la radio.

> When you say you have done an activity in the perfect tense, try to give your opinion about the activity using *c'était* (it was), e.g. *J'ai lu un livre, mais c'était ennuyeux. J'ai fait la cuisine, c'était amusant.*
>
> **Astuce**

5 🗨 With a partner, ask and answer these questions about what you do at home.

▨ Quelle sorte de musique aimes-tu?

▨ Est-ce que tu joues d'un instrument de musique?

▨ Qu'est-ce que tu aimes lire?

▨ Qu'est-ce que tu aimes regarder à la télé?

▨ Tu aimes jouer aux cartes et à des jeux de société?

▨ Qu'est-ce que tu as fait le week-end dernier pour t'amuser à la maison?

▨ Qu'est-ce que tu as fait pour aider tes parents?

▨ Tu as passé un bon week-end? Pourquoi (pas)?

Je joue Je lis	souvent / rarement / de temps en temps	du piano / de la guitare / de la clarinette. un roman / des magazines.
Je regarde	la télé / des DVD	tous les jours / presque tous les jours.
Le week-end / Samedi dernier,	j'ai mangé une pizza / joué aux cartes / préparé le dîner / nettoyé ma chambre.	
Plus tard,	j'ai rencontré / retrouvé mes amis et nous avons joué aux cartes / chanté ensemble / regardé un film.	
Je l'ai trouvé / J'ai trouvé ça / C'était	très / assez / un peu	ennuyeux / monotone / barbant / fatigant / amusant / marrant / intéressant / utile.

Quelle sorte de musique aimes-tu?

J'adore le rap, mais je n'aime pas tellement le hip-hop.

kerboodle!

Les loisirs

Le deltaplane: un sport dangereux?

Pauline, tu fais du deltaplane depuis l'âge de 14 ans. C'est un sport dangereux, non?

C'est une activité à risques, comme la plongée sous-marine ou le rugby, mais il y a moins d'accidents que dans l'alpinisme ou l'escalade. Le principal danger, c'est quand on atterrit. La première fois, je suis arrivée assez vite et le choc était un peu dur.

Quelles sont les qualités nécessaires?

Il faut être en bonne forme et ne pas avoir une mauvaise vue. Il faut pouvoir rester vigilant et actif à chaque instant. La force physique n'est pas importante, c'est la technique et l'expérience qui sont indispensables.

Pourquoi fais-tu du deltaplane?

C'est à cause de mon père. Il fait du deltaplane depuis dix ans et m'a encouragée à l'essayer. Un jour, je suis allée le voir et j'ai tout de suite voulu en faire.

L'objectif d'un vol, c'est d'abord la durée: c'est de rester le plus longtemps en l'air. Voler, c'est une sensation inoubliable. Une fois que j'ai atterri, je veux recommencer tout de suite.

Quels sont les inconvénients de ce sport?

Le matériel est assez cher. Le port du casque est obligatoire. J'ai payé 200 euros pour mon nouveau casque. Et s'il fait mauvais, mon père ne me permet pas de partir.

Est-ce que tu recommandes ce sport?

Oui, mais il faut une formation intensive avec un moniteur. Elle peut durer jusqu'à deux semaines. Certains n'aiment pas attendre si longtemps avant de partir et ils décident de faire autre chose.

---

1 **V** In the article, find the French for the following.

1 to land   a_____
2 bad eyesight   m_____ v_____
3 physical strength la f_____ p_____
4 the length   la d_____

5 to fly   v_____
6 unforgettable   i_____
7 compulsory   o_____
8 training   la f_____

2 Choose the correct word or phrase to make each sentence true according to the article.

1 Selon Pauline, le deltaplane est plus / moins / aussi dangereux que l'alpinisme.

2 Le plus grand danger, c'est quand on commence son vol / est en train de voler / revient sur terre.

3 La technique est plus / moins / aussi importante que la force physique.

4 L'objectif principal, c'est de faire un vol court / long / rapide.

5 À la fin d'un vol, Pauline veut se reposer / oublier le vol / recommencer l'expérience.

6 Un des inconvénients de ce sport, c'est la qualité / la quantité / le coût du matériel.

7 Pauline ne peut pas partir sans la permission de son père / quand il fait chaud / avec un casque.

8 Certains abandonnent le deltaplane parce qu'ils ont peur / sont impatients / sont en mauvaise santé.

3a 🎧 Listen to five people talking about what they did last weekend and what they intend to do next weekend and link each person to the correct activity.

1	Olivier	4 Jasmine	a le cinéma	d le théâtre
2	Richard	5 Julie	b le cyclisme	e le foot
3	Danielle		c la musique	

3b 🎧 Listen again and answer the questions in English.

1 Why does Olivier have to stay at home next weekend?

2 Do you think Richard enjoyed going to the match? Why?

3 What was Danielle's problem last weekend?

4 What was the drawback of the meal for Jasmine?

5 What did Julie watch last weekend and why?

4a 🄶 Select the correct past participle.

1 Je m'appelle Jacqueline. Je suis allé / allée / allés au bord de la mer.

2 Est-ce que tu es sorti / sortie / sortis hier soir, Anne-Marie?

3 Ils sont venu / venus / venues en retard.

4 Nous sommes resté / restée / restés trop longtemps.

4b 🄶 Change the infinitive in each sentence into a perfect tense verb.

1 Les filles arriver avant nous.

2 Elle tomber dans la rue.

3 Vous retourner à quelle heure, les garçons?

4 Il partir sans me dire au revoir.

5 🖊 🔊 Write an account of a busy weekend.

▪ Say where you went on Saturday afternoon.

▪ Say what you did on Saturday night.

▪ Say where you went on Sunday.

▪ Talk about something you did that you will do again and why.

▪ Talk about something you did that you will not do again and why.

▪ Say what you thought of the weekend.

Samedi après-midi / soir,	je suis allé(e) au cinéma / au stade / à la piscine / en ville.	
Dimanche,	je suis sorti(e) avec mes ami(e)s.	
Je veux y retourner	parce que	je me suis très bien amusé(e) / j'ai trouvé la journée tellement passionnante.
Je n'irai plus au stade		c'était trop cher / j'ai trouvé le match ennuyeux.
J'ai trouvé le week-end	marrant / amusant / relaxant / fatigant / ennuyeux / stressant.	

Perfect tense with *être* **🄶rammaire** *page 181*

Some verbs take *être* instead of *avoir*. The past participle of an *être* verb has to agree with the subject of the sentence, e.g. *Elle est tombée* – She has fallen / She fell. Other verbs in this group are: *aller, sortir, descendre, arriver, rester, venir, monter, naître, mourir, entrer, retourner, partir.*

Also learn about the perfect tense of reflexive verbs and the perfect tense in the negative.

See page 70 ➡

🖊 Show your knowledge of different time frames by combining two tenses in the same sentence. The first part (what you normally do) is in the present tense and the second part (the exception) is in the perfect tense.

Normalement, je vois des films français, mais samedi, j'ai vu une comédie anglaise avec des sous-titres. **🄢tratégie**

You don't always have to write about things that you have done. In order to extend your answer, you can add some negative expressions, e.g. *Je suis allé à la piscine avec mes copains, mais je n'ai pas nagé.* **Astuce**

L'argent et le shopping

Objectifs

Talking about money and shopping

Direct object pronouns

Using all three time frames

Un nouveau centre commercial

Le nouveau centre commercial Clair-Soleil a ouvert ses portes au public mercredi matin. Musique discrète, décor moderne et coloré, escaliers roulants rapides. Un immense centre avec cinq restaurants et une cinquantaine de magasins extrêmement variés: de l'équipement de sport à la maison, en passant par la décoration, le jardinage ou l'habillement, il y en a pour toute la famille. Il y a même un coin jeux (pour les petits) et des distributeurs automatiques (pour les plus grands).

Avec l'arrivée du nouveau centre, les petits commerçants à proximité ne sont pas contents. Ils ont peur de perdre leurs clients. À Aubejean, plusieurs commerçants de la ville ont déjà annoncé leur intention de vendre leur boutique.

Selon le maire, «Il faut améliorer le centre-ville. Il faut proposer aux visiteurs plus de choses à faire en ville. Faisons la différence sur le service et la qualité de nos produits.» Mais Alain Maurois, qui est propriétaire d'une boucherie-charcuterie à Aubejean, est beaucoup moins sûr: «Parking gratuit, variété de magasins pour le client, centre ouvert les jours fériés, c'est attractif. Mais dans le centre-ville il n'y aura plus de magasins traditionnels comme l'épicerie, la boulangerie ou la pâtisserie. Ce centre va les détruire complètement.»

1a 📖🎧 Read the first paragraph and decide whether the statements are true (T), false (F) or not mentioned (?).

1 Le nouveau centre va bientôt ouvrir ses portes au public.

2 On ne peut pas manger dans le centre.

3 On peut y acheter des vêtements.

4 Le centre se trouve près de l'autoroute.

5 Les enfants peuvent jouer au centre commercial.

1b 📖🎧 Read the next two paragraphs and choose T, F or ?.

1 Tout le monde est satisfait de l'ouverture du centre.

2 Plusieurs commerçants vont peut-être fermer leur magasin.

3 Il faut payer pour garer sa voiture au centre commercial.

4 Alain Maurois est plutôt pessimiste.

5 Il travaille comme boucher depuis vingt ans.

2 🎬🎧 Watch or listen to Sections A and B and correct the mistakes in the following sentences.

A 1 Laurie receives 20 euros pocket money per week.

2 She buys clothes, make-up and jewellery.

3 She thinks the shopping centre has cheap prices but not much choice.

4 Nathan earns money by going to the supermarket for his parents.

5 He wants to buy himself a new bike.

B 6 Maude bought a new guitar last month.

7 At the moment she is not going to the shops at all.

8 Simon likes receiving presents.

9 He thinks small shops are more expensive and less varied.

10 In the shopping centre, there are not many people.

3 **G** Rewrite the sentences, replacing the highlighted words with a pronoun: *le*, *la*, *l'* or *les*.

1 Je vends les livres au marché.
2 Il achète les magazines en ville.
3 Elle déteste le centre commercial .
4 Il a perdu le plan .
5 Vous mettez la veste ?
6 Nous achetons la voiture .

4a Work with a partner. Decide whether each of these answers about money and shopping is in the past, present or future. Then work out the questions for these answers.

▨ Je reçois dix livres par semaine.

▨ Je reçois mon argent de mes parents et de mes grands-parents.

▨ Je mets dix livres par semaine à la banque.

▨ Le week-end dernier, j'ai fait du jardinage pour mes parents.

▨ J'ai acheté un pantalon, une chemise et une nouvelle paire de chaussures.

▨ J'aime mieux les grands magasins.

▨ Je vais acheter des cadeaux pour ma famille.

4b Ask each other the questions. Adapt the answers to talk about yourself and add some information in a different time frame.

> Tu reçois de l'argent de poche?

> Je reçois dix livres par semaine.

> Je reçois cinq livres par semaine, mais je vais recevoir six livres après mon anniversaire au mois d'avril.

Je reçois mon argent	de mes parents / quand je fais du travail chez moi / pour mon anniversaire.	
Je mets dix livres par semaine à la banque	parce que j'ai l'intention de … / je veux …	
J'ai acheté	un nouveau … / une nouvelle … / un cadeau pour …	
J'aime mieux les petits magasins / centres commerciaux	parce qu'	il y a moins / plus de choix.
	parce que	le service est bon / meilleur.
		c'est plus / moins cher.
Récemment, je suis allé(e) au / à la …	pour acheter …	
Je vais acheter …	pour Noël / l'anniversaire de ma mère.	

Grammaire — page 177

Direct object pronouns

Direct object pronouns replace the noun and the article. In English we use the words 'it' and 'them'. The French for 'it' can be *le*, *la* or *l'* and for 'them' is *les*. The direct object pronoun in French is placed before the verb.

Je vends le vélo. ➡️ *Je le vends.*

Il achète les chaussures. ➡️ *Il les achète.*

Elle aime la boutique. ➡️ *Elle l'aime.*

Also learn about demonstrative pronouns.   *See page 70* ➡️

Stratégie

> Try to use all three time frames when speaking – past, present and future. You could describe a visit to the shops in the past tense and give information about your likes and dislikes in the present tense. Then talk about what you intend to do on your next shopping trip. Can you find two examples each of the past, present and future tenses in the reading passage on page 62?

Astuce

Don't forget that there are various ways to express the future: the future tense; *aller* + infinitive; or if you are not definitely certain you will do the things you mention, *j'ai l'intention de* or *je voudrais* + infinitive.

La taille zéro et ses effets

A On entend souvent parler de la taille zéro américaine. C'est à la mode en ce moment et on voit des mannequins et des vedettes très très minces. Selon plusieurs experts, c'est la mode qui est à l'origine du problème de l'image de la fille et de l'anorexie. La presse pour adolescentes est pleine de photos de top models, d'articles sur les régimes, les produits de beauté et les maisons de couture.

B Beaucoup de jeunes lectrices veulent imiter ces mannequins et les magazines leur donnent l'impression que c'est en perdant des kilos qu'elles vont devenir belles. Les jeunes filles deviennent anorexiques ou boulimiques car elles voudraient être comme les top models.

C Une étude publiée dans la revue française *Forum Santé* en janvier révèle que les adolescentes qui lisent des articles sur les régimes ont deux fois plus de chances d'avoir des troubles alimentaires cinq ans plus tard.

D La réalité de l'anorexie est affreuse. Dans son livre *Ce matin, j'ai décidé d'arrêter de manger*, Justine raconte comment, à 14 ans, elle a commencé un régime «pour être belle» et a fini par perdre 36 kilos.

E Pour vendre les vêtements des couturiers on idéalise les personnes qui les portent, mais certaines villes ont décidé de combattre ce problème. Les mannequins trop minces ou trop jeunes ne sont plus admis aux défilés. Quand notre reporter a cherché l'avis du ministre de la Santé, il lui a répondu: «L'image de la femme idéale dans les magazines de mode n'existe pas. On aime toutes les filles, grosses ou maigres, grandes ou petites.»

1a 📖🎧🔍 Read the article and choose a title for each paragraph.

1   Ban on models who are too thin
2   Images of very thin celebrities
3   A personal account of the effects of anorexia
4   Results of a recent study
5   Starting a diet to look better

> 📖 **Stratégie**
> When you come across a word you do not recognise, you need to use the context and the surrounding words you do know to work out the meaning. In a sentence such as *l'homme porte un gilet chic*, you can reasonably assume that *gilet* is an item of clothing because a man is **wearing** it and it is described as **smart**.

1b 📖🎧🔍 Answer the following questions in English.

1   According to experts, what is to blame for anorexia?
2   How do models and fashion magazines influence young girls?
3   What is the finding of the study in *Forum Santé*?
4   What effect did anorexia have on Justine?
5   What is the view of the Minister of Health?

2 ⓥ Use the table to design an elegant or a tasteless outfit.

une veste	noir(e)(s)			en jean
un pantalon	violet(te)(s)		large(s)	en laine
une jupe	orange(s)	clair	long(ue)(s)	en soie
des chaussettes	rose(s)	foncé	court(e)(s)	en coton
une chemise / un chemisier	gris(e)(s)		étroit(e)(s)	en cuir
une cravate	vert(e)(s)			en velours

> The words *clair* (light) and *foncé* (dark) can be added to a colour, e.g. *bleu clair* (light blue), *vert foncé* (dark green). When you do this, the adjective does not agree with the noun, e.g. *une veste bleu foncé.*

3 🎧 Listen to all four speakers and find two expressions for each one.

1 Julien
2 Émy
3 Annabelle
4 Hugo

a des vêtements noirs
b des vêtements trop grands
c des vêtements élégants
d des vêtements rétro
e la tête couverte
f les couleurs vives
g la bonne qualité
h les piercings

4 ⓖ Work with a partner. First decide whether a direct pronoun or an indirect pronoun is needed. Then choose the correct one from the selection given.

1 Je n'aime pas ses amis, je ne lui / les / leur parle jamais.
2 C'est l'anniversaire de ma sœur. Je la / le / lui offre des fleurs.
3 Elles n'aiment pas les bottes. Elles la / les / leur détestent.
4 Il m'a envoyé une lettre. Je vais lui / le / leur répondre bientôt.
5 La jupe qu'elle a achetée est affreuse. Il faut la / le / lui dire la vérité.
6 Cette chemise ne me va pas du tout. Je vais le / la / lui mettre à la poubelle.

> ### ⓖ Indirect object pronouns
>
> These are words that **replace** the indirect object.
>
> *Je parle à Pierre.* – I'm talking to Pierre. ➡ *Je lui parle.* – I'm talking to him.
>
> *Pierre* is the indirect object and this word is replaced by the indirect object pronoun *lui* (him). Check out the list of direct and indirect object pronouns in the grammar section.
>
> Also revise the verbs of liking / disliking which are followed by the infinitive.   *See page 71* ➡
>
> **Grammaire** *page 177*

5 ✏ Work in a group to design a new school uniform.

Student A designs the boys' uniform, Student B the girls' uniform, Student C the PE uniform and Student D writes about why the new uniform is an improvement. Describe the items of clothing of your new uniform.

▦ Describe the style, materials and colours.

▦ Say why you have chosen these items of clothing.

▦ Say why the new uniform will be an improvement.

When you have finished, present your work to the rest of the class.

Les élèves vont On va	mettre / porter	un jogging / un pantalon / un jean / un blouson / des baskets.
Le pantalon est		en cuir / en coton / en laine / en jean.
La robe est		uni(e) / à rayures / à carreaux / à pois / à fleurs.
Les chaussures sont		long(ue)(s) / court(e)(s) / large(s) / étroit(e)(s).
On doit porter un pantalon parce que c'est		confortable / plus chic / pratique / plus chaud en hiver.
L'uniforme va		améliorer la discipline / donner une bonne impression aux autres / nous donner le sentiment d'appartenir à un groupe.

2.5 Les nouvelles technologies

Objectifs

Talking about new technology

Superlative adjectives

Justifying your opinions

---

1 ⓥ Match each verb with a phrase you could use it with.

1 envoyer	4 écouter	a de la musique sur un lecteur mp3	d des textos
2 écrire	5 regarder	b des renseignements	e un e-mail
3 appeler	6 chercher	c plusieurs chaînes	f avec un portable

Je cherche l'avis des autres. Moi, je ne peux pas vivre sans mon téléphone portable. J'envoie des textos à toutes mes amies et le portable est indispensable pour appeler mes parents si je suis en retard. Avec mon nouveau portable, je peux regarder des vidéoclips et écouter les derniers hits. C'était le meilleur modèle dans le magasin. J'utilise mon portable assez souvent quand je sors avec mes copines. Que pensez-vous des nouvelles technologies?

Maudit

Je trouve Internet très utile pour chercher des renseignements quand je fais mes devoirs. Je trouve le traitement de texte utile parce que mon écriture est difficile à lire. Je suis bloggeur et j'ai reçu plus de 10 000 visites sur mon site. Je participe à des forums et je me suis fait de nouveaux amis grâce à Internet. C'est aussi la forme de communication la plus rapide et le meilleur moyen de rester en contact avec les autres. J'envoie des e-mails tous les jours et je consulte régulièrement ma boîte aux lettres électronique. Je ne peux pas vivre non plus sans ma console de jeu. Je passe des heures à jouer à des jeux vidéo.

Jacquesadit

Pour mon anniversaire, mes parents m'ont offert le lecteur mp3 que je leur avais demandé. Je l'ai choisi parce qu'il a un écran tactile et la plus grosse mémoire possible. Dans ma chambre, j'ai maintenant la télé par satellite. Je peux regarder plus de cent émissions différentes. L'année prochaine, j'espère recevoir un nouveau lecteur DVD pour ma chambre.

Praline2

2a 📖🎧 Match the pieces of equipment (A–F) with the bloggers.

1 Maudit   2 Jacquesadit   3 Praline2

2b 📖🎧 Who says the following?

1 Je me sers d'Internet pour faire mes devoirs.
2 Il y a un grand choix de chaînes.
3 Je peux télécharger de la musique.
4 L'e-mail est très utile.

5 Grâce aux nouvelles technologies, j'ai rencontré de nouveaux copains.
6 J'ai créé mon propre site.
7 Mes parents sont rassurés.

3 🎧 Link the letters of the items you hear (a–h) to the concerns (1–6). You can use the same letter more than once.

1 health issues	**3** irritating noise	**5** lack of variety
2 crime	**4** false identity issues	**6** expense

4 **G** Write sentences using the comparative and the superlative, following the example given. Some ideas for adjectives are given below.

Exemple: La radio <u>est plus amusante que</u> le cinéma, mais la télé <u>est la plus amusante</u>.

1 les portables … les lecteurs mp3 … les blogs
2 la lecture … la musique … le sport
3 le portable … Internet … la télé
4 les journaux … les magazines … les romans
5 les films d'amour … les films d'horreur … les comédies

dangereux	**meilleur**	**pratique**	**intéressant**
relaxant	**marrant**	**utile**	**pire**	**amusant**

5 💬 🌐 With a partner, answer these questions about new technology. A plays the part of someone who loves new technology, while B dislikes it. When your partner has given their opinion, ask them *pourquoi?* or *pourquoi pas?*

▦ Tu utilises souvent un téléphone portable?

▦ Quels sont les avantages ou les dangers d'Internet?

▦ Que penses-tu de la télé par satellite ou par câble?

▦ Est-ce que tu utilises un lecteur mp3?

▦ Est-ce que tu envoies souvent des messages électroniques?

> **Grammaire** — page 174
>
> **Superlative adjectives**
>
> To say something is 'the most', add *le / la / les + plus* before the adjective.
>
> *C'est la chaîne la plus intéressante.* – It's the most interesting channel.
>
> Two exceptions are *le meilleur / la meilleure* (best) and *le / la pire* (worst).
>
> *C'est le meilleur modèle.* – It's the best model.
>
> Also learn about using the pronoun *on* with impersonal expressions. *See page 71* ➡️

> **Stratégie**
>
> 💬 When you have given your opinion, try to give a reason for your view. Useful phrases for adding a reason are *parce que*, *puisque* and *car*. Jacquesadit says, *Je trouve le traitement de texte utile.* What reason does he give for this?

> **Astuce**
>
> When you use adjectives in French, try to add a quantifier such as *très*, *assez* or *trop*. *C'est trop cher, c'est assez utile*, etc.

Tu utilises souvent un téléphone portable?

Oui, assez souvent.

Pourquoi?

J'appelle souvent mes parents et j'envoie des textos à mes amis.

	Avantage	Désavantage
(téléphone) portable	On peut envoyer des textos / contacter ses parents / ses amis facilement.	C'est trop cher. Quand ça sonne, ça m'énerve.
Internet	On peut l'utiliser pour faire du shopping / les devoirs.	On peut passer trop de temps devant l'ordinateur.
télé par satellite	Il y a plus de choix / beaucoup d'émissions.	Il y a beaucoup de mauvaises / vieilles émissions, par exemple …
lecteur mp3	C'est agréable / pratique d'écouter …	Ils sont chers.
messagerie électronique	C'est rapide / facile.	On dit des choses stupides. C'est inutile.

Free time and the media

On a porté les vêtements de nos parents pour une bonne cause

Ma mère adorait ce style géométrique.»

Pour Marc et Sylvie, c'était le look des années soixante-dix.

«Je porte un vieux jean, une chemise indienne blanche et des sandales. Je n'ai pas les cheveux longs comme les avait mon père à mon âge.»

«Moi, j'ai une jupe longue en coton, un chemisier bleu clair et beaucoup de bijoux.»

A Vendredi dernier, les élèves du lycée ont collecté beaucoup d'argent pour une bonne cause. Ils ont organisé une présentation de la mode des années passées.

Philippe et Francine décrivent leur look, des années soixante:

«Moi, je porte une chemise rose, une cravate large à fleurs et un pantalon blanc.»

«Moi, c'est une robe très courte noire et blanche.

Et Monsieur Hourcade, le professeur qui les a encouragés? Il a présenté le spectacle en portant des vêtements du style préféré de son père, celui des années cinquante: un pantalon étroit, une veste longue bleu marine et des bottes en cuir!

B Ils veulent acheter des équipements de sport pour les élèves d'une école au Cameroun. Un des professeurs de sport, Guy Hourcade, a visité le Cameroun en avril. Pendant son séjour, il a passé une journée dans une petite école près de son hôtel. En rentrant en France, il a demandé à ses élèves de penser à des idées pour aider les élèves de cette école, car ils adorent le sport, mais ils n'ont pas d'équipement. Le résultat: cette soirée amusante. L'idée, c'était d'emprunter à ses parents des vêtements de leur jeunesse. Le père ou la mère a payé cinq euros si son fils ou sa fille a porté ses vêtements dans le spectacle du lycée. Beaucoup de parents sont venus voir le spectacle, et les étudiants ont préparé des boissons et des gâteaux qu'ils ont vendus.

1a 📖🎧 Read Section A. Who wore the following?

1 white trousers
2 a short dress
3 an Indian shirt
4 leather footwear
5 something pink
6 something with a flowery design
7 jewellery
8 clothes from the 1950s
9 something pale blue
10 tight trousers

> **AQA** *Examiner's tip*
>
> You can sometimes work out the meaning of less familiar words or phrases from your existing knowledge of French. For example, you will probably know the meaning of the noun *fleur* in the phrase *à fleurs*, which means 'flowery'.

1b 📖🎧 Read Section B. Which four sentences are true?

1 The money raised will pay for sports equipment.
2 Guy Hourcade spent a week in an African school.
3 He wrote to his students from Africa.
4 He told his students how to raise the money.
5 The students were paid to wear their parents' clothes.
6 They had a big audience.
7 They also raised money by selling refreshments.

> **Vocabulaire**
>
> | | |
> |---|---|
> | *la botte* | boot |
> | *emprunter* | to borrow |
> | **peut-être** | perhaps |
> | *quand même* | all the same |
> | *le séjour* | stay |

2a 🎧 Listen to Section A and put the following activities in the order that Solange did them at the weekend (1–5).

a homework
b reading
c shopping
d a party
e a film

2b 🎧 Listen to Section B. Complete the sentences in English.

1 Solange bought _____.
2 Her mother thinks they are _____.
3 Delphine bought _____.
4 Her mother thinks it is _____.
5 Patrick has invited Delphine _____.
6 Delphine is unlikely to see Patrick often because _____.
7 Solange thinks that Patrick will _____.

> **Grammaire** *page 177*
>
> The following sentences are used in the conversation:
> *Je vais les porter.*
> *Je vais la porter.*
> Why does one use *les* and the other *la*? What do they each refer to?
> For more information about these sorts of pronouns, refer to the grammar section.

G Free time and the media

Adverbial time expressions; perfect tense with negatives and reflexives; demonstrative pronouns

1 Pay attention to the tense in each sentence and complete it using a word from the grammar box – use each word only once. Then translate the sentences into English.

1 Qu'est-ce qu'on fait _____?

2 Qu'est-ce que tu as acheté _____?

3 _____, on va regarder le DVD.

4 Tu as _____ dépensé tout ton argent?

5 Elle leur donnera le cadeau _____ -demain.

6 J'ai envoyé ce message _____ -hier

2 Translate the following sentences into French, using the verbs in brackets. Pay particular attention to the word order.

1 She woke up. (se réveiller)

2 We went for a walk. (se promener)

3 They met at the swimming pool. (se rencontrer / masculine)

4 You didn't buy a present. (acheter / tu)

5 My sister never got bored. (s'ennuyer)

6 I didn't try any more. (essayer)

3 Choose between *ça*, *ce* or *c'* to complete the following sentences.

1 _____ n'est pas très cher ici! Super!

2 J'ai fait des économies, _____ est fantastique!

3 _____ ne va pas, j'ai dépensé tout mon argent!

4 _____ est trop cher ici, je n'ai pas assez d'argent.

5 Est-ce que j'aime faire les magasins? Bof, _____ va.

6 On me donne dix euros par mois et _____ n'est pas assez!

7 J'aime aller au marché, parce que _____ est très pratique.

8 Faire les courses, tu aimes _____?

Adverbial time expressions

Grammaire page 176

Verb tenses usually give you a clue as to whether people are talking about the past, present or future. The following phrases help too:

déjà (already), *avant-hier* (the day before yesterday), *hier* (yesterday), *aujourd'hui* (today), *demain* (tomorrow), *après-demain* (the day after tomorrow).

Most of these expressions go at the beginning or end of the sentence. Be careful with *déjà*, which goes in the middle of the sentence: *Tu es déjà arrivé?* – Have you already arrived?

Perfect tense with negatives and reflexives

Grammaire page 181

Pay attention to the word order of negatives in the perfect tense. The *ne* and *pas* go on each side of the auxiliary (*avoir* or *être*).

Elle a crié. (She screamed.) ➡ *Elle n'a pas crié.* (She didn't scream)

The same applies to other negatives: *Elle n'a jamais deviné. (She never guessed.)*

With reflexive verbs, the *ne* goes before the reflexive pronoun (*me, te,* etc.).

Je me suis ennuyée. (I got bored.) ➡ *Je ne me suis pas ennuyée. (I didn't get bored.)*

Demonstrative pronouns

Grammaire page 178

Ce means 'that', 'it', 'they' or 'those'. It is always followed by a form of *être*. It is shortenend to *c'* in front of a vowel. If the verb that follows is not *être*, use *ça* or *cela*.

C'est un fruit. Ce sont des légumes. – It's a fruit. They are vegetables.

Cela also means 'that'. It is often shortened to *ça*. *Tu aimes ça?* – Do you like that?

It is used in various phrases:
Ça va? – Are you okay?
Ça ne fait rien. – It doesn't matter.

Verbs of liking and disliking + infinitive; pronoun *on* with impersonal expressions

4 Use infinitives to complete the captions to go with each set of pictures.

1 Je déteste _____, je préfère _____.

2 J'aime _____, mais je préfère _____.

3 Je n'aime pas _____, je préfère _____.

4 Je déteste _____, je préfère _____.

5 Replace each infinitive with the correct form of the verb. In each case, note whether *on* means 'we' or the impersonal 'you' / 'people'.

1 Qu'est-ce qu'on faire ce soir?
2 On regarder un film ensemble, si tu veux.
3 Est-ce qu'on pouvoir se faire des amis sur Internet?
4 On dire que les téléphones portables sont dangereux, mais on ne savoir pas vraiment.
5 Si on rester trop longtemps devant son ordinateur, on avoir mal aux yeux.
6 On sortir ? On aller où?

> **Grammaire** *page 179*
>
> ## Verbs of liking and disliking + infinitive
>
> When *j'aime, je déteste* or *je préfère* is followed by a verb, the second verb is in the infinitive.
>
> *J'aime porter une robe.*
> I like wearing a dress.
>
> *Je déteste faire les magasins.*
> I hate going shopping.
>
> *Je préfère aller à la patinoire.*
> I'd rather go ice skating.

> **Grammaire** *page 177*
>
> ## Pronoun *on* with impersonal expressions
>
> *On* often means 'we' and can be used for making suggestions, or talking about what you are doing.
>
> *On va au cinéma ce soir?* – Shall we go to the cinema this evening?
>
> *On s'amuse bien.* – We are having a great time.
>
> On can also mean 'you' or 'one' or 'people' in an impersonal expression.
>
> *Comment dit-on «hat» en français?* – How do you say 'hat' in French?
>
> *On peut utiliser l'Internet à la bibliothèque.* – You can use the internet in the library.

Vocabulary

 V

Free time and the media

Ce que j'ai fait chez moi ➡ *pages 58–59*

les	actualités (f)	the news
	aider	to help
la	bande dessinée	comic book / strip cartoon
	bavarder	to chat
	comme d'habitude	as usual
les	échecs (m)	chess
	en ce moment	at the moment
	ensemble	together
	ensuite	then
	faire (fait)	to do / to make
	faire la grasse matinée	to lie in
	faire du jardinage	to do the gardening
	faire la lessive	to do the washing
	feuilleter	to flick through
	le feuilleton	soap (TV series)
	gagner	to win / to earn
	il y a	ago (time)
	lire (lu)	to read
(avoir)	mal à la tête	(to have a) headache
de	mauvaises notes (f)	bad marks
	normalement	usually
	pleurer	to cry
	promener le chien	to walk the dog
	ranger	to tidy / to put away
le	roman	novel
le	soir	(in) the evening
le / la	voisin(e)	neighbour

Les loisirs ➡ *pages 60 – 61*

l'	alpinisme (m)	mountaineering
	atterrir (atterri)	to land
s'	amuser	to enjoy yourself / to have fun
le	casque	helmet
	chanter	to sing
le	clavier	keyboard

la	comédie	comedy
le	deltaplane	hang-gliding
le	dessin animé	cartoon (film)
l'	escalade (f)	rock climbing
les	loisirs (m)	leisure activities
	marquer un but	to score a goal
le	moniteur	sports trainer
	oublier	to forget
	perfectionner	to improve
la	plongée sous-marine	diving
les	sous-titres (m)	subtitles
en	version originale	in the original language (films)
le	vol	flight
	voler	to fly / to steal

L'argent et le shopping ➡ *pages 62–63*

	acheter	to buy
l'	aire de jeux (f)	playground
	améliorer	to improve
l'	argent de poche (m)	pocket money
la	boucherie	butcher's
la	boulangerie (f)	baker's (bread)
la	boutique	shop
le	cadeau	present
le	centre commercial	shopping centre
la	charcuterie	pork butcher's / delicatessen
	cher(-ère)	dear / expensive
	chercher	to look for
le	choix	choice
le / la	commerçant(e)	shopkeeper
le	coût	cost
	dépenser	to spend (money)
l'	épicerie (f)	grocer's
	faire des économies (f)	to save up
	faire du lèche-vitrine	to go window shopping
le / la	fana	fan / enthusiast

	gratuit(e)	free (no cost)
l'	*habillement (m)*	clothes
le	*jeu vidéo*	computer game
le	*magasin*	shop
le	*maquillage*	make-up
la	*pâtisserie*	baker's (pastries, cakes)
le	*prix*	price
la	*promotion*	promotion / special offer
	recevoir (reçu)	to receive
la	*réduction*	reduction
les	*soldes (m)*	the sales
	trop de monde	too many people
	varié(e)	varied
	vendre (vendu)	to sell
les	*vêtements (m)*	clothes

1 **V** Find pairs of words with similar meanings in the two columns.

1	les vêtements		a	le commerçant
2	un frigo		b	certain
3	une boutique		c	gratuit
4	le propriétaire d'un magasin		d	des animations
			e	l'habillement
5	il ne faut pas payer		f	une aire de jeux
6	des distractions		g	un appareil électroménager
7	un endroit où les enfants peuvent jouer		h	un magasin
8	sûr			

La mode ➡ pages 64–65

les	*chaussettes (f)*	socks
le	*chemisier*	blouse
	chic	smart
en	*coton*	(made of) cotton
la	*couture*	high fashion
en	*cuir*	(made of) leather
	décontracté(e)	relaxed
le	*défilé (de mode)*	fashion show
	étroit(e)	tight / narrow
	gros(se)	fat
en	*laine*	woollen

	large	loose-fitting / broad
	maigre	thin
le	*mannequin*	model
	mettre (mis)	to put (on)
	mince	slim
la	*mode*	fashion
le	*pull à capuche*	hooded top
le	*régime*	diet
la	*taille*	size
le	*trouble alimentaire*	eating disorder
la	*vedette*	star / celebrity

Les nouvelles technologies ➡ pages 66–67

le	*bloggeur*	blogger
la	*boîte aux lettres électronique*	(email) inbox
la	*chaîne*	channel (TV)
la	*console de jeu*	games console
l'	*écran tactile (m)*	touch screen
l'	*émission (f)*	programme (TV)
	en ligne	online
	envoyer	to send
l'	*étranger(-ère) (m / f)*	stranger (also, foreigner)
le	*jeu (les jeux)*	game / game show
le	*lecteur DVD*	DVD player
le	*lecteur mp3*	mp3 player
le	*moteur de recherche*	search engine
	nouveau (nouvelle)	new
l'	*ordinateur (m)*	computer
le	*(téléphone) portable*	mobile (phone)
les	*renseignements (m)*	information
la	*série*	series
le	*site*	site (internet)
	sonner	to ring (phone, bell)
	télécharger	to download
	le texto	text (message)
	le traitement de texte	word processing

2.6 Vive les vacances!

Les vacances préférées des Français ...

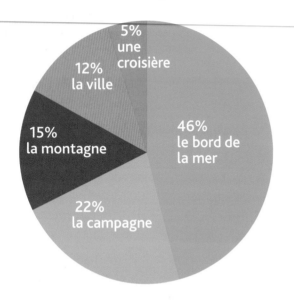

5%
une croisière

12%
la ville

15%
la montagne

46%
le bord de
la mer

22%
la campagne

La montagne est la destination favorite de 15% des personnes interviewées. C'est surtout pour pratiquer les sports d'hiver. Le seul inconvénient pour les skieurs: quelquefois il ne neige pas!

12% disent qu'ils aiment passer des séjours courts en ville. Ces gens aiment la culture et le shopping. Ils aiment moins le bruit et la pollution.

Seulement 5% des Français rêvent de faire une croisière. On visite beaucoup de villes intéressantes, mais le mal de mer n'est pas très agréable.

L'avis de nos lecteurs

Richard, 17 ans

Quand j'étais petit, j'aimais le bord de la mer. Je nageais dans la mer, je bronzais sur le sable mais maintenant, en été, je trouve qu'il y a trop de personnes sur les plages et on dit que bronzer est mauvais pour la santé.

Béatrice, 16 ans

L'année dernière, je suis allée à la campagne au centre de la France. Il n'y avait pas grand-chose à faire, c'était vraiment barbant et il a plu presque tous les jours. L'année prochaine, on va retourner au bord de la mer.

La destination préférée des Français reste toujours le bord de la mer. Ils aiment nager dans la mer ou simplement se relaxer. Un problème: il y a souvent beaucoup de touristes en août.

22% des Français aiment mieux passer leurs vacances à la campagne pour le calme et les paysages. C'est une destination qui devient de plus en plus populaire, mais pour les enfants c'est moins intéressant.

1a 📖📖🎧 Read the main article. Note an advantage and a disadvantage for each destination.

Destinations: seaside   countryside   mountains   city break   cruise

1b 📖📖🎧 Read the readers' opinions and answer the questions in English.

1 Why did Richard like the seaside?

2 What does he think of it now?

3 What did Béatrice think of the countryside?

4 Where will she go next year?

2a 🎧 Listen to Section A and decide which two statements are true.

1 Océane aime se détendre en vacances.

2 Elle aime nager dans la mer.

3 Elle n'a jamais fait de sports nautiques.

4 Elle préfère passer ses vacances en France.

5 Elle adore goûter des plats étrangers.

2b 🎧 Listen to Section B and decide which two statements are true.

1 Olivier ne veut pas faire de tâches ménagères quand il est en vacances.
2 Il y avait beaucoup de soleil quand il a fait du camping.
3 Il ne s'entend pas bien avec ses parents.
4 Il doit économiser de l'argent pour partir en vacances avec ses amis.
5 Il voudrait bien faire le tour du monde.

3 **G** Match up the sentence beginnings and endings and complete the verbs in the imperfect tense.

1 Je suis resté à la maison
2 Maintenant, j'aime aller à la plage, mais
3 J'ai bronzé à la plage et
4 Je n'ai pas nagé parce que
5 Ils sont tombés plusieurs fois
6 Nous avons bu une limonade

a l'eau ét_____ trop froide.
b quand ils fais_____ du ski.
c parce qu'il pleuv_____.
d parce que nous av_____ soif.
e c'ét_____ relaxant au soleil.
f avant j'aim_____ mieux la campagne.

4 🗨 🌐 In five minutes go round the class and ask as many people as possible these questions about holiday preferences. Make a note of your findings.

▪ Où est-ce que tu aimes partir en vacances et pourquoi?
▪ Quelle sorte de logement préfères-tu? Pourquoi?
▪ Comment est-ce que tu aimes voyager? Pourquoi?
▪ En vacances, qu'est-ce que tu aimes faire pendant la journée?

▪ Et le soir?
▪ Tu aimes mieux les vacances en famille ou avec des amis? Pourquoi?
▪ Où es-tu parti(e) l'année dernière? C'était comment?
▪ Comment seront tes prochaines vacances? Pourquoi?

Report what you have found out to someone else.

The imperfect tense

This tense is used to describe what was happening, what used to happen or what something was like.

Quand j'étais petit, j'aimais le bord de la mer. – When I was small, I liked the seaside.

Remove the *-ons* from the present tense *nous* form of the verb and add the following endings: *-ais, -ais, -ait, -ions, -iez, -aient*.

***jou**ons* ➡ *jou + ais* ➡ *je jouais*

Être is irregular – *j'étais*.

Also learn about using the correct preposition when talking about going 'to' or being 'in' countries.

See page 84 ➡

Grammaire page 182

🗨 When speaking French, avoid making up words you do not know. Use only what you are sure is correct. If you are talking about holidays, for example, and you forget the French word for campsite, it is better to say *j'ai logé dans un hôtel* than to make up something which may be wrong.

Stratégie

When you are starting a written or spoken task, try to use an imperfect tense to set the scene before using the perfect, e.g. *Samedi dernier, il faisait mauvais, donc j'ai décidé de faire les magasins.*

Il y avait ('there was' or 'there were') is a very useful imperfect form.

Astuce

Alison aime partir en Espagne parce qu'il y fait chaud. Elle préfère loger dans un hôtel. Elle préfère voyager en train.

Je préfère / J'aime	partir à la campagne / au bord de la mer / à la montagne		j'aime les vacances tranquilles / faire de la voile.
J'aime mieux loger	dans un hôtel / un terrain de camping / une villa	parce que / qu'	c'est plus confortable / pratique.
J'aime	bronzer / visiter les monuments / aller au restaurant		je trouve ça relaxant / fascinant.
Je préfère partir avec	mes parents / mes amis		ils paient pour moi / j'ai plus de liberté.
Je suis allé(e)	en Italie / au Canada / aux Caraïbes		le climat est très agréable.

Des projets de vacances

1 **V** Put these expressions into chronological order, starting with *l'année dernière*.

l'année dernière	le week-end dernier	il y a trois mois
demain	le week-end prochain	dans trois mois
l'été prochain	hier	aujourd'hui

Les vacances des Français

Les Français ont la réputation de ne pas aimer le travail, de ne penser qu'aux loisirs. Ces jugements sont certainement un peu inexacts, mais il est vrai de dire que la plupart des Français sont très attachés à leurs vacances.

La destination la plus populaire en hiver est la montagne: pendant les vacances de février, une semaine dans une station de ski est le rêve de beaucoup de Français. Mais en août, plus de 35 millions de Français partent en vacances et reviennent au bord de la mer, dans les stations balnéaires des côtes de la Méditerranée ou de l'Atlantique, à la recherche du soleil.

Pour ceux qui aiment le calme, il reste la campagne. On peut y faire des promenades, aller à la pêche dans les rivières, nager dans les lacs, redécouvrir l'histoire d'une région, admirer les paysages. On a remarqué que ce «tourisme vert» est devenu plus populaire récemment. Encore plus de touristes vont retourner à la campagne à l'avenir car le milieu rural est à la mode.

En général, les Français n'aiment pas traverser les frontières et préfèrent rester dans leur pays. Seulement 15% des Français ont visité un pays étranger pendant leurs vacances et ce nombre va diminuer en raison de l'impact négatif de l'aviation sur l'environnement. La plupart de ces séjours se passent dans un pays voisin, surtout l'Espagne. Les Français aiment revoir les belles plages espagnoles.

A

B

C

2a 📖🎧👁 Read the article and look at pictures A, B and C. In which order are they mentioned in the article?

2b 📖🎧👁 According to the article, are these statements true (T), false (F) or not mentioned (?)?

1 Les Français apprécient les sports d'hiver.
2 La côte de la Méditerranée est plus populaire que la côte Atlantique.
3 Il n'y a rien à faire à la campagne.
4 En général, les Français aiment mieux partir à l'étranger.
5 25% des Français ne partent pas en vacances.
6 Les Français prendront moins souvent l'avion.

📖 Many adjectives beginning with *in-* (such as *inexact*) are the equivalent of the English 'un-' or '-less', e.g. *inconfortable* (uncomfortable), *inutile* (useless). Look out for these when reading or listening to French. Verbs beginning with *re-* (such as *retourner*) often mean to do something again, e.g. *revenir* (to come back), *revoir* (to see again). How many can you find in the article?

Stratégie

3 🎧 Fill in the table with the correct destinations (a–d) and activities (e–l). Note down the correct letters for each person.

	Destination last year	Activities last year	Destination this year	Activities this year
Maxime				
Clémentine				
Anaïs				

> **Astuce**
>
> When doing listening activities which require noting different types of information, you will find it easier to listen twice, focusing on just one aspect of the task each time. In this case, listen once for destinations and once for activities.

a	seaside	b	mountains	c	city break	d countryside
e	shopping	f	water sports	g	walking	h theme park
i	cycling	j	museums	k	reading	l sunbathing

4 **G** Working with a partner, put the verbs in brackets into the correct tense (perfect or future).

1 L'année dernière, je _____ _____ en Suisse, tandis que cette année, je _____ la Grèce. (aller, visiter)

2 Il y a deux ans, j'_____ _____ mes vacances aux États-Unis mais cet été, j'_____ en France. (passer, aller)

3 J'_____ toujours _____ mes parents en vacances mais l'année prochaine, je _____ avec un groupe d'amis. (accompagner, partir)

4 Je n'_____ rien _____ l'année dernière, tandis que cette fois, je _____ certainement du shopping. (acheter, faire)

5 Je _____ l'avion cette année parce que j'_____ _____ en train au mois de mars et c'était trop long. (prendre, voyager)

6 Je _____ une chambre dans un hôtel parce que l'année dernière, j'_____ _____ dans une auberge de jeunesse, ce qui était affreux. (réserver, loger)

> **Grammaire** pages 181, 183
>
> ### Combining perfect and future tenses
>
> This is a good way to include more complex structures in your work. If you start with the perfect tense, you could use the connectives *mais* and *tandis que* to introduce the future part. If you start with the future, you could use the linking term *parce que*.
>
> *L'année dernière, je suis parti en vacances en famille mais cette année, je partirai sans mes parents.*
>
> Also learn about using *quand* with the future tense.   *See page 84* ➡

5 ✏ Compare last year's holiday with your plans for this year.

- ▮ Include where you stayed last year and what you intend to do this year.

- ▮ Describe what you did and what you intend to do.

- ▮ Describe last year's destination and give your opinion about it.

- ▮ Describe this year's destination and say why you have chosen it.

- ▮ Say who you went with last year and who you are going with this time.

> **Astuce**
>
> To compare things when speaking or writing in French, try to use connective phrases such as *cependant, pourtant, tandis que* and *en revanche*.

L'année dernière, je suis allé(e) … et j'ai logé dans …,	pourtant cette année, j'irai … et je logerai dans …
L'été dernier, j'ai fait / joué / visité …,	tandis que cette année, je ferai / jouerai / visiterai …
L'année dernière, il y avait / il n'y avait pas de …	Je l'ai trouvé / J'ai trouvé ça …
Cette année, il y aura … / la destination sera …	J'ai choisi cet endroit parce que …
La dernière fois que je suis parti(e) en vacances, j'y suis allé(e) avec …,	cependant / en revanche, la prochaine fois j'irai avec…

Qu'est-ce que vous voudriez faire en vacances?

A Vous avez toujours un guide à la main, vous cherchez donc les sites, les musées et les lieux des grands événements historiques (les champs de bataille, les cavernes et les grottes).

B Vous voulez vous sentir mieux. Au début de votre séjour, essayez un traitement dans notre station thermale. Plus tard dans la semaine, vous pouvez vous baigner en eau salée ou avant votre départ, pourquoi ne pas essayer un massage.

C Louez un de nos bateaux bien équipés et naviguez doucement sur le canal. Vous pourrez vous relaxer en regardant les jolis paysages ou vous pourrez faire les magasins dans les grandes villes qui se trouvent au bord du canal.

D Tu as moins de 14 ans? Tu t'ennuies avec tes parents? Viens dans notre centre de vacances. Alpinisme, escalade, moto-neige, parapente: essaie une nouvelle activité chaque jour. Ne bronze pas idiot! C'est interdit.

E Venez voir les grands artisans de la région travailler le bois. Ils font souvent le même travail de père en fils. Si vous préférez, dégustez les plats traditionnels de la région.

1a Read the text and choose an appropriate title for each paragraph (A–E).

1 Vacances sur l'eau
2 Vacances terroir et traditions
3 Vacances culturelles
4 Vacances actives
5 Vacances de bien-être

1b Complete each sentence with a word chosen from the list.

1 C'est une bonne idée de visiter des sites et des musées si vous vous intéressez à l'_____ .
2 La station thermale est recommandée si on veut rester en bonne _____ .
3 Pendant les vacances sur le canal, on a la possibilité de faire du _____ .
4 Dans le centre de vacances, il y a un grand choix d'_____ intéressantes.
5 Dans beaucoup de régions, on peut essayer la _____ locale.

activités   cuisine   histoire   shopping   santé

2a 🎧 Listen and match each picture with the correct speaker. Write R (Rosalie), A (Alex) or M (Morgane).

2b 🎧 Listen again and note what the speaker thinks of the following. Is their attitude positive (P), negative (N) or mixed (P / N)?

1 Rosalie – water sports
2 Rosalie – walking in the woods
3 Alex – fishing
4 Alex – school work
5 Morgane – theme parks
6 Morgane – barge holidays

3 🅖 Complete each sentence with a verb in the conditional. Choose from the infinitives in the list.

1 S'il faisait froid, je _____ à la maison.
2 S'il avait assez d'argent, il _____ du ski.
3 Si on me donnait le choix, je _____ à la plage.
4 Si mes parents gagnaient à la loterie, nous _____ aux États-Unis.
5 Si possible, elle _____ en Inde.
6 Pendant nos vacances idéales, nous _____ des plats traditionnels.

| manger | partir | bronzer | rester | aller | faire |

> **Grammaire** page 183
>
> **The conditional**
> When you want to say what you **would** do, you use the conditional. To form the conditional, you use the same stem as the future tense, but with the imperfect tense endings. For most verbs the stem is the infinitive, e.g. *jouer* ➡ *je jouerais*. But remember the irregular forms, e.g. *avoir* ➡ *j'aurais*.
>
> *J'irais à la pêche au bord d'un lac tranquille.* – I would go fishing by a peaceful lake.
>
> Also learn about using the correct singular form of the imperative.
> *See page 85* ➡

4 📝 🌐 Describe a disastrous holiday and what you would do differently next time.

▧ Give some details about the holiday (when, where, who with).
▧ Say what went wrong on the holiday.
▧ Say where you would like to go next time and why.
▧ Say how you would make improvements.

Il y a deux ans / l'année dernière,	je suis allé(e) à / en …	avec …
	on a logé dans / à …	pendant …
Au début de la semaine,	je suis tombé(e) et je me suis cassé …	
Deux jours plus tard,	ma sœur a …	
Il pleuvait tous les jours. / Le temps était affreux.		
La prochaine fois,	je voudrais visiter / aller à …	
On logerait dans / à …	au lieu de …	parce que …
Je ne ferais pas de	randonnées / parachutisme	
Je n'irais pas à la	pêche	

> **Stratégie**
> 📝 Make your work more interesting by adding a sequence to your account. You can use the days of the week (*lundi, j'ai nagé dans la mer, mardi, j'ai fait une excursion*). Expressions such as *le lendemain* (the next day) or *deux jours plus tard* (two days later) are also useful. Don't forget the simple expressions *le matin*, *l'après-midi* and *le soir*.

> **Astuce**
> Try to use less obvious time expressions such as *la veille* (the day before) and *au bout de cinq jours* (after five days).

Objectifs
Getting around
The pronoun *y*
Listening for gist

2.9 Les excursions

On vous propose …

A

Bienvenue à bord notre bateau au design contemporain avec climatisation, pour une heure quarante-cinq minutes de croisière. Vous allez découvrir un Paris majestueux à travers la verrière panoramique. Amusez-vous pendant notre nouvelle soirée musicale! Dîner servi entre 19h00 et 20h30 (50 euros en sus). Départ du pont de l'Alma, accessible en métro (à cinq minutes du pont).

B

Visitez la maison et le jardin de l'artiste impressionniste Claude Monet. Départ de votre hôtel en car grand tourisme. Déjeuner au restaurant à Giverny. Continuation vers Rouen et visite guidée de la ville. Vous y serez logé dans un hôtel 2**. Dîner et logement compris.

C

Nous vous proposons un vol à bord d'un hélicoptère privé d'une durée de 15 min, 30 min ou 45 min. Un vol en hélicoptère inoubliable. Une fois dans les airs, vous allez découvrir les monuments de Paris: la tour Eiffel, la Défense, etc.! Pour deux personnes (les enfants ne sont pas admis à bord).

1a 📖🎧 Match each picture (1–3) with the correct advert (A–C).

1b 📖🎧 Read the adverts and decide if the information in the sentences below is true (T), false (F) or not mentioned (?).

1 On fait la promenade sur la Seine dans un vieux bateau.
2 Le déjeuner en bateau n'est pas compris dans le prix.
3 La visite de la maison de Monet dure une heure.
4 On passe la nuit à Rouen.
5 L'hélicoptère part près de la tour Eiffel.
6 Les enfants ne peuvent pas faire le vol en hélicoptère.

2a 🎧 🌐 Listen to the journey descriptions (1–5). Which is the means of transport mentioned in each one?

la voiture　le train　le bateau
l'avion　le bus

2b 🎧 🌐 All five travellers had negative experiences. Give two reasons why in each case.

3 Ⓖ Rewrite the sentences, replacing the highlighted words with the pronoun *y*.

1　Je suis allé au centre-ville en bus.
2　Nous sommes arrivés au camping deux heures plus tard.
3　J'ai bronzé à la plage toute la journée.
4　Il a mangé au restaurant presque tous les soirs.
5　Nous sommes montés dans le train avec tous nos bagages.
6　Il a décidé d'aller à la gare en taxi.

4 🗨 With a partner, answer these questions about getting around on holiday.

▮　Comment as-tu voyagé quand tu es parti(e) en vacances et pourquoi?
▮　Le voyage a duré combien de temps?
▮　Qu'est-ce que tu as fait pendant le voyage?
▮　Tu as fait des excursions en vacances? Qu'est-ce que tu as visité?
▮　Tu as loué un vélo / fait des randonnées?
▮　Quel est ton moyen de transport préféré et pourquoi?

The pronoun *y* **Grammaire** *page 177*

The indirect object pronoun *y*, usually translated as 'there', is used to replace a place already mentioned, e.g. *J'adore nager à la piscine. J'y vais une fois par semaine.*

Note that *y* is always placed between the subject and the verb in the present tense. In the perfect tense, place it before *avoir* or *être*, e.g. *J'y suis allé(e).*

Also learn about using the plural form of the imperative. *See page 85* ➡

Astuce When speaking in French, you can use exclamations to make what you say more interesting: *quel dommage!* (what a shame!), *quelle surprise!* (what a surprise!), *quelle horreur!* (how awful!), *quelles vacances!* (what a holiday!).

Comment as-tu voyagé quand tu es partie en vacances et pourquoi?

J'ai voyagé en avion parce qu'on arrive à destination plus vite, mais on dit que c'est mauvais pour l'environnement.

L'année dernière, quand je suis parti(e) en vacances,	j'ai voyagé en voiture / avion / train	parce que c'est plus pratique / très rapide / pas trop cher.
Le voyage a duré	environ trois heures.	
On est arrivés	à l'heure / en retard.	
Pendant le voyage,	j'ai lu un livre / joué aux cartes.	
Je l'ai trouvé / J'ai trouvé ça	ennuyeux / fatigant / assez agréable.	
J'ai fait une excursion en car / loué un vélo	et j'ai visité un château / fait une promenade.	
C'était	(assez / très) intéressant / ennuyeux.	
J'aime mieux voyager en avion / voiture	parce que c'est plus rapide / confortable / pratique,	mais c'est assez fatigant / plus cher que le train.

Holidays

A

Vannes, le 26 février

Monsieur,

Je viens de rentrer de mon séjour de deux semaines en Martinique et je voudrais vous faire les réflexions suivantes:

Il n'y avait pas de représentant de votre organisation à l'aéroport et nous avons dû attendre deux heures dans le car à l'aéroport avant de partir pour l'hôtel.

Nous avons réservé une chambre à deux lits avec salle de bains. En arrivant, nous avons trouvé une chambre à un grand lit sans salle de bains.

Selon la brochure, l'hôtel est très près de la mer. En réalité, elle était au moins à vingt minutes à pied.

La plage était sale à cause de la pollution du port juste à côté.

La brochure indiquait qu'il y avait des distractions tous les soirs. Le samedi, il y a eu une soirée disco, mais c'est tout.

Les excursions étaient mal organisées et souvent, elles ont été annulées sans explication.

À cause de tout ceci, je trouve que vous devriez nous rembourser une partie de la somme que nous avons payée avant de partir.

Je vous prie de recevoir, monsieur, l'expression de mes salutations distinguées,

J. Crougneau

J. Crougneau

B

Nantes, le 3 mars

Monsieur,

Nous sommes désolés d'apprendre que vos vacances en Martinique ne vous ont pas plu.

En effet, notre représentant était malade à ce moment-là, et c'est à cause de cela que vous avez eu des problèmes. D'habitude, il est bien organisé, mais cette fois-ci:

Le chauffeur du car n'avait pas la liste des hôtels de ses clients et a dû téléphoner au bureau.

La nouvelle réceptionniste de l'hôtel n'a pas trouvé votre réservation avec votre demande de chambre.

On a demandé au patron de l'hôtel d'organiser les excursions, mais lui aussi était malade.

Nous nous en excusons et vous prions d'accepter un chèque de 200 euros que vous trouverez avec cette lettre.

En espérant pouvoir vous être utile, nous vous prions, monsieur, de recevoir l'expression de nos sentiments les meilleurs,

R. Guyot

R. Guyot

Martinique – destination idéale pour toute la famille!

AQA *Examiner's tip*

At GCSE, you will not have to produce this type of formal letter, and you do not need to fully understand all the language used. For example, the last sentence is just an elaborate way of concluding, and is not vital to understanding. Focus on the main body of the letter to find the information you need.

1a 📖🎧 Read letter A and decide whether the following statements are true (T), false (F), or not mentioned (?).

1 The journey from the airport to the hotel took two hours.

2 They were expecting a room with a bath.

3 The beach was very close to the hotel.

4 The beach was polluted.

5 The hotel had an indoor swimming pool.

6 There was entertainment on Saturday evening.

7 They went on excursions every day.

8 They expect a complete refund of the price of their holiday.

1b 📖🎧 Read letter B, the response from the travel company. Choose the correct endings for the sentences.

1 The holiday representative did not meet the family because …
   a he was on holiday.
   b he was ill.
   c he was late.

2 The coach driver delayed leaving the airport because …
   a the coach had broken down.
   b he had to wait for another plane to arrive.
   c he did not know exactly where he had to go.

3 There were problems with the hotel room because …
   a the new receptionist did not know what the family wanted.
   b the new receptionist did not know what the rooms were like.
   c some of the rooms were not available.

4 The excursions should have been organised by …
   a the holiday representative.
   b the receptionist.
   c the hotel owner.

5 The cheque for 200 euros …
   a is included with the letter.
   b will be sent later.
   c was sent earlier.

6 In general, Monsieur Guyot …
   a is apologising for the problems.
   b is not willing to take responsibility for the problems.
   c is trying to argue that there was nothing really wrong.

> **Grammaire** page 184
>
> In both letters, the pronoun *on* is used when it is not clear exactly **who** did the action, or when the passive would be used in English. *On a demandé au patron* could be translated as 'the owner was asked'.
>
> For more information on the use of *on*, see page 71.

2a 🎧 Mr Crougneau's daughter Maëlle is telling her friend Rosanne about how she spent her birthday while in Martinique. Listen to Section A and choose the four pictures that match her experience (1–4).

2b 🎧 Listen to Section B and answer the questions in English.

1 How high does sugar cane grow?
2 Why do the birds perch on the sugar cane?
3 What was Maëlle's opinion of the visit to see rum being made? Give two reasons.
4 Why did her father buy some rum?
5 Where did she mention seeing bananas?
6 What surprised her about the coffee beans?
7 What suggests that she prefers chocolate to coffee?

> **AQA Examiner's tip**
>
> It is sometimes difficult to understand cognates or near cognates (words that are the same or similar to English) in listening passages because of their different pronunciation. Think about the context of an unfamiliar word. It may help you to recognise it. Listen to the words *rhum, canne, exotique, insectes*. Can you pick out any more?

> **Grammaire**
>
> In the last part of the conversation, Maëlle uses *ne … que* to describe something she **only** did once. For more information on this form of the negative, see page 186. ➡

> **Vocabulaire**
>
> | | |
> |---|---|
> | *annuler* | to cancel |
> | *la canne à sucre* | sugar cane |
> | *goûter* | to taste |
> | *le grain de café* | coffee bean |
> | *malgré* | in spite of |
> | *le rhum* | rum |

kerboodle!

(G) Holidays

'To' or 'in' countries / towns / regions; *quand* + future tense; *quand* + imperfect tense

1 Complete each sentence with *à, au, aux* or *en*.

1 Ils habitent _____ France.
2 Tu es déjà allé _____ États-Unis?
3 Elles voudraient aller _____ Bruxelles.
4 Je suis née _____ pays de Galles.
5 Il y a des auberges de jeunesse _____ Paris?
6 On nous recommande de partir _____ Suisse.
7 On peut aller _____ Belgique en Eurostar.
8 Elle a passé trois mois _____ Maroc.

> **Grammaire** page 188
>
> **'To' or 'in' countries / towns / regions**
> The French word for 'in' and 'to' can be *à, au, aux* or *en*.
>
> | | |
> |---|---|
> | *à* + villages, towns or cities | *à Paris* – in / to Paris |
> | *en* + names of feminine countries | *en France* – in / to France |
> | *au* + names of masculine countries | *au pays de Galles* – in / to Wales |
> | *aux* + plural nouns | *aux États-Unis* – in / to the United States |

2 Decide whether the verbs in brackets need to be in the future tense or the present. Complete each sentence using the correct form.

1 Quand ils _____ la ville, ils iront au musée d'art moderne. (visiter)
2 Quand on _____ au Maroc, je t'enverrai une carte postale. (aller)
3 Quand je _____ en Suisse, c'est pour voir mes parents. (aller)
4 Il _____ les photos quand vous rentrerez d'Écosse. (voir)
5 Quand tu _____ là-bas, tu pourras admirer la mer. (être)
6 Quand j' _____ de l'argent, je pars en vacances! (avoir)
7 Je _____ en vacances quand je serai plus riche. (partir)
8 Quand tu _____ à la gare, il sera huit heures. (arriver)

> **Grammaire** page 189
>
> **Quand + future tense**
> Use the future tense after *quand* to express something due to happen in the future.
>
> *Quand j'irai à Boulogne, je mangerai du poisson.* – When I go to Boulogne, I'll eat fish.
>
> However, use the present tense to express a general statement.
>
> *Quand je vais à Boulogne, je mange du poisson.* – When I go to Boulogne, I eat fish.

3 Find the correct ending for each sentence, then fill the gaps by choosing verbs from the list.

1 Quand j'_____ petite,
2 Quand ils _____ un but,
3 Quand ma sœur s'_____,
4 Quand on _____ en Irlande,
5 Quand tu _____ en vacances,
6 Quand il _____ à la poissonnerie,

a il se levait à cinq heures.
b j'allais souvent à Paris.
c elle jouait aux cartes.
d tu voyageais en train.
e il faisait toujours beau!
f tout le monde criait.

> **Grammaire** page 189
>
> **Quand + imperfect tense**
> Use the imperfect tense after *quand* to describe what was happening, what used to happen or what something was like.
>
> *Quand j'habitais à Paris, j'allais souvent au cinéma.*
>
> For more on the imperfect tense, see page 75.

allait   ennuyait   étais   marquaient   partais   travaillait

Singular imperatives; plural or formal imperatives

4 Translate the sentences into English. They all contain singular imperatives (commands).

Exemple: Visite le port! – Visit the harbour!

1 Loue un vélo!
2 Va à la pêche!
3 Va voir le château.
4 Ne me quitte pas!
5 Prends un bateau!
6 Reviens en train!
7 N'oublie pas de composter les billets!

Grammaire *page 183*

Singular imperatives

Use the imperative when giving orders or instructions.

Use the *tu* form when you speak to someone your own age or someone you know very well.

Va à la piscine! – Go to the swimming pool.

Achète un billet! – Buy a ticket.

5 Rewrite all the sentences from activity 4 using the plural or formal form of the imperative.

Exemple: Visitez le port!

6 Rewrite the following sentences. Replace the infinitives with the correct form of the imperative (as shown in brackets) and replace the symbols with words.

Grammaire *page 183*

Plural or formal imperatives

Use the *vous* form when speaking to someone you don't know very well or to more than one person. The *vous* form normally ends in -*ez*, except *faites* (from *faire*).

Allez au camping! – Go to the campsite.

Tournez à gauche. – Turn left.

Exemple: Prendre un . (tu)

Prends un vélo!

1 Tourner à . (tu)

2 Voyager en ! (vous)

3 Réserver un confortable! (tu)

4 Ne stationner pas devant la . (vous)

5 Éviter de prendre l' . (vous)

6 N' oublier pas ta . (tu)

Holidays

Vive les vacances! ➡ *pages 74–75*

	barbant(e)	boring
le	*bord de la mer*	seaside
	bronzer	to sunbathe / to get a tan
la	*campagne*	countryside
le	*camping*	campsite
la	*croisière*	cruise (holiday)
la	*cuisine*	cooking / cuisine (national)
	étranger(-ère)	foreign
à l'	*étranger (m)*	abroad
	il y avait	there was / were
le	*mal de mer*	seasickness
la	*méduse*	jellyfish
la	*mer*	sea
la	*montagne*	mountain(s)
	nager	to swim
	passer	to spend (time)
le	*paysage*	landscape / scenery
la	*plage*	beach
	pleuvoir (plu)	to rain
le	*séjour*	stay (in a place)
le	*sport d'hiver*	winter sport
le	*terrain de camping*	campsite
la	*vue*	view

1 ⓥ **Link each holiday destination to an activity you might do there.**

1	le bord de la mer	a	faire du ski
2	la montagne	b	visiter les musées
3	la campagne	c	bronzer à la plage
4	la ville	d	passer des vacances sur un bateau
5	une croisière	e	faire une promenade dans la nature

Des projets de vacances ➡ *pages 76–77*

	aller à la pêche	to go fishing
l'	*Atlantique (m)*	the Atlantic
l'	*auberge (f) de jeunesse*	youth hostel
le	*champ*	field
la	*côte*	coast
	décoller	to take off (plane)
	faire les magasins	to go shopping
	faire de la planche à voile	to go windsurfing
	faire des randonnées	to go hiking
	faire de la voile	to go sailing
la	*forêt*	forest
la	*frontière*	border (between countries)
l'	*hiver (m)*	winter
	injuste	unfair
	louer	to rent / to hire
la	*Méditerranée*	the Mediterranean
le	*milieu rural*	rural environment
le	*parc d'attractions*	theme park
le	*pays étranger*	foreign country
le	*pays voisin*	neighbouring country
	redécouvrir	to rediscover
	remarquer	to notice
le	*soleil*	sun
la	*station balnéaire*	seaside resort
la	*station de ski*	ski resort
le / la	*touriste*	tourist
le	*trajet*	journey / trip
le	*travail*	work

Que faire en vacances? ➡ *pages 78–79*

se	*baigner*	to bathe / to swim
le	*bateau*	ship / boat
	bouger	to move
	bien équipé(e)	well equipped / with good facilities
au	*début*	at the beginning
la	*détente*	relaxation / chilling out
s'	*ennuyer*	to get bored / to be bored
le	*gîte*	self-catering accommodation
(s')	*inquiéter*	to worry
	salé(e)	salty
se	*sentir*	to feel
la	*station thermale*	spa resort
le	*terroir*	local area

2 **Ⓥ** Match each word or phrase with its English translation.

1 un événement historique
2 les champs de bataille
3 une grotte
4 un traitement
5 la chasse
6 un artisan
7 le parachutisme

a hunting
b parachuting
c a craftsman
d a historical event
e a cave
f battlefields
g a treatment

Les excursions ➡ *pages 80–81*

	à l'heure	on time
l'	*aire (f) de repos*	stopping area (off the motorway, with basic facilities)
l'	*arrêt (m) (d'autobus)*	bus stop
	attendre (attendu)	to wait
l'	*autoroute (f)*	motorway
les	*bagages (m)*	luggage
	bienvenue	welcome
la	*climatisation*	air conditioning
	compris(e)	included
la	*correspondance*	change (on train journey)
	découvrir (découvert)	to discover
	durer	to last
l'	*essence (f)*	petrol
les	*feux rouges (m)*	red lights (traffic lights)
la	*gare*	railway station
la	*gare routière*	coach or bus station
la	*ligne*	line / route
le	*métro*	the underground (in Paris)
le	*passage à niveau*	level crossing
le / la	*passager / passagère*	passenger
le	*prix*	price
le	*retard*	delay
la	*route*	road
la	*salle d'attente*	waiting room
	sauf	except
la	*station de taxi*	taxi rank
la	*traversée*	crossing (e.g. the Channel)
le	*trottoir*	pavement
la	*visite guidée*	guided tour

2 🗩 En vacances

You are on holiday in France. You have agreed to take part in a survey about holidays.
Your teacher will play the part of the person carrying out the survey and will ask you the following:

1 personal details
2 details about your accommodation
3 why you chose the area
4 what you did yesterday
5 what you have planned for today
6 where you intend to holiday next
7 **!**

! Remember you will have to respond to something that you have not yet prepared.

1 **Personal details**
   - Say your name and spell it. Say when and where you were born.
   - Say how you travelled, how long it took and what you did during the journey.
   - Say how long you are staying for and ask what's on in the area during your stay.
   - Give details about your family and their areas of special interest.

2 **Details about your accommodation**
   - Say where your hotel is located and give a short description of it.
   - Describe the hotel facilities – inside and outside.
   - Describe your room and compare it to your room at home.
   - Say what you think of the standard of accommodation and whether it is good value for money.

3 **Why you chose the area**
   - Give two reasons why you chose the area.
   - Say what you did last year for your summer holiday.
   - Compare it to your own area at home and to your last holiday destination.
   - Say which area you prefer and give reasons.

AQA Examiner's tips

Start with *Je m'appelle …* and then say *Mon prénom s'écrit …* and *mon nom de famille s'écrit …*
Use *prendre* or *durer* to say how long the journey took.
Start your question with *Qu'est-ce qu'il y a … ?* Asking a question yourself makes it seem more like a real conversation, and can help you to gain extra marks.

AQA Examiner's tips

Now, start your plan. Write a maximum of six words. Here are some suggested words for the first section: *nom, anniversaire, voyage, séjour, famille, loisirs.*
Remember that you need to write five or six words for each of the points mentioned in the task description (top left), but that you must not write more than 40 in total.
Don't use unnecessary words such as articles or prepositions on your plan.

AQA Examiner's tips

Use *à l'intérieur* and *à l'extérieur* for inside and outside.
Use *plus / moins / aussi … que* when comparing rooms.
You will need to use adjectives to describe things. If you are describing feminine items, make sure you use the feminine form of adjectives, e.g. *petite* for *chambre*, *haute* for *qualité*, etc. The expression for good value is *bon marché*, but you may prefer to say *pas trop cher*.

AQA Examiner's tips

Show that you can use complex grammatical structures such as *choisir de* + verb, *j'ai aimé / je n'ai pas aimé* + verb.
Link up opinions and reasons using *car, parce que* and *par contre*.
Use words that suggest something to you on your plan. You can use proper nouns, so you might include the names of holiday destinations. The aim is to remind you of what you are going to say next.

4 What you did yesterday

- Say where you went yesterday morning and what you did.
- Say what you thought of it and give reasons for your opinion.
- Say what you did for the rest of the day and compare it to what you normally do at home.
- Say what other members of your family did and what they thought of it.

AQA Examiner's tips

Normalement and *d'habitude* are followed by a verb in the present tense.

Check how to use *avoir* and *être* in the perfect tense when referring to other people. See grammar section page 181.

To give your opinion, use the perfect tense, e.g. *J'ai pensé que …, j'ai trouvé que …* followed by the imperfect (usually *c'était*).

You will have the task card in front of you. Therefore, you do not need to write words such as *hier* on your plan. Use the task card plus your plan to remind you what to say next.

5 What you have planned for today

- Say what your own plans for today are (morning, afternoon and evening).
- Say why you chose those activities.
- Say what you will do if it rains or if you are prevented from doing what you have planned.
- Say what others in your family want to do today and mention alternatives in case that proves impossible.

AQA Examiner's tips

Use various ways of introducing a future event, e.g. *je vais / je voudrais / j'espère / j'ai l'intention de …*

When talking about what others want to do, be careful with the verb forms, e.g. *il va, ils vont.*

You can show initiative by relating your chosen activities for the day to your usual areas of interest, e.g. *D'habitude, chez moi, je …*

Take care! The title of this section is in the past tense (what you have planned for today), but most of what you say is likely to be in the future or using a construction that suggests the future, e.g. *j'espère.*

6 Where you intend to holiday next

- Say where you intend to holiday next, mentioning the type of holiday and accommodation.
- Give one or two reasons for your choice.
- Say how long you would like to go for and why that particular length of time.
- Say what you would like to do or visit there and why.

AQA Examiner's tips

Show that you can handle using a variety of tenses within the same section, in this case future for the first bullet point, present and past for the second bullet point, conditional for the last two bullet points.

When six words are not enough to illustrate what you want to say, try to select words that will remind you of more than one idea.

Remember that you can use visuals as well as words on your plan.

7 ! The conclusion to the survey might be about:

- how the resort could be made more appealing to various groups of people
- what you think the area has to offer compared to other areas
- the impact of tourism on the local environment
- what you think of a new housing development project targeted at tourists.

AQA Examiner's tips

Choose the two options which you think are the most likely, and for each of these, note down three different ideas. In your plan, write three words that illustrate each of the two most likely options. For the first option you might choose: *adultes, jeunes, familles.*

Remember to check the total number of words you have used. It should be 40 or fewer.

You should now have completed your plan and prepared your answers. Give your plan to your teacher for feedback. Compare your answers with the online sample version – you might find some useful hints to make yours even better.

kerboodle!

2 Mes loisirs

You are writing an email to your French friend Stéphanie who has asked you:

1. what you do with your free time when you stay in
2. what you do when you go out
3. how much money you receive and who from
4. how you like spending your money
5. if you have a mobile phone
6. if you are interested in fashion
7. if you are sporty.

> **AQA Examiner's tips**
>
> Start with *J'aime beaucoup écouter ...*
> Don't use many names (groups, singers) or titles of TV programmes in English. Explain what they are instead, e.g. *J'aime beaucoup les émissions de sport ...*
> Use *J'ai invité ... chez moi* to say you had a friend round, then remember to use *nous* (we) and the correct verb endings.
> Show your knowledge of the perfect tense by using a combination of verbs that take *avoir* and *être*, including reflexive verbs, e.g. *j'ai regardé ..., nous sommes montées ..., nous nous sommes couchés ...*

1. **What you do with your free time when you stay in**
   - Write about music that you listen to and play.
   - Write about how much TV you watch, your favourite programmes and what you watched last night.
   - Mention what you like and don't like doing on the computer.
   - Mention what happened last time you had a friend round.

> **AQA Examiner's tips**
>
> Now, start your plan. Write a maximum of six words. Here are some suggested words for the first section: *musique, instrument, télé, ordinateur, copine.*
> Use fewer than six words if it is enough to illustrate what you intend to say. You may find it useful to have spare words later on in the task. Don't forget that the maximum number for the whole task is 40.

2. **What you do when you go out**
   - Include where you go and what you do.
   - Mention when you go and who with.
   - Describe what happened last time you went out.
   - Explain the potential problems linked with young people staying out late at night.

> **AQA Examiner's tips**
>
> Rather than just naming the person / people you go out with, explain what they are like and how you get on with them, e.g. *Je m'entends bien avec ... parce que ...*
> You could introduce the last section with *Quand les jeunes sortent tard le soir, ...*
> Add up to six words to your plan.

3. **How much money you receive and who from**
   - Say how much money you receive per week or per month, and whether it is pocket money or money that you earn.
   - Say whether you think it is enough, and why or why not.
   - Compare the pocket money you get with what your brothers / sisters / friends get.
   - Say how much you would like to get ideally and say why.

> **AQA Examiner's tips**
>
> Use *je dois* + verb to say what you have to do to earn your pocket money.
> Think of various ways of expressing your opinion, e.g. *Je pense que c'est ... / À mon avis, c'est ... / Je trouve que c'est ...*
> In your plan, use just one word from a phrase if it is enough to remind you what it refers to, e.g. *poche* is probably enough to remind you that the topic is pocket money, not just 'pocket'.

4 How you like spending your money

- Include how much you regularly save, what for and when that is to happen.
- Mention what you like buying with your money and who it is for.
- Give details of how you spent your money last month and what you thought of what you bought.
- Describe what you would do if you won the lottery.

Use *j'aime m'acheter …* to say what you like buying for yourself.

Start the last bullet point with *Si je gagnais la loterie, je voudrais …*

What you write in your plan is likely to reflect your own experience and, therefore, means something to you and you only. It is best for you to keep your plan to yourself and not to borrow someone else's.

5 If you have a mobile phone

- Say that you have a mobile phone and how you got it.
- Describe what it can do and what you like doing with it.
- Include how much you spend on it monthly and who pays for it.
- Give your opinion of your mobile and how it compares to your previous mobile.

If you were given your mobile, start your sentence with (*Mon père*) *m'a donné …*

Use *mon ancien portable* to refer to your previous mobile. If your new mobile has more features, you might want to say *Avec mon nouveau portable, je peux aussi …*

Remember that the word for better is *meilleur*, and worse is *pire*.

6 If you are interested in fashion

- Say what clothes you like wearing and describe them.
- Say whether fashion is important to you and why.
- Describe a fashionable item you bought recently and say how much it cost.
- Explain why it is difficult to keep up with fashion.

Use colours and materials to describe clothes, e.g. *vert / verts / verte / vertes* (make sure you choose the correct version), *en coton / en cuir*, etc.

Use *suivre la mode* for 'to keep up with fashion'.

In your plan, you may want to use grammatical markers to help you remember what tense you should use at that point, e.g. *récemment*.

7 If you are sporty

- Mention which sports you like and dislike and say why.
- Include how far and how frequently you walk and / or cycle in order to keep fit.
- Say whether your diet helps your fitness and what you should avoid eating.
- Say whether it is important to play sport and be fit and say why.

When writing about a sport, don't forget the article, e.g. 'I like football' is *J'aime le foot*. However, if you use *jouer*, the next word is usually *au*, e.g. *Je joue au foot*.

Introduce the idea of what you do to keep fit with *Pour garder la forme, je …*

See if you can recall everything you want to cover in your response to the task using just your plan. If you find it too hard to remember everything, you may want to change some of the words in it.

You should now have completed your plan and prepared your answers. Give your plan to your teacher for feedback. Compare your answers with the online sample version – you might find some useful hints to make yours even better.

2

1 Choose the correct phrase to end this sentence:

Quand je reste à la maison, j'aime …

a sortir. c passer du temps chez ma copine.

b lire. d jouer au foot au parc.

2 Choose the correct phrase to end this sentence:

Au ciné, j'adore …

a les dessins animés. c faire de l'équitation.

b les romans. d jouer de la guitare.

3 Choose the correct phrase to end this sentence:

Avec un téléphone portable on ne peut pas …

a appeler ses amis. c faire des photocopies.

b prendre des photos. d envoyer des textos.

4 Which of the following refers to a holiday by the sea?

a On a fait du ski nautique.

b On a fait des sports d'hiver.

c On est resté dans une petite ferme en pleine campagne.

d On est resté dans un hôtel près de la tour Eiffel.

5 Which of the following contains a verb in the imperfect tense?

a J'ai l'intention de passer mes vacances en Italie.

b J'ai bronzé au bord de la piscine.

c Il pleuvait beaucoup, quelle horreur!

d J'aimerais acheter des souvenirs.

6 Choose the correct French translation of this sentence:

I'll go to the United States by plane.

a Je vais partir au pays de Galles en avion.

b Il ira aux États-Unis en deltaplane.

c Elle voyagera en Amérique en avion.

d Je prendrai un vol pour les États-Unis.

Le sais-tu?

Le vélo est le sport le plus pratiqué en France. Est-ce que tu connais le nom de la grande course cycliste qui se passe chaque été en France? Les Français ont un surnom pour le vélo, ils l'appellent *la petite reine* (the little queen).

Le sais-tu?

Est-ce que tu sais que Paris est une des premières destinations touristiques du monde?

90% des Français ne partent pas à l'étranger, ils restent en France pour leurs vacances. Au mois d'août, presque tout le monde part en vacances. Il y a donc des embouteillages sur les autoroutes françaises. Est-ce que tu connais des villes touristiques françaises?

3 Home and environment

Home and local area

Special occasions celebrated in the home

Home, town, neighbourhood and region, where it is and what it is like

Environment

Current problems facing the planet

Being environmentally friendly within the home and local area

3.1 On fait la fête
- Combining perfect and imperfect tenses
- Including negative expressions

3.2 Ma maison
- Using *depuis* and *pendant*
- Qualifiers and intensifiers

3.3 Là où j'habite
- Adjectives with special forms
- Clues about size and quantity

3.4 Des mondes différents
- Passive voice and *on*
- Percentages and fractions

3.5 La pollution
- *Il faut* + infinitive or subjunctive
- Pronunciation of similar words

3.6 Planète en danger
- Common subjunctive expressions
- Fluency techniques

3.7 L'environnement et ma ville
- Expressions of sequence
- Recognising words from ones already known

Compass points; house types and locations

1a 📖🎧 Look at the map to check which three of the statements are true. Correct the statements that are false.

1 Calais est dans le sud de la France.
2 Bruges est dans le nord de la Belgique.
3 Marseille est dans le sud de la France.
4 Genève est dans l'est de la Suisse.
5 Bordeaux est dans le sud-est de la France.
6 Rennes est dans le nord-ouest de la France.

1b ✏ Write four more sentences describing the positions of other cities on the map.

2a 📖🎧 Read what Théo says about his friends and relatives, then match each statement with the correct person.

«Quand je suis chez mon père, j'habite un appartement moderne en centre-ville. Chez ma mère, c'est une petite maison individuelle dans la banlieue de Nantes. Ma copine Nadia habite un vieil appartement en centre-ville et elle rêve d'un chalet à la montagne! Moi, je préférerais une grande maison au bord de la mer. La campagne aussi, c'est sympa. Ma grand-mère habite une petite maison dans un village du sud-est de la France. J'aime bien aller chez elle.»

Vocabulaire	
le centre	centre
l'est (m)	east
le nord	north
l'ouest (m)	west
le sud	south

Vocabulaire	
l'appartement (m)	apartment / flat
la banlieue	suburbs
la campagne	countryside
grand(e)	large
la maison	house
la montagne	mountain(s)
petit(e)	small
vieux / vieille	old
la ville	town / city

1 Son appartement est moderne.
2 Cette personne habite à la campagne.
3 Sa maison idéale est au bord de la mer.
4 Sa maison est située à Nantes, à l'extérieur du centre-ville.
5 Cette personne aimerait habiter à la montagne.

a Nadia, une copine de Théo
b la grand-mère de Théo
c la mère de Théo
d le père de Théo
e Théo

2b 🗨 Work in pairs. Partner A makes a statement about one of the people above (a–e) and where they live. Partner B says whether it is true or false and, if it is false, makes a correct statement. Then swap over.

> La mère de Théo habite en centre-ville.

> C'est faux! Elle habite dans la banlieue de Nantes.

Grammaire

Remember how to talk about the kind of area where people live.

en ville	in town
en banlieue	in the suburbs
à la campagne	in the country(side)
au bord de la mer	at the seaside

Rooms in house; furniture and prepositions

1a  Read Rose's email about her new house, then answer the questions below.

De:	Rose
À:	Théo
Sujet:	Ma nouvelle maison

Au rez-de-chaussée, il y a l'entrée, un petit salon et puis une super grande cuisine. Il y a aussi des toilettes et puis l'escalier pour monter au premier étage où il y a un grand salon, un petit bureau et la chambre de mes parents. Au deuxième étage, il y a ma chambre, la chambre d'Émilie et puis la salle de bains. Il n'y a pas de cave, mais nous avons un immense jardin avec une belle cabane!

1 Where is her parents' bedroom?

2 How many bedrooms are there?

3 How many sitting rooms are there?

4 Where is the main bathroom?

5 Where is the toilet?

6 Where is the study?

Vocabulaire

le bureau	office / study
la cabane	shed / hut
la cave	cellar
la chambre	bedroom
la cuisine	kitchen
le premier / deuxième étage	first / second floor
le rez-de-chaussée	ground floor
la salle à manger	dining room
la salle de bains	bathroom
le salon	sitting room
les toilettes (f)	toilet

1b ✎ Adapt Rose's email to give a description of your own house or a house of your dreams.

2a Look at the picture and correct the description. There are four mistakes.

J'ai rangé ma chambre! La table (où est mon ordinateur) est devant la fenêtre. Mes livres sont sur les étagères. Mon cartable est sous la table. Mes baskets sont à côté du lit. Mon portable et mon mp3 sont dans mon cartable. J'ai mis ma guitare entre l'armoire et la fenêtre, et le chat est derrière la porte!

Théo

2b 🗩 Work in pairs. Partner A makes a statement about Théo's bedroom. Partner B says whether it is true or false and, if it is false, corrects it. Then swap over.

La guitare est sous le lit.

C'est faux! Elle est dans l'armoire.

Vocabulaire

l'armoire (f)	wardrobe
la commode	chest of drawers
à côté de	next to
dans	in
derrière	behind
devant	in front of
entre	between
l'étagère (f)	shelf
la fenêtre	window
le lit	bed
l'ordinateur (m)	computer
la porte	door
sous	under
sur	on

Helping at home; daily routine

1a 📖🎧 Read about what Théo does to help at home, then choose the correct caption for each picture.

> Chez ma mère, je range ma chambre une fois par mois et je passe l'aspirateur dans la maison une fois par semaine. Par contre, je ne fais jamais la vaisselle, car nous avons un lave-vaisselle. Ma mère fait souvent la cuisine. C'est mon beau-père qui fait les courses deux fois par semaine. Mes petits frères rangent leur chambre de temps en temps et, quelquefois, ils mettent la table. C'est tout.
>
> Chez mon père, je fais souvent le ménage. C'est mon père qui fait les courses et la cuisine. Il adore ça! Moi, je mets la table et je fais la vaisselle.

Théo

1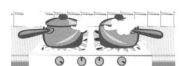
    a Théo est chez son père.
    b Théo est chez sa mère.

2
    a Le père de Théo adore faire la cuisine.
    b Le beau-père de Théo adore faire la cuisine.

3
    a On est chez le père de Théo.
    b On est chez la mère de Théo.

1b ✏️ Describe who does what in your household and when. Use Théo's description to help you.

2a 📖🎧 Read and complete Alice's email complaining about her twin sister, Manon.

2b ✏️ Write a caption for each picture. Use Alice's email to help you.

Vocabulaire

une fois par semaine/mois	once a week/ month
jamais	never
quelquefois	sometimes
rarement	rarely
souvent	often
de temps en temps	from time to time
tous les jours	every day

Vocabulaire

les courses (f)	the shopping
la cuisine	the cooking
le ménage	the housework
mettre la table	to lay the table
nettoyer	to clean
ranger sa chambre	to tidy one's bedroom
la vaisselle	the washing up

Grammaire *page 181*

Remember that reflexive verbs have an extra pronoun (*me, te, se*, etc.).

se réveiller	**to get up**
je me réveille	I get up
tu te réveilles	you get up
il / elle / on se réveille	he / she / one gets up

Refer to the list of reflexive verbs on page 110 to help you with activities 2a–b.

> Je partage ma chambre avec ma sœur jumelle, Manon, et c'est l'horreur!
>
> Manon _____ lève à six heures et demie. Moi, je _____ lève à sept heures et quart. Manon se douche et elle _____ habille, puis elle prend son petit déjeuner très lentement. Moi, je _____ lave et je _____ brosse les dents très vite. Je _____ habille et hop! je pars au collège.
>
> Le soir, Manon _____ couche à dix heures. Moi, je _____ _____ vers onze heures. Après le dîner, j'_____ de la musique dans notre chambre. Mais Manon n'est pas contente: elle veut dormir! C'est énervant!

Home activities; perfect tense

1a 📖🎧 Read about Mimi's typical day and put the pictures into the correct order.

D'habitude, je me réveille à six heures et demie et j'écoute la radio au lit pendant une demi-heure. Après, je vais à la piscine où je nage pendant une heure. Après, je prends une douche. Ensuite, je rentre à la maison et je prends mon petit déjeuner. Normalement, entre neuf heures et quatorze heures, je suis toujours dans mon studio. Là, je joue de la guitare, je chante et j'écris des chansons.

À treize heures, je vais dans la cuisine, je mange une salade et je bois un café. L'après-midi, je me maquille et je sors. Je vais chez ma grand-mère tous les jours. En général, je suis chez elle entre trois heures et cinq heures … Le soir, je vais chez mes copains, on écoute de la musique, on discute et on s'amuse bien.

Vocabulaire

après	after that
bien s'amuser	to have a good time
la chanson	song
ensuite	then
entre … et …	between … and …
en général	generally
d'habitude	usually
se maquiller	to put make-up on
normalement	normally
pendant	during

1 **2**  **3** **4**  **5**  **6**

1b 💬 Work in pairs. Partner A pretends to be Mimi and says one thing she does on a typical day. Partner B says whether the statement is true or false. Then swap over.

> Normalement, je nage pendant deux heures.

> Faux!

2a 📖 Read Mimi's blog about last Friday. Copy all the phrases that are not part of her normal routine.

Vendredi dernier, je me suis réveillée à six heures et demie et je me suis levée tout de suite. Je suis allée à la piscine. Ensuite, je me suis douchée, mais je n'ai pas pris de petit déjeuner. Je me suis maquillée et je suis sortie. Je suis allée à Paris pour enregistrer une émission de télévision.

Vocabulaire

l'émission (f) de télévision	TV programme
enregistrer	to record

Grammaire — page 181

To talk about what happened in the past, use the perfect tense:

1 *avoir* + past participle – with most verbs
   j'ai nagé

2 *être* + past participle – with *aller, venir, sortir, rester*, etc.
   je suis sorti(e)

3 *être* + past participle – with refelexive verbs: *se réveiller, s'amuser*, etc.
   je me suis réveillé(e)

Remember – with *être* verbs, if the subject is feminine, add an *e* to the past participle.

Il est sorti et elle est rentrée!

2b ✏️ Yesterday, Mimi was back to her normal routine. Answer the following questions on her behalf.

1 Tu t'es réveillée à quelle heure?
2 Tu as nagé pendant combien de temps?
3 Qu'est-ce que tu as fait dans ton studio?
4 Qu'est-ce que tu as mangé?
5 Qu'est-ce que tu as fait l'après-midi?
6 Qu'est-ce que tu as fait le soir?

Objectifs

Special occasions celebrated in the home

Combining perfect and imperfect tenses

Including negative expressions

Noël et le jour de l'an

Tu aimes Noël, Marc?

Bien sûr. J'ai un petit frère de cinq ans et une petite sœur de sept ans, et eux, ils croient toujours au père Noël. Moi, je pense que je n'y croyais plus à leur âge. Le matin du vingt-cinq, ils réveillent tout le monde entre quatre et cinq heures! On descend tous pour admirer ce que le père Noël a apporté et les petits commencent à ouvrir leurs cadeaux tout de suite. Moi, maintenant, je fais partie des adultes, et pour ne pas rompre le charme de l'occasion, je joue le jeu de quelqu'un qui croit encore au père Noël. Plus tard, comme chaque année, ma mère prépare le repas traditionnel de Noël. Je l'aide un peu parce qu'il y a beaucoup de choses à faire. En général, on n'est jamais seuls à table. Mes deux cousins arrivent en fin de matinée avec leurs parents et on passe le reste de la journée à faire la fête.

Tu réveillonnes?

Pour la Saint-Sylvestre, c'est-à-dire la veille du jour de l'an, oui. L'année dernière, comme j'avais seize ans, mes parents m'ont permis de sortir et de réveillonner chez un de mes copains. Je n'avais jamais réveillonné avec des copains avant. C'était génial! On s'est retrouvé en début de soirée chez Luc. Ses parents l'avaient laissé réarranger le garage pour pouvoir y faire la fête. On était à peu près une vingtaine et on a dansé, chanté et mangé jusqu'au lever du jour. Au moment où on se disait «bonne année» à minuit, les parents de Luc sont venus voir si tout se passait bien. C'est là que j'ai rencontré Marine qui est toujours ma petite amie maintenant. Les réveillons, à mon avis, c'est extra.

---

1  Read the text and decide whether these statements are true (T), false (F) or not mentioned (?).

A 1 Marc's brother and sister still believe in Father Christmas.
  2 Marc also believed in Father Christmas when he was their age.
  3 Now he pretends to believe, in order not to break the magic for his brother and sister.
  4 His father helps with preparing the Christmas meal.
  5 His aunt and uncle's family arrive just after lunch.

B 6 On réveillonne le soir du trente et un décembre.
  7 À peu près trente personnes ont réveillonné chez Luc l'année dernière.
  8 Les parents de Luc ont préparé le garage pour la fête.
  9 Les parents de Luc ont fait la fête avec leurs amis.
  10 Marc a rencontré sa petite amie à la fête.

2a Listen to Section A and answer the questions in English.

  1 Why was this birthday celebration different from usual?
  2 What does Rachid think about Moroccan cuisine?
  3 Explain two of the three problems that arose.

2b 🎧 Listen to Section B and find the correct ending for each sentence.

1 Quand on ne mange pas pendant la journée,
2 Quand on fait la fête pendant trois jours,
3 Avant, Rachid allait chez
4 L'oncle et la tante de Rachid n'ont pas dormi
5 Rachid et ses cousins ont couché
6 Rachid s'est bien entendu avec

a c'est la fête de l'Aïd.
b ses cousins.
c c'est le Ramadan.
d dans la même chambre.
e dans une chambre.
f ses grands-parents.

3 **G** Complete the sentences by replacing the infinitives with the correct form of the imperfect and perfect tenses.

1 Pendant que je **manger** au restaurant, on m' **voler** mon porte-monnaie.
2 Quand elle **dormir**, sa mère **téléphoner** pour lui dire bon anniversaire.
3 Comme il **faire** mauvais à Noël, nous **rester** à la maison.
4 Je **arriver** au moment où mon père **préparer** un repas pour la fin du Ramadan.
5 Nous **visiter** le Louvre quand nous **être** à Paris à Pâques.

> ### Combining perfect and imperfect tenses
> You can use the imperfect and perfect tenses in the same sentence, saying what was happening (imperfect) and what happened (perfect). Use words like *quand* (when), *pendant* (during) and *comme, car, parce que* (because) to link them:
>
> *Pendant que nous mangions, un groupe a joué de la musique.*
>
> Also learn about indefinite adjectives such as *chaque* and *quelque*. *See page 108* ➡️
>
> **Grammaire** pages 181, 182

4 🖊️ 🌐 Write a message to your friends on a social networking site, telling them about your birthday.

Mention:

▪ when your birthday is and how old you are
▪ how you normally spend your birthday (where, what you do)
▪ what you did for your last birthday (using the imperfect and perfect)
▪ what you thought of it (using *faire*, *avoir* and *être* in the imperfect)
▪ what your favourite festival is and why
▪ how you spent that festival last year.

> 🖊️ Improve your marks for your written work by including what you **don't** do as well as what you do. As well as *ne … pas*, use expressions such as *ne … jamais* (never) and *ne … plus* (no more, not any more).
>
> **Stratégie**

Mon anniversaire, c'est le …		
Normalement, pour mon anniversaire	je reste à la maison / on va au restaurant.	
Pour mon anniversaire,	j'ai reçu … / j'ai mangé … / je suis allé(e) …	
C'était	génial / barbant / agréable.	
Ma fête préférée, c'est	Noël / Pâques / l'Äid	parce que …
Je préfère (Noël) parce que	je reçois … / on mange … / on va ….	
Cette année / l'année dernière,	j'étais …. / on était … / on a mangé …. / on est allés …	
J'ai passé Noël	à la maison / en France / chez mes grand-parents.	
Il faisait froid / beau.	Il neigeait / pleuvait. Il y avait du vent.	

> When you are writing about events in the past, think carefully about the meaning of each sentence to help you decide which verbs should be in the perfect tense and which should be in the imperfect tense.
>
> **Astuce**

Objectifs

Comparing homes

Using *depuis* and *pendant*

Qualifiers and intensifiers

La nouvelle maison de Mani!

Le rappeur Mani Mustafa nous présente sa maison

Salut! J'habite depuis six mois dans une maison très spacieuse qui est située dans le centre de Marseille. C'est une grande ville industrielle qui se trouve au bord de la mer, dans le sud de la France, et il fait toujours beau en été. Ma maison a été construite dans les années quatre-vingt-dix, donc elle est assez moderne, avec huit chambres, deux salles de séjour, trois salles de bains, une grande piscine et une petite salle de musculation. Je suis né au Sénégal, où j'ai habité pendant plusieurs années. Je suis parti quand j'avais seize ans et j'habite en France depuis huit ans.

La maison de Jazmine

Nous allons maintenant visiter le village d'origine de Mani, qui se trouve près de Dakar, la capitale du Sénégal. On rencontre la famille de Jazmine, qui nous invite chez elle. On a donc la possibilité de vous montrer une maison comme celle où Mani habitait dans sa jeunesse. La différence est étonnante! Il n'y a que deux chambres, et pour aller aux WC il faut aller derrière la maison. Il n'y a pas de robinet non plus, il faut aller à la pompe au bout de la rue. Jazmine est allée au café du village avec ses copines hier soir, où elles ont regardé une émission au sujet de son héros Mani, et aujourd'hui elle rêve d'avoir une maison comme la sienne.

1 📖🎧 Read about Mani's and Jazmine's houses and decide which four sentences are true. Correct the others in French.

1 À Marseille, il fait beau temps en juillet et en août.
2 Mani n'a pas de salle pour faire du sport dans sa maison.
3 Mani habite assez près de Marseille.
4 Il habite dans sa maison depuis six ans.
5 Mani a plusieurs salles de bains.
6 Il a quitté le Sénégal quand il avait huit ans.
7 La maison de Jazmine est moins confortable que celle de Mani.
8 Les robinets et les toilettes sont derrière la maison.
9 Jazmine a vu Mani à la télé hier soir.
10 Jazmine n'aime pas beaucoup la maison de Mani.

2a 🎧 Listen to Section A and select the correct word to complete each sentence.

1 The garden has a huge pool / summerhouse / lawn.
2 Marc watched a DVD of a football match / film / gig.
3 The games room is under / in / behind the house.
4 Marc has been living in his house for fifteen months / weeks / years.
5 He says he will never / hopes to / will definitely have a big house one day.

2b 🎧 Listen to Section B and answer the questions in English.

1 What are the two main differences between Laurence's and Marc's homes?

2 Why is Laurence not happy with her sleeping arrangements?

3 What is her comment about a cellar?

4 What did she like about her previous accommodation?

5 What disadvantage does Laurence's garden have and why doesn't she mind this?

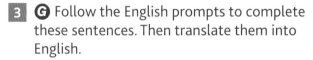

3 **G** Follow the English prompts to complete these sentences. Then translate them into English.

1 J'ai habité à Marseille _____. (for three years)

2 Grég habite dans cette maison _____. (for six months)

3 J'habite dans mon appartement _____. (for a year)

4 Nous sommes dans la salle à manger _____. (for an hour)

5 Elle a regardé la télé dans la salle de séjour _____. (for two hours)

6 J'habite en France _____. (since I was born)

> ### Using *depuis* and *pendant*
>
> *Depuis* can mean 'for' or 'since'. In English we use the past tense, but in French use the present tense.
>
> *J'habite ici depuis ma naissance.* – I have been living here since I was born.
>
> *J'habite ici depuis six ans.* – I have been living here for six years.
>
> For a completed activity in the past, use the perfect tense and *pendant*.
>
> *J'ai habité là-bas pendant cinq ans.* – I lived there for five years.
>
> Also learn about using *être situé(e)* and *se trouver* to indicate where something is.   *See page 108* ➡️
>
> **Grammaire**   *page 188*

4 💬 🔊 Interview a celebrity like Mani Mustafa. Partner A asks the questions. Partner B is the celebrity and gives answers that have as much detail as possible. Then swap over.

- Où habites-tu exactement?
- Tu y habites depuis quand?
- Elle est comment, ta maison?
- Tu aimes y habiter?
- Où as-tu habité avant?
- Où voudrais-tu habiter?

> 💬 When using adjectives, remember to add qualifiers and intensifiers such as *très* (very), *un peu* (a bit), *assez* (quite), *trop* (too) and *vraiment* (really). Example: *C'est assez amusant.*
>
> Practise saying in French: 'a bit tired', 'very ill', 'really cool', 'quite rich'.
>
> **Stratégie**

Où habites-tu exactement?

J'habite dans une grande maison à côté de la mer en Floride, aux États-Unis.

J'habite dans	une assez grande maison / un très petit appartement	
	près de … / dans le centre de …	
J'y habite depuis	trois ans / ma naissance.	
Nous avons	une salle de bains / une salle à manger / six chambres.	
Dans la salle de séjour / le jardin,	il y a	une table / une douche / des fleurs.
Je trouve que ma maison est très / assez …		
J'aime / Je n'aime pas habiter ici parce que …		
Avant, j'ai habité …	pendant … ans.	
Je voudrais habiter …	parce que …	

> If you want to give an opinion about what something was like, remember to use the imperfect, e.g. *c'était assez difficile.*
>
> **Astuce**

Ma ville

A Je m'appelle André et j'habite à Genève, une grande ville suisse. Cette ville est toute près de la frontière française, et on y parle français. C'est une ville très historique qui a été fondée pendant l'époque romaine, mais qui est maintenant un des plus grands centres financiers du monde. C'est une ville verte, située au bord d'un très grand lac, avec beaucoup de jardins publics. J'habite dans une maisonnette au centre-ville, pas loin du lac.

Qu'est-ce qu'on peut faire à Genève? Les montagnes ne sont pas loin, donc en hiver on peut faire du ski. Je suis content d'habiter ici parce que j'adore skier, mais ce week-end, il n'y a pas assez de neige, alors ce que je vais faire, c'est du VTT à la campagne. Quand je ne fais pas de sport, j'aime jouer du saxophone. Au mois de juillet, il y aura un festival de jazz à Montreux, près de Genève, et je vais y participer avec d'autres jeunes musiciens.

B Je suis Maha. J'habite dans un petit appartement au cinquième étage d'un HLM aux Buttes-Chaumont, dans le 19ème arrondissement de Paris. C'est un quartier de Paris qui était assez riche à une époque mais qui est maintenant un peu démodé. Je trouve que c'est un immeuble avec plein de problèmes.

L'appartement est déjà trop petit pour moi et mes frères, et bientôt il y aura un nouveau bébé! C'est vrai que c'est plus animé ici qu'à la campagne, mais c'est aussi plus bruyant. Il y a beaucoup de difficultés aussi, par exemple des ados qui ont fait des graffitis partout dans le quartier. Ça, c'est quelque chose que je ne ferais jamais, et mes frères non plus. Le problème principal, c'est qu'il n'y a pas assez de choses à faire pour les jeunes. Pour améliorer la situation, on devrait construire un centre culturel ou sportif où on pourrait aller s'amuser le soir.

1a Read Section A and choose the correct word to complete each statement.

1 Genève est une petite / vieille / nouvelle ville.
2 À Genève on parle français / anglais / espagnol.
3 Genève a beaucoup de parcs / de montagnes / d'usines.
4 André va jouer dans un festival de tennis / musique / sports d'hiver.

1b Read the whole text and decide who the statements are about. Complete each sentence with the name André or Maha.

1 xxxxx n'habite pas en France.
2 Ce n'est pas tellement joli où xxxxx habite.
3 Là où xxxxx habite, c'est plus calme qu'à Paris.
4 xxxxx aime la campagne et aussi la musique.
5 La famille de xxxxx sera bientôt plus grande.
6 Quelques jeunes posent des problèmes près de chez xxxxx.

2a 🎬 🎧 🔍 Watch or listen to the conversation between three friends. Which town does each adjective refer to, Avignon (A) or Vitrolles (V)?

1 polluée
2 sale
3 animée

4 touristique
5 industrielle
6 belle

🎬 Listen for clues about size and quantity. Examples on this spread include *une centaine* (about a hundred) and *une maisonnette* (a little house). Use expressions such as *environ* and *à peu près* (both meaning 'about').

Stratégie

2b 🎬 🎧 🔍 Watch or listen again. According to the conversation, which three statements refer to Avignon and which refer to Vitrolles?

1 Le père d'Arnaud y travaille maintenant.
2 On peut voir un film dans le centre-ville.
3 Il y a des endroits où on peut aller danser.
4 Il y a trop de voitures qui passent au centre.
5 La plupart des amis d'Arnaud y habitent.
6 Il y a beaucoup de magasins.

3 🅖 Fill in the gaps in the table.

Masculine singular	Masculine + vowel	Feminine singular	Masculine plural	Feminine plural	Translation
beau	*bel*	_____	*beaux*	_____	beautiful
nouveau	_____	*nouvelle*	_____	*nouvelles*	new
vieux	*vieil*	*vieille*	_____	_____	_____

Adjectives with special forms

The adjectives *beau*, *nouveau* and *vieux* come before the noun. There is a special masculine form when the noun begins with a vowel or a silent *h*:

un bel endroit – a beautiful place

un vieil hôtel – an old hotel

le nouvel an – the new year

These forms are similar to the feminine forms: *belle*, *vieille* and *nouvelle*.

Also learn about the use of *en* as a pronoun.

See page 108 ➡️

Grammaire page 173

4 ✏️ Write a website about your home town or village (or a fictional home town). If you are working alone, construct the home page only. If you are working in a group, you can each work on different pages and link them via the home page.

Have a look on the internet for some French tourist office websites to give you ideas.

Astuce

Include on the home page:

■ where your town or village is situated

■ what the climate is like

■ what sort of place it is (e.g. busy, quiet, touristy)

■ what there is (principal buildings etc.)

■ what you can and can't do there

■ an event coming up in the future.

On the link pages:

■ add short accounts by local people, saying how long they have lived there, why they like living there, and something they have done there recently.

J'habite	à (Avignon) / au centre-ville / en banlieue / à la campagne.	
C'est dans	le nord / l'est / le centre / le sud-ouest	de la France.
C'est un(e) grand(e) / petit(e) / joli(e)	ville / village / banlieue	moderne / industriel(le) / pittoresque / touristique / calme / animé(e).
À (Avignon) il y a	une cathédrale / un château / des grands magasins / des cinémas.	
Ici on peut	aller au cinéma / jouer au golf.	
Hier, j'ai … / je suis …	Demain, je vais …	
J'aime / Je n'aime pas habiter là	parce que c'est intéressant / ennuyeux.	

kerboodle!

Des mondes différents

A La vie saharienne

Dans le Sahara algérien, la langue officielle est le français. Le climat y est aride et très chaud toute l'année. La végétation est pratiquement non existante. C'est un monde de sable avec des oasis où il y a des points d'eau. Certains arbres poussent bien. Des maisons ont été construites près de ces points d'eau. Il n'y a pas beaucoup de gens qui habitent là tout le temps.

Beaucoup de Sahariens ont une vie de nomade. Ils vivent sous une tente et portent des vêtements amples qui leur permettent de ne pas avoir trop chaud. Le moyen de transport le plus usuel est le chameau. C'est un animal qui n'a pas besoin de beaucoup d'eau et qui peut transporter les objets des nomades. Les habitants de l'oasis se réunissent le soir pour parler.

La vie en banlieue

Les banlieues des grandes villes sont pleines de cités. Le HLM est la norme. Dans chacun de ces immeubles vivent des centaines de familles. On a construit des appartements qui sont en général trop petits. Ce sont souvent ceux qui ne peuvent pas acheter de maison qui habitent là. La concentration de population dans les HLM est une des causes des problèmes que l'on voit dans les banlieues. Le manque d'espaces verts, la pauvreté, les tensions raciales, tout cela contribue à la frustration de beaucoup d'habitants de la banlieue parisienne en particulier.

Dans la région parisienne, il pleut assez souvent. Il fait rarement très chaud ou très froid. Les gens vivent beaucoup à l'intérieur et ne sont pas souvent en plein air. Quand ils sortent en voiture, ils se retrouvent souvent dans des embouteillages, donc l'air est très pollué. La vie des cités est assez triste.

1a 📖🎧 Read Section A and answer the questions, giving descriptions in English.

1　What does the Sahara desert look like?
2　What does an oasis look like?
3　How do people travel?
4　How do people dress and why?
5　What happens in the evening?

1b 📖🎧 Read Section B. Decide whether, according to the text, the statements are true (T), false (F) or not mentioned (?).

1　Most people who live in the suburbs are in high-rise blocks of flats.
2　Some people buy their flat.
3　The climate makes people want to spend a lot of time outdoors.
4　Life on a Parisian housing estate can be bad for your health.
5　Air pollution is caused by cars.

2a 🎧 ❂ Listen to Section A. Which three of these statements are true?

1　Henri lives on the island of La Réunion in the Indian Ocean.
2　The weather is cool in July there.
3　The weather is very hot in January.
4　Henri doesn't want to live there in the future.
5　Half the population are of local origin.

> 🎧 You need to recognise the following uses of numbers:
>
> ■ fractions: *un quart* (a quarter), *un tiers* (a third), *la moitié* (half)
>
> ■ temperature: *trente degrés*
>
> ■ percentages: *cinquante pour cent*
>
> ■ decimals: *2,3 – deux virgule trois* (2.3 – two point three).
>
> Try to say in French: 'half of the time'; '22 degrees'; '20 per cent'; 'three quarters of the population', '4.5'.
>
> ❂ **Stratégie**

2b 🎧 🔊 Listen to Section B. Which three of these statements are true?

1 Caroline lives in a village in western Canada.
2 The climate there is very cold in winter, with wet, warm summers.
3 The air is clear and unpolluted.
4 They have snow for six months of the year.
5 Her village has a good feeling of community.

La vie dans des pays et régions francophones

3 🄶 Work with a partner. Partner A reads out a sentence, and Partner B says a sentence that means the same, but using *on* instead of the passive.

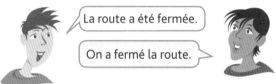

> La route a été fermée.

> On a fermé la route.

1 Des appartements ont été construits.
2 J'ai été invité à manger.
3 La vaisselle a été faite.
4 Les touristes sont accueillis.
5 Les snowmobiles sont utilisés quand la route est fermée.

The passive voice and *on*

The passive is used to say what is being done to someone or something. Use the appropriate tense of *être* plus the past participle:

J'ai été invité(e). – I was invited.

La maison sera vendue. – The house will be sold.

It is much more common to convey the same meaning by using *on*.

On fait les lits. – The beds are made.

On parle français. – French is spoken.

Also revise prepositions of place.   *See page 109* ➡️

Grammaire page 184

---

4 🗨 Work in a group to describe the region where you live. Each person should select one or two of the bullet points below.

Astuce
You could use your IT skills to help you research and present your description to the rest of the class.

Describe:

- what kind of area it is
- where it is near
- the population
- the climate and its effects on lifestyle
- some geographical features (rivers, mountains, etc.)
- housing and industry
- problems and possible solutions
- any other details you would like to include.

C'est	une belle région / une région industrielle / rurale / montagneuse.
C'est près de …	
La population est …	
En hiver / été, le climat est chaud / froid / sec / pluvieux.	
Il y a	une rivière / des montagnes / des châteaux.
	beaucoup de grandes maisons / petits appartements / des HLM.
L'industrie principale est	l'agriculture / le tourisme.
Les problèmes sont	le climat / la pauvreté / les tensions raciales.

Home and local area

• Bastia

La Corse

De: Guillaume
À: Joël
Sujet: La Corse

Salut Joël!

A Comment ça va à Lyon? Ici en Corse, depuis notre arrivée, c'est toujours le désordre!

Voici une copie des projets pour une partie de notre maison.

Au rez-de-chaussée

1 La cuisine (à gauche de la porte d'entrée): de nouveaux placards bleus, il y aura une nouvelle cuisinière (achetée par le client). Les murs seront blancs et le plancher en bois naturel (ce qui est le cas maintenant).

2 La pièce à côté de la cuisine sera pour la machine à laver. On va garder la porte qui donne sur le jardin.

3 Les deux petites pièces en face de la cuisine deviendront un grand salon avec une table et des chaises dans le coin pour remplacer la salle à manger. Il faut installer un plancher en bois. Les murs seront jaunes. Il y aura de petits tapis sur le plancher (que le client a apportés de sa maison de Lyon, ainsi que les meubles).

B Nous sommes arrivés il y a quinze jours. Mon père a commencé son nouvel emploi dans un lycée de Bastia. Moi, je me suis installé au collège et je me suis vite fait quelques amis en classe, alors ça va. Mon petit frère Damien va à une école primaire du village, mais il est très timide et il a trouvé les premiers jours un peu difficiles.

Le village où nous habitons est très petit et il n'y a pas beaucoup de choses pour les jeunes, sauf la plage. Ma mère aime le village, car elle dit que c'est moins dangereux que les grandes villes, mais le problème, c'est notre maison. Comme tu le vois sur la photo, c'est une jolie maison traditionnelle, mais il y a beaucoup de travail à faire. Il faut rénover la cuisine et la salle de bains. La douche ne marche pas (mais on peut prendre un bain!) et nous avons seulement un four à micro-ondes pour préparer les repas.

Heureusement, le maçon-décorateur va commencer son travail lundi prochain. Tout sera fini avant ton arrivée en juillet.

À bientôt, Guillaume

1a 📖🎧 Read the description of the plans for the ground floor of Guillaume's house in Section A. For each room labelled with a letter on the plan, note the following in English.

1 What it will be used for
2 Any colour schemes mentioned
3 Any features or fittings that the builder will add or has been asked to preserve. Do not include things that the family will provide.

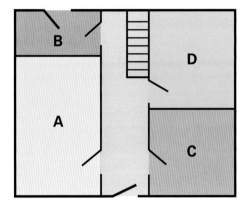

In order to complete activity 1a, you need to understand a number of prepositions of place. How many different ones can you spot? For more information, see page 109.

Grammaire page 188

1b 📖🎧 Read Section B and answer the questions in English.

1 How long has Guillaume been in Corsica?
2 Where does his father work?
3 Who has not settled in easily at school, and why?
4 Why does Guillaume's mother like the village where they live?
5 What disadvantage does Guillaume mention about the village?
6 Which parts of the house need most work?
7 Give two examples of difficulties they are coping with in the house.
8 When does the builder hope to finish his work?

2a 🎧 Listen to Section A. Guillaume is talking to Joël about his move from Lyon to Corsica. Indicate whether the following are easier (✓) or more difficult (✗) to do in Corsica than in Lyon, or about the same (–).

1 Taking part in water sports
2 Going to see a film
3 Travelling by bus
4 Playing football
5 Outdoor activities
6 Visiting his grandparents
7 Going skiing

2b 🎧 Listen to Section B and answer the questions in English.

1 What did Guillaume's father particularly dislike about living in the town? Give two details.
2 What two leisure interests will he be able to pursue in Corsica?
3 What is his opinion of his new journey to work? Give two reasons.
4 Why is it more difficult to go to the supermarket in Corsica?
5 What are the two disadvantages of the shops in the village?
6 What has Damien's father bought for him, and why?
7 What problem will Damien have in the winter?

Vocabulaire	
l'épicerie (f)	grocery shop
l'île (f)	island
le placard	cupboard
la plupart de	most of
rénover	to renovate
sauf	except

G Home and local area

Indefinite adjectives *chaque* and *quelque*; *être situé* and *se trouver*; *en* as an indirect object pronoun

1 Choose between *quelque(s)* and *chaque* to complete the following sentences.

1 Il fait son lit _____ matin.
2 Il y a _____ usines dans ma région.
3 Elle a gardé une clé pour _____ porte.
4 J'ai oublié _____ chose dans le bureau.
5 Il a visité _____ immeubles horribles.
6 Il y a un ordinateur dans _____ chambre.
7 J'ai _____ beaux meubles dans le salon.
8 Elle a mis _____ fleurs dans _____ pièce.

2 Replace all the highlighted verbs with a suitable form of *être situé* or *se trouver*. The two are practically interchangeable, but use a mixture for variety. Don't forget to make the verbs and past participles agree with the subject.

L'hôtel Villa Caroline 1 **est** dans un environnement de rêve, car il 2 **est** en face d'une plage extraordinaire. La piscine 3 **est** sur une magnifique pelouse. Nos chambres 4 **sont** au cinquième étage, elles sont calmes et confortables. On peut prendre l'ascenseur pour descendre au sous-sol où 5 **il y a** un parking. Le soir, on prend un bateau pour aller s'amuser dans les bars et les boîtes de nuit qui 6 **sont** sur une petite île.

3 Rephrase the answers to these questions, using *en* to replace the words that have been crossed out.

1 Il y a combien de **pièces** dans ta maison? Il y a huit ~~pièces~~.
2 Vous avez combien de **chambres**? Nous avons trois ~~chambres~~.
3 Il y a combien de **salles de bains**? Il y a deux ~~salles de bains~~.
4 Il y a un **garage**? Non, je n'ai pas besoin ~~de garage~~.
5 Vous avez un **jardin**? Oui, nous avons un ~~jardin~~.
6 Vous mettez **des fleurs** aux fenêtres? Oui, nous mettons ~~des fleurs~~!

Indefinite adjectives *chaque* and *quelque*

The adjective *chaque* means 'each' or 'every'. It is always singular.
chaque jour – every day
chaque pièce – each room
The adjective *quelque(s)* means 'some'. You are more likely to use it in the plural.
quelques fleurs – some flowers
It is, however, useful to know the phrase *quelque chose* – something.

Grammaire page 174

Être situé and se trouver

For variety, you can often replace *être* with verbs such as *se trouver* (to be found) or *être situé* (to be situated).
Le parking se trouve au sous-sol. The car park can be found in the basement.
Don't forget to make *situé* agree with the subject.
Les églises sont situées sur une colline. The churches are situated on a hill.

Grammaire page 185

En as an indirect object pronoun

The pronoun *en* is used to avoid repeating a noun introduced with a number or *du / de la / de l' / des*. It goes before the verb.
Il y a deux salles de bains? Non, il y en a trois!
Are there two bathrooms? No, there are three (of them)!

Grammaire page 177

Prepositions of place; *depuis* + imperfect tense

4 Look at the picture and complete the descriptions using prepositions from the grammar box.

1 Mon immeuble se trouve _____ église.
2 Mon appartement est situé _____ pharmacie.
3 Le parking se trouve _____ pharmacie.
4 La pharmacie est _____ jardin public.
5 Il y a de belles fleurs _____ pelouse.
6 Le jardin public est _____ terrain de sport.

Grammaire page 188

Prepositions of place

When using the following prepositions make sure you use the correct form of *du, de la, de l'* or *des* depending on the noun that follows.

à côté de	next to
près de	near
en dessous de	under
au-dessus de	above
en face de	opposite
au milieu de	in the middle of

For example:

près de l'église	near the church
en face des toilettes	opposite the toilets

5 Choose the correct translation for each sentence.

1 On a fait le ménage pendant une heure.
  a We had been cleaning for an hour.
  b We cleaned for an hour.
2 Il a fait du bricolage pendant une semaine.
  a He did some DIY for a week.
  b He does DIY for weeks.
3 Il lavait le mur depuis une heure quand on est arrivé.
  a He washed the wall for an hour before we arrived.
  b He had been washing the wall for an hour when we arrived.
4 Je lisais depuis deux heures quand la musique a commencé.
  a I had been reading for two hours when the music began.
  b I was reading for two hours after the music began.
5 Elle dormait depuis deux heures quand le réveil a sonné.
  a She had been asleep for two hours when the alarm rang.
  b She slept for two hours after the alarm rang.
6 Tu as dansé pendant trois jours?!
  a You had been dancing for three days?!
  b You danced for three days?!

Grammaire page 188

Depuis + imperfect tense

In French, use the imperfect to describe an action that had been going on in the past and was still going on until a given time.

Tu chantais depuis une heure quand elle est arrivée. – You had been singing for an hour when she arrived.

Compare with: *Tu as chanté pendant trois jours.* – You sang for three days.

Home and local area

Reflexive verbs ➡ *page 96*

se	brosser les dents	to brush one's teeth
se	coucher	to go to bed
se	doucher	to have a shower
s'	habiller	to get dressed
se	laver	to have a wash
se	lever	to get up
se	réveiller	to wake up

On fait la fête ➡ *pages 98–99*

l'	anniversaire (m)	birthday
la	boîte de nuit	night club
la	boum	party
la	fête	party / celebration
le	grenier	attic
d'	habitude	usually
le	jour de l'an	New Year's Day
le	jour férié	public holiday
les	lits (m) superposés	bunk beds
	Noël	Christmas
le	Nouvel An	New Year
	Pâques	Easter
	réveillonner	to celebrate on Christmas Eve or New Year's Eve
la	Saint-Sylvestre	festival of 31 December
la	Saint-Valentin	Valentine's Day
la	Toussaint	All Saints Day

1 V Which festival is being described? Look on pages 98–99 and in the list above.

1 Il y a souvent un arbre dans la maison.
2 C'est une fête musulmane qui dure trois jours.
3 Il y a des œufs en chocolat.
4 C'est le début de l'année.
5 On envoie une carte à la personne qu'on aime.
6 C'est le dernier jour de l'année.
7 C'est le premier novembre.

Ma maison ➡ *pages 100–101*

le	canapé	sofa
	donner sur	to look out over
le	fauteuil	armchair
	entouré(e)	surrounded
la	fontaine	fountain
la	haie	hedge
la	moquette	carpet
la	naissance	birth
l'	herbe (f)	grass
l'	immeuble (m)	building / block of flats
le	jardin	garden
la	musculation	weight training
la	pelouse	lawn
la	pièce	room
la	pompe	pump
le	quartier	area of a town
le	robinet	tap
la	salle de séjour	living room / sitting room
le	sous-sol	basement
	spacieux(-euse)	spacious
le	volet	shutter

2 V Match the words with their definitions.

1 le rez-de-chaussée
2 le fauteuil
3 la pelouse
4 la salle de bains
5 la campagne
6 le canapé

a C'est en dehors de la ville, il y a des bois et des champs.
b C'est fait pour s'asseoir confortablement.
c C'est dans le jardin. Quand on s'en occupe, on coupe l'herbe.
d C'est l'étage en dessous du premier étage.
e C'est la pièce où on se lave.
f C'est fait pour plus d'une personne. C'est pour s'asseoir.

Là où j'habite ➡ *pages 102–103*

	améliorer	to improve
	animé(e)	lively
l'	*arrondissement (m)*	administrative district of Paris
la	*banlieue*	suburb
	bruyant(e)	noisy
le	*centre culturel*	cultural centre
le	*centre sportif*	sports centre
à une	*époque*	at one time
la	*forêt*	forest
	historique	historical
le / la	*HLM*	block of high-rise council flats
le	*jardin public*	park / public garden
le	*jardin zoologique*	zoo
le	*magasin*	shop
	pittoresque	picturesque
l'	*usine (f)*	factory

3 ⓥ Work in a group. Imagine you are moving house to a different town. Which of these adjectives would make you feel it was the right town for you? Choose your top five and put them in order. Give reasons for your first, second and last choices.

pittoresque	touristique	animée
fleurie	industrielle	calme
historique	moderne	

Des mondes différents ➡ *pages 104–105*

	ailleurs	elsewhere
l'	*arbre (m)*	tree
le	*chameau*	camel
la	*cité*	housing estate
	construire (construit)	to build
	créole	creole
l'	*endroit (m)*	place
l'	*espace (m) vert*	park
l'	*habitant (m)*	inhabitant
	pluvieux(-euse)	rainy
	pousser	to grow
	respirer	to breathe
se	*réunir (réuni)*	to meet up
le	*sable*	sand
	sec (sèche)	dry
la	*vie*	life
	vivre (vécu)	to live

4 ⓥ Match up the vocabulary items with their definitions.

1 une cité
2 ailleurs
3 un chameau
4 le climat
5 la banlieue
6 se réunir

a un animal qu'on trouve dans le désert
b un groupe de maisons ou d'appartements dans le même quartier
c le temps qu'il fait dans une région
d se retrouver ensemble
e à un autre endroit
f les quartiers d'une grande ville qui ne sont pas dans le centre

La pollution

Deux environnements différents

J'ai habité Paris pendant quatre ans quand j'étais étudiante. Dans le centre de Paris et dans d'autres grandes villes, il y a beaucoup de pollution parce qu'il y a trop de circulation: les camions qui font des livraisons, les voitures qui polluent avec leurs gaz d'échappement, les embouteillages pendant les heures d'affluence.

Pour résoudre en partie ce problème, il faut qu'on construise plus de zones piétonnes et plus d'espaces verts. Peut-être que la ville de Paris devrait faire payer les automobilistes pour avoir le droit d'entrer dans la ville. C'est une manière de réduire le nombre de véhicules et donc la pollution de l'air.

Dans certaines zones industrielles, les usines rejettent leurs déchets toxiques dans nos rivières. Cela crée une pollution qui tue des milliers de poissons. Comme les rivières se jettent dans la mer, cela explique en partie pourquoi les bords de mer sont aussi pollués.

La pollution est un problème moins grave sur l'île de Ré. Moi, je prends le TGV pour aller à La Rochelle, près de l'île de Ré. Sur l'île, les piétons et les cyclistes sont les bienvenus et l'air n'est pas pollué. Plus de

100 kilomètres de pistes fléchées ont été construits pour les cyclistes. Il faut utiliser un vélo si on veut se déplacer! C'est un endroit calme où la pollution de l'air et le bruit ne sont pas des problèmes alarmants.

Sur l'île de Ré la protection de l'environnement est considérée comme quelque chose d'important. Par exemple, l'utilisation des conteneurs pour les bouteilles et autres produits recyclables est obligatoire et il est interdit de jeter ses déchets par terre. J'y habiterai un jour, j'espère. À mon avis, c'est le plus bel endroit de la France.

1a 📖🎧 Read the article and write the numbers of the following topics in the order in which they are mentioned.

1 Throwing litter
2 Building more pedestrian precincts
3 Traffic jams
4 Facilities for cyclists
5 River pollution
6 Where the writer used to live

1b 📖🎧 Read the whole article again and decide which three statements are true according to the article.

1 The writer is not particularly concerned about water pollution.
2 She is in favour of creating more green spaces in Paris.
3 Recycling is compulsory on the Île de Ré.
4 The writer does not recommend cycling on the Île de Ré.
5 The Parisian authorities should consider charging motorists for entering the city.

2a 🎧 🔊 Listen to Section A and answer these questions in English.

1 What two advantages of cycling does Suliman mention?
2 What two advantages of using a car does Virginie mention?
3 But what is the disadvantage?
4 How does she justify travelling by car?

> 🎧 When listening, you will find that, although French and English words can look very similar, they are often pronounced quite differently. Listen again to words such as *collège, rapide, confortable* and *environnement*.
>
> Say the following words to a partner: *création, chimique, problème, bouteille, circulation.* Your partner should listen and work out the equivalent English pronunciation.
>
> **Stratégie**

2b 🎧 🌐 Listen to Section B. Decide which three of these statements are true and correct the other three in French.

1 Michel prend l'autobus parce que c'est confortable.
2 Marc pense que les camions sont bruyants.
3 Les autoroutes sont interdites aux camions le dimanche.
4 Les camions ne sont pas nécessaires.
5 Les avions sont les plus gros pollueurs.
6 Dorothée pense que les voitures ne polluent pas plus que les trains.

3 🅖 Rewrite these sentences, replacing the infinitive with the subjunctive form.

Exemple: Il faut consommer moins d'énergie. ➡ Il faut qu'on consomme moins d'énergie.

1 Il ne faut pas jeter les déchets par terre.
2 Il faut recycler les bouteilles.
3 Il faut utiliser le vélo.
4 Il faut aller au lycée à pied.
5 Il faut être prudent.
6 Il faut faire plus d'efforts.

4 ✏ Write a letter to a French friend explaining your views on local transport and its impact on the environment.

Mention:

- ▪ how you and your family get around
- ▪ whether you think this is environmentally sound
- ▪ a recent journey you have been on
- ▪ what public transport is like
- ▪ what has to be done to improve matters.

Je vais au travail / au collège / en ville / à (Paris)	à vélo / à moto / à pied / en train / en autobus / en voiture.
Hier / Pendant les vacances, je suis allé(e) (à Paris)	
C'est bon / mauvais pour l'environnement parce que	ça pollue / fait trop de bruit / consomme trop d'énergie.
À Paris / La Rochelle, il y a	une zone piétonne / des embouteillages / des pistes cyclables / trop de circulation / de bons transports en commun.
Il n'y a pas assez de / d'	zones piétonnes / espaces verts.
Pour améliorer la situation,	il faut qu'on (construise / fasse) …

🅖rammaire *pages 183, 185*

Using *il faut* with an infinitive or the subjunctive

After *il faut* (you have to) you can use either the infinitive or the form called the subjunctive.

The subjunctive form of *-er* verbs is the same as the present tense, e.g. *il faut qu'on recycle*.

But *-ir* and *-re* verbs change. You need to learn some irregular subjunctive forms.

Infinitive	Subjunctive
Il faut …	*Il faut …*
aller	*qu'on aille*
être	*qu'on soit*
jeter	*qu'on jette*
faire	*qu'on fasse*
construire	*qu'on construise*

Also revise the use of the definite article.   *See page 120* ➡

Astuce

When writing, always try to add extra information and reasons using connectives such as *parce que*.

1 ⓥ Find the French for these words in the article. Use the anagrams to help you.

1 greenhouse effect   le chantfeufémer de la natèple   5 to reduce   rudeiré

2 global warming   l'fefte de reser   6 inconvenient   agêntn

3 scientist   le siquitnefcie   7 flood   l'ointannodi

4 climate change   le gemchentan quetlaimic

Planète en danger

A La destruction de la planète est un problème mondial. En Terre Adélie (la partie française de l'Antarctique), la glace est en train de fondre. Nos émissions de dioxyde de carbone contribuent à l'effet de serre. Le résultat de cet effet est le réchauffement de la planète.

B Le niveau de la mer monte et les vagues menacent les Maldives. Les îles sont seulement à un mètre au-dessus de la mer, et on pense que le niveau de la mer va monter de deux mètres avant la fin du siècle.

C Chaque année, il y a de nouveaux records de températures. Partout dans le monde, il y a de plus en

plus d'inondations, de tempêtes et de tornades. Beaucoup de scientifiques pensent que la pollution mondiale provoque un effet de serre et entraîne le réchauffement de la planète, et donc le changement climatique.

D En 1998, le protocole de Kyoto réunit beaucoup de pays qui décident collectivement un plan d'action. Les objectifs sont de réduire les émissions de dioxyde de carbone entre 2008 et 2012. Bien que plus de cent cinquante

pays signent cet accord à ce moment-là, les États-Unis, la Chine et l'Inde, tous des gros pollueurs, refusent de signer.

E L'association Les Amis de la Terre nous donne à tous les conseils suivants.

- Bien que ce soit gênant, essayez de ne pas utiliser votre voiture.
- À condition qu'il ne fasse pas trop froid, réduisez votre consommation de gaz et d'électricité.
- Bien que ce ne soit pas la solution de facilité, évitez de voyager en avion.

Allons-nous arriver à sauvegarder notre planète pour les générations futures? Il est important de faire quelque chose avant qu'il ne soit trop tard.

2a 📖🎧 Read the text and match up the five paragraphs of the article (A–E) with the headings below.

1 How scientists explain climate change   4 Rising seas

2 The melting of ice fields   5 A partly successful solution

3 What individuals can do

2b 📖🎧 Read the text again and answer the questions in English.

1 According to the text, what causes global warming?

2 What is the threat to the Maldives?

3 What other examples of climate change are there in the text?

4 What is the importance of the Kyoto protocol?

5 What do Friends of the Earth ask individuals to do to help with the problem?

3a 🎧 Listen to Section A of the radio documentary. Which three of these statements are true?

1 Laurent est chef d'un projet de recherches.
2 La Côte d'Ivoire est une forêt d'Afrique.
3 L'équipe a passé les trois derniers mois dans le département d'Adiaké.
4 L'équipe de Greenpeace-France comprend trois personnes.
5 L'équipe de Greenpeace-France a travaillé dans la forêt tropicale.

3b 🎧 Listen to Section B and decide which three statements are true.

1 La protection de la forêt tropicale est importante pour le bien-être de notre planète.
2 On détruit la forêt pour construire des maisons pour la population locale.
3 On brûle la forêt pour faire de la place pour des champs.
4 Les forêts disparaissent à une vitesse alarmante.
5 En 2100, la moitié de la forêt tropicale mondiale sera probablement détruite.

4 **G** Re-read the text *Planète en danger*. Find and note down the French for these five phrases. All contain verbs using the subjunctive.

1 Before it is too late
2 Although more than 150 countries sign this agreement
3 Provided it is not too cold
4 Although it is inconvenient
5 Although it is not the easy solution

> **Grammaire** — page 183
>
> **Common subjunctive expressions**
>
> The subjunctive is used after various expressions, as well as after *il faut*. Below are three that you should learn.
>
> *avant que* – before
>
> *bien que* – although
>
> *à condition que* – provided that
>
> *Il est important de faire quelque chose avant qu'il ne soit trop tard.* – It is important to do something before it is too late. See also page 121 ➡
>
> Also learn about indefinite pronouns such as *tout le monde* and *personne*. See page 120 ➡

5 💬 🌐 Work in a small group. Pick an environmental cause to champion. Say why you think it is the most serious environmental problem. Mention one possible solution to the problem. Your group can give a presentation to the rest of the class.

> **Stratégie**
>
> 💬 Here are some techniques to help you if you don't know exactly how to say what you want to express.
>
> ▪ Replace words you don't know with *chose* or *truc* (thing).
> ▪ If you don't know an expression, describe something similar, e.g. use *cent ans* if you've forgotten *siècle* (century).
> ▪ Ask *Comment dit-on _____ en français?*
> ▪ Stall with words such as *alors, ben, eh bien.*

La cause	du changement climatique,	c'est	la pollution.
	de l'effet de serre,	ce sont	les émissions de gaz toxiques.
	du réchauffement de la planète,		
Nous trouvons que c'est le problème le plus grave parce que ….			
Pour protéger l'environnement,	il faut qu'on	arrête le déboisement des forêts.	
		fasse des économies de gaz, d'eau et d'électricité.	
	il ne faut pas qu'on	utilise la voiture ou l'avion, si possible.	

> **Astuce**
>
> You can suggest improvements by saying *il faut qu'on* … plus the subjunctive.

3.7 — L'environnement et ma ville

Objectifs
- Local issues and action
- Expressions of sequence
- Recognising words from ones already known

1 **Ⓥ** Scan through the leaflet below and find the French terms to fit these definitions.

1 Something to make you smell nice
2 What you should carry your shopping in
3 Something you might be given coffee in
4 Annoying stuff that comes through the letter box
5 Something that you can compost

Des conseils écologiques

A

Le dentifrice en flacon pompe, les déodorants en aérosol et les biscuits sont emballés dans de l'aluminium, puis dans du carton et finalement dans du plastique. Les emballages coûtent cher. De plus, tout cela finit inutilement dans nos poubelles et contribue aux montagnes de déchets que l'on voit dans les décharges publiques. Personne n'aime habiter à proximité d'une de ces décharges. Pour éviter qu'elles ne se multiplient, il faut limiter les déchets qu'on met à la poubelle.

B

■ D'abord, pour faire ses achats, il faut qu'on emporte un sac recyclable au lieu de prendre les sacs en plastique des supermarchés (dont 170 millions ont été distribués aux caisses françaises l'année dernière!).

■ Puis, quand on boit un café pendant la pause au travail, on devrait prendre une tasse en porcelaine au lieu d'utiliser trois ou quatre gobelets en plastique. Le plastique est pratiquement indestructible.

■ On peut mettre un panneau «Pas de publicité merci!» sur sa boîte aux lettres pour éviter les prospectus et les journaux gratuits. Si vous en recevez quand même, n'oubliez pas de les recycler.

■ Ensuite, on doit recycler tous ses déchets et ordures (papier, magazines, emballages, bouteilles). Afin de faciliter le recyclage, chaque ville a des centres de recyclage et souvent les éboueurs ramassent aussi les sacs de choses recyclables posés devant la maison.

■ Finalement, on peut recycler les résidus alimentaires qu'on peut utiliser plus tard dans le jardin sous forme de compost. On peut alors cultiver des légumes biologiques.

2a 📖🎧🌐 Read Section A of the leaflet. Two of the statements given below are correct. Which ones?

Section A is about …

1 wrapping products carefully so as not to waste them.
2 using too many plastic bin liners.
3 limiting the rubbish that has to go to landfill sites.
4 the problem of living near a landfill site.
5 the cost of packaging.

2b 📖🎧🌐 Read Section B and answer the questions in English.

1 What are you advised to take to the supermarket, and why?
2 What's environmentally friendly about a china cup?
3 Why would you put a sign on your letter box?
4 What two things do local councils do to encourage people to recycle?
5 What should you do with leftover organic waste?

> **📖 Stratégie**
> You can often recognise new words because of their similarity to words you already know. Some examples from this page are:
>
> Verb: *acheter*   Noun: *achat*
> Verb: *recycler*   Noun: *recyclage*
>
> Find: a noun connected with *emballer* (to package), and a verb and an adverb connected with *utile*.

3a 🎧 Listen to four young people talking about environmental action. Note the numbers of the pictures in the order they are mentioned.

3b 🎧 Listen again. Who might say each of the sentences below? Alex (A), Brigitte (B), Charlotte (C), Damien (D) or the reporter (R)?

1 C'est un problème grave parce que ça ne se recycle pas.
2 On n'a rien laissé par terre. On a tout recyclé.
3 Quand il fait trop chaud à l'intérieur, on dépense de l'énergie inutilement.
4 De toute façon, j'aime bien marcher.
5 Mes parents aussi sont contents du résultat. Après tout, l'électricité est chère.

4 🄶 Complete each sentence by inserting a suitable expression of sequence or duration.

1 _____, pour aller en ville, j'ai pris le bus. (first)
2 _____, j'ai acheté des légumes biologiques. (then)
3 _____ midi _____ 14 heures, je me suis promenée dans le parc. (between … and)
4 _____, je suis allée au centre de recyclage. (after that)
5 J'étais en ville _____ cinq heures en tout. (for)
6 _____, je suis rentrée à la maison à pied. (finally)

> ### Expressions of sequence and duration
> To list a sequence of events, use *d'abord* (firstly), *puis* (then), *ensuite* (then), *après ça* (after that) and *finalement* (finally).
>
> Find examples of these in the reading text on page 116.
>
> Other useful time expressions: *entre … et …* (between … and …), *pendant … semaines / heures* (for … weeks / hours).
>
> Also learn about the use of emphatic pronouns such as *toi* and *vous*.   *See page 121* ➡
>
> **Grammaire** *page 176*

5 🖊 Write an article about environmental issues in your local area and what can be done about them.

Mention:

◼ a problem that used to exist and was solved through local action
◼ one or two typical problems to do with cars, pollution or energy saving
◼ what some irresponsible people do
◼ a few things that could be done to improve the situation.

> **Astuce**
> Try to add in a few original ideas of your own. Use a dictionary and try to be adventurous.

Les produits sont emballés	dans du plastique / du papier / de l'aluminium.
Avant, je / j'	jetais les bouteilles / les déchets par terre.
	utilisais des sacs en plastique.
À l'avenir, je vais	utiliser des sacs en coton.
	baisser la température chez moi.
	éteindre la lumière quand je quitterai une pièce.
	recycler les déchets / les bouteilles.
	aller au centre de recyclage.
On devrait	aller au collège / en ville / au travail à vélo / à pied.
	utiliser les transports en commun.

Environment

Problèmes sur la côte de l'Afrique

Obasi, un jeune journaliste nigérien, décrit l'environnement où il habite.

A

La côte ici, près de Calabar, est interdite au public à cause du niveau de pollution. La fumée des usines pollue l'atmosphère et ces usines rejettent des produits chimiques dans la rivière près d'ici. Résultat: le ciel est toujours gris, l'eau est toxique et dangereuse. Il y a aussi des déchets plastiques partout sur la plage. Ce sont des emballages qu'on pourrait recycler. Et, en plus, le bruit des trains qui transportent les marchandises des usines jour et nuit est insupportable! Dans cet environnement, la santé des habitants se dégrade et des poissons sont morts.

B

Le gouvernement dit que c'est la faute des patrons américains qui dirigent les usines installées ici. Ce sont les patrons qui autorisent le déversement de produits toxiques dans la rivière et dans l'atmosphère. Avant, les patrons ne venaient jamais ici et ne s'intéressaient pas à ces problèmes, mais récemment il y a eu une visite d'un nouveau directeur. Quand il a vu les problèmes, il a promis d'investir de l'argent pour moderniser les usines. Il y a quelques semaines, un ingénieur est arrivé des États-Unis. Il va organiser ces changements:

«Nous allons commencer par les problèmes de la rivière. En installant un équipement moderne, contrôlé par ordinateur, il n'y aura plus de produits chimiques rejetés dans la rivière. Dans deux ans, vous verrez encore une fois des oiseaux et des poissons dans cette région.»

La réponse de la mairie?

«Bien qu'on soit heureux de recevoir cette aide, nous devons continuer à demander aux patrons de ne pas oublier leur responsabilité envers nos habitants. J'ai peur que ce soit une action isolée. Nous avons besoin aussi d'un air propre et d'une plage sans déchets.»

1a 📖🎧 Read Section A of the report about a heavily polluted area of the West African coast. In which order are the following referred to?

1 Noise pollution
2 The fish population
3 Polluted water

4 Air pollution
5 Discarded rubbish
6 Local health problems

1b 📖🎧 Read Section B. Decide whether the statements are true (T), false (F) or not mentioned (?).

1 The government takes responsibility for the pollution.
2 The American owners used to take an active role in the running of the factories.
3 New ICT systems will monitor the factory's output into the river.
4 Wildlife has already started to return to the area.
5 The mayor gives the changes a cautious welcome.
6 The beach will be clear of rubbish in two years' time.

2a 🎧 Listen to Section A of a radio report at a recycling centre. Which of the slogans below applies to each person interviewed (1–5)?

a Turn all your garden waste into compost!
b A tonne of recycled plastic saves more that 700 kilos of crude oil!
c Our recycling centre is near the shops. Arrive with your rubbish! Leave with your shopping!
d Cardboard can be recycled up to ten times!
e Old textiles are still useful!

2b 🎧 Listen to Section B and choose the correct ending for each sentence.

1 When the interviewer turns down the heating, his wife is likely to …
  a put on extra clothes.
  b turn it up again.
  c agree with what he has done.
2 He will save water in the summer by …
  a recycling washing up water in the garden.
  b installing a shower.
  c washing clothes less often.
3 He tries to encourage his children to …
  a watch less television.
  b spend less time on the computer.
  c switch off equipment that they are not using.

4 He thinks low energy bulbs are …
  a expensive.
  b attractive.
  c a waste of time.
5 He uses his daughter's old bed as an example of …
  a how he recycles everything.
  b how he would like to recycle more.
  c why he thinks recycling is pointless.
6 He also argues with his family about …
  a how often they go out.
  b using the car to go out.
  c using public transport.

Grammaire *page 183*

At the end of the reading text, in the quotation from the local council, there are two examples of the subjunctive. The expression *j'ai peur que* is another expression that is followed by the subjunctive, in addition to those you have already met. Can you pick out the subjunctive verbs in the final paragraph? For more help with the subjunctive, see pages 113 and 115.

AQA *Examiner's tip*

In activity 2b most of the options look possible, so you will need to concentrate on the details to work out the correct answers. Make sure that you listen carefully to the context of key words you hear before you decide on an answer.

Vocabulaire

chimique	chemical
le déversement	dumping
diriger	to direct / to manage
en veille	on stand-by
éteindre	to turn off
rejeter	to discharge / to pour

Grammaire *page 177*

The final speaker in the listening activity uses examples of object pronouns, e.g. *je l'ai jeté*. Did you notice any others? For more information, see pages 63 and 65.

(G) Environment

Use of the definite article; indefinite pronouns

1a Translate the following sentences into English. Compare the use of the definite article in French and in English.

1 Je n'aime pas les grosses voitures.
2 J'utilise les transports en commun.
3 Je préfère les sacs en coton.
4 Je dis «oui» à la paix.

1b Translate these sentences into French.

1 I like nature and animals.
2 I say 'no' to war.
3 I recycle rubbish.
4 I refuse plastic bags.

2a How can we save the planet? Choose between *personne ne / n'*, *tout le monde* and *la plupart* to complete the sentences describing an ideal world.

1 _____ des gens vont au travail à vélo.
2 _____ pollue les rivières.
3 _____ recycle ses déchets.
4 _____ va au collège en voiture.
5 _____ utilise des sacs en coton.
6 _____ des gens font des économies d'eau.

2b Select sentences from activity 2a as captions for pictures a–c and then write your own caption for picture d.

Use of the definite article | Grammaire page 172

- *le* (masculine singular)
- *la* (feminine singular)
- *l'* (singular in front of a vowel or a silent h)
- *les* (plural)

The definite article is used in French far more frequently than its equivalent 'the' in English, especially:

when talking about likes and dislikes:
Je déteste les sacs en plastique.
   – I hate plastic bags.

when referring to abstract things:
la guerre et la paix
   – war and peace.

Indefinite pronouns | Grammaire

The French for 'nobody' is *personne*. In a sentence, it is followed by *ne* in front of a verb or *n'* before a vowel, and it doesn't need *pas*. The French for 'everybody' is *tout le monde*. Both are followed by a verb in the singular.

Tout le monde veut sauver la planète.
– Everyone wants to save the planet.

Personne ne jette ses déchets.
– Nobody throws their rubbish away.

La plupart means 'most' and is followed by a verb in the plural.
La plupart des gens recyclent leurs déchets.
– Most people recycle their rubbish.

Emphatic pronouns *toi*, *vous*, etc.; the subjunctive

3 Complete each sentence with the correct emphatic pronoun from the grammar box.

1 _____, j'utilise des sacs en coton.
2 Mais _____, tu prends des sacs en plastique.
3 _____, il va à l'école en voiture.
4 Mais _____, elle prend le bus.
5 _____, nous éteignons la lumière.
6 _____, vous dépensez trop d'énergie.
7 _____, ils jettent leurs déchets sur le trottoir.
8 _____, elles les mettent à la poubelle.

4a Replace the infinitives with a subjunctive. Which two of these statements do you most agree with?

1 Il faut qu'il y **avoir** plus de pistes cyclables.
2 À condition que tout le monde **faire** un effort, tout ira bien.
3 Il faut absolument qu'on **arrêter** d'utiliser les sacs en plastique.
4 Bien que la planète **être** en danger, on ne recycle pas assez.
5 À condition qu'on **économiser** l'énergie, il n'y aura pas de problème.
6 Avant qu'il ne **jeter** ses déchets, dis-lui de les recycler.
7 Il faut que tout le monde **construire** des maisons écolos.
8 Il faut qu'on **consommer** moins d'énergie.

> ## Ⓖ Grammaire — page 178
> ### Emphatic pronouns *toi, vous,* etc.
> In English if you want to emphasise something you do or don't do, you just say it a bit more forcefully. When you write it you sometimes put it in italics or underline it. French people put 'me', 'you', 'him' or 'her' at the beginning of the sentence to emphasise it. For example:
>
> *Moi, je recycle toutes mes bouteilles.* – <u>I</u> recycle <u>all</u> my bottles.
>
> *Toi, tu ne recycles rien.* – <u>You</u> don't recycle <u>anything</u>.
>
> Use the following pronouns for emphasis:
>
> *moi* with *je, toi* with *tu, lui* with *il, elle* with *elle, nous* with *nous, vous* with *vous, eux* with *ils, elles* with *elles.*

> ## Ⓖ Grammaire — page 183
> ### The subjunctive
> Remember to use the subjunctive after the following phrases:
>
> | | |
> |---|---|
> | *avant que* | before |
> | *bien que* | although |
> | *à condition que* | provided that |
> | *il faut que* | it is necessary that. |
>
> Useful subjunctive forms:
>
> | | |
> |---|---|
> | *faire* | qu'il / elle / on fasse |
> | *être* | qu'il / elle / on soit |
> | *avoir* | qu'il / elle / on ait |
> | *construire* | qu'il / elle / on construise |
>
> *Il faut qu'on fasse attention.* – We must be careful.

4b Select sentences from activity 4a as captions for pictures a–c and then write your own caption for picture d.

Environment

La pollution ➡ *pages 112–113*

le	*bruit*	noise
le	*camion*	lorry
la	*circulation*	traffic
	conduire (conduit)	to drive
les	*déchets (m)*	rubbish / waste
se	*déplacer*	to get around
	émettre (émis)	to emit
l'	*embouteillage (m)*	traffic jam
l'	*environnement (m)*	the environment
les	*gaz (m) d'échappement*	exhaust fumes
l'	*heure (f) d'affluence*	rush hour
	jeter	to throw (away)
le	*moyen de transport*	means of transport
la	*piste cyclable*	cycle track
la	*poubelle*	(dust)bin
	réduire (réduit)	to reduce
les	*transports (m) en commun*	public transport
	utiliser	to use
la	*zone piétonne*	pedestrian zone

1 **V** Match up the vocabulary items with their definitions.

1	un embouteillage	4	les déchets
2	une zone piétonne	5	l'autoroute
3	la poubelle	6	les gaz d'échappement

a C'est pour les voitures. C'est payant en France.

b On y met tout ce dont on ne veut plus qui n'est pas recyclable.

c Ça arrive quand la circulation est trop dense ou quand il y a eu un accident.

d C'est interdit aux voitures et aussi à tous les autres véhicules.

e Le dioxyde de carbone émis par les voitures par exemple.

f C'est ce qu'on jette à la poubelle.

Planète en danger ➡ *pages 114–115*

	augmenter	to increase
le	*conseil*	advice
la	*consommation*	consumption
le	*changement climatique*	climate change
la	*Côte d'Ivoire*	the Ivory Coast
le	*déboisement*	deforestation
	détruire (détruit)	to destroy
	disparaître (disparu)	to disappear
l'	*effet (m) de serre*	greenhouse effect
l'	*équilibre (m)*	balance
l'	*équipe (f)*	team
le	*feu*	fire
	fondre	to melt
la	*forêt tropicale (humide)*	rainforest
	gênant(e)	inconvenient / annoying
	gêner	to be a nuisance
l'	*inondation (f)*	flood
	mondial(e)	global
la	*planète*	planet
	produire (produit)	to produce
le	*réchauffement de la planète*	global warming
le	*siècle*	century
la	*tempête*	storm
la	*vague*	wave (water)

L'environnement et ma ville ➡ *pages 116–117*

	baisser	to lower
	biologique	organic
la	boîte (en carton)	(cardboard) box
le	centre de recyclage	recycling centre
la	circulation	traffic
le	coton	cotton
	cultiver	to grow
la	*décharge publique*	rubbish dump
les	déchets (m)	waste
l'	*éboueur (m)*	dustman
l'	emballage (m)	packaging
l'	environnement (m)	the environment
	éteindre (éteint)	to switch off
	jeter	to throw (away)
la	lumière	light
	ramasser	to collect / to pick up
les	ordures (f)	rubbish
le	pétrole	oil
la	piste cyclable	cycle route
	pollué	polluted
la	poubelle	dustbin
le	problème	problem
	propre	clean
	protéger	to protect
se	rappeler	to remember
	recyclable	recyclable
le	sac	bag
	sale	dirty
	sans plomb	unleaded
	sauver	to save
la	Terre	(the) Earth
les	transports en commun (m)	public transport
la	zone piétonne	pedestrian area

Le temps

l'	averse (f)	(rain) shower
	briller	to shine
le	brouillard	fog
la	chaleur	heat
	chaud	hot
le	ciel	sky
le	climat	climate
	couvert	overcast
le	degré	degree
	doux	mild
l'	éclair (m)	lightning
l'	éclaircie (f)	sunny spell
	ensoleillé	sunny
	faire beau	good weather
	faire mauvais	bad weather
le	froid	cold
	geler	to freeze
la	glace	ice
	humide	humid
la	météo	weather forecast
	mouillé	wet
la	neige	snow
	neiger	to snow
le	nuage	cloud
	nuageux	cloudy
l'	ombre (f)	shade
l'	orage (m)	thunderstorm
	orageux	stormy
	pleuvoir	to rain
la	pluie	rain
	sec	dry
le	soleil	sun
la	température	temperature
la	tempête	storm
le	temps	weather
le	tonnerre	thunder
	tremper	to soak
le	vent	wind

3 ◯ Chez moi

You are talking to your French friend about your house and your town. Your teacher will play the part of your friend and will ask you:

1 where you live and what your house is like
2 who lives in your house
3 what your room is like
4 about meal times
5 what you do to help round the house
6 what your local town is like
7 !

! Remember you will have to respond to something that you have not yet prepared.

1 Where you live and what your house is like
- ▥ Say where you live and what you think of the area.
- ▥ Say what your house is like and how long you have lived there.
- ▥ Say how many rooms it has and which is your favourite.
- ▥ Describe your ideal house.

2 Who lives in your house
- ▥ Say who lives in the house and give physical descriptions.
- ▥ Describe their characters and say who you get on with.
- ▥ Say who you don't get on with and why.
- ▥ Talk about your pets and say who looks after them.

3 What your room is like
- ▥ Describe your room and say what you like about it.
- ▥ Say whether you share your room and what you think of this arrangement.
- ▥ Give details of what is in your room and what you would like to have in your room.
- ▥ Say what you like doing in your room and why.

AQA Examiner's tips

Start with *J'habite ...*
Use *j'y habite depuis ...* to say how long you have lived there.
Préféré is an adjective but also a past participle. As an adjective, use it after the noun it qualifies, e.g. *Ma pièce préférée ...*
Remember that you can only write verbs as the infinitive or the past participle on your plan.

AQA Examiner's tips

Now, start your plan. Write a maximum of six words for each of the seven sections that make up the task. Here are some suggested words for the first section: *où – opinion, description, pièces, jardin, idéal.*
Remember that you can use hyphens to remind you that two words belong together, but they still count as separate words.

AQA Examiner's tips

Use *je ne m'entends pas bien avec ...* to say who you don't get on with.
Use *s'occuper de ...* for 'to look after'.
On your plan, words that have an apostrophe, e.g. *s'occuper*, only count as one word.

AQA Examiner's tips

To emphasise that it is you (and no one else) who chose the colour scheme, the curtains, etc. in your room, use *C'est moi qui ai choisi ...*
Use prepositions such as *en face de, à côté de, près de* and *sur* to say where things are in relation to each other in your room.
Remember to develop each of the six areas suggested by the six words on your plan.
Remember that you can use words and visuals on your plan. Although the number of words is limited, you can draw as many visuals as you like.

4 About meal times

- Say at what times you have meals and what you like eating.
- Say whether you have your meals as a family and who prepares them.
- Say what your favourite meal is and what you don't like eating.
- Talk about the last time you went out for a meal (when, where, what you ate, your opinion of it).

If you don't have set meal times at home, be creative and make them up!

Use *prendre* + food or drink as an alternative to using *manger* or *boire*. Take care, as it is an irregular verb. See the verb table on page 195.

For the last point, you will need to use the perfect tense – see grammar section page 180. To say what it was like, use the imperfect, e.g. *c'était, il y avait*.

On your plan, use words that suggest something to you, e.g. the name of the restaurant.

5 What you do to help round the house

- Describe what you do to help round the house and how frequently you do it.
- Say whether you get pocket money for helping and, if so, how you like to spend it.
- Say what other members of the household do to help and whether the workload is shared fairly.
- Say what you did and didn't do to help in the house last weekend.

There is a difference in spelling between the *je* form and the *il / elle* form of the verbs in phrases such as *je fais / elle fait la vaisselle, je mets / il met la table, je sors / il sort la poubelle*. But there is no difference in the way they sound.

Some of the verbs you will need have irregular past participles, e.g. *faire, mettre*, so make sure you learn them.

If *sortir* is followed by a direct object, it takes *avoir* instead of *être* in the perfect tense, e.g. *J'ai sorti la poubelle*.

6 What your local town is like

- Describe the town centre and say what you like about it.
- Say what facilities there are for young people and also for tourists.
- Say when you intend to go to town next and what you would like to do.
- Talk about your ideal town and compare it to where you live.

As an alternative to *il y a*, use *pouvoir* in different forms, e.g. *on peut / les touristes peuvent / les jeunes peuvent*.

Use the conditional to talk about your ideal town, e.g. *Dans ma ville idéale, il y aurait* ... See grammar section page 183.

Avoid using the word *ville* on your plan. As the question is 'What is your town like?' it is clear that everything you will say in this section will be about your town.

7 ! At this point you may be asked:

- if there are environmental problems in your local town and, if so, what they are and what could be done to solve them
- if you prefer living in town or in the countryside and what the advantages and disadvantages are of each
- if you intend to continue living in the same area or if you would like to move, and what you would gain and lose if you moved
- if you prefer living in a small town or a large town and why.

Choose the two options which you think are the most likely, and for each of these, note down three different ideas. In your plan, write three words that illustrate each of the two most likely options. For the first option you might choose: *circulation, déchets, recyclage*.

Remember to check the total number of words you have used. It should be 40 or fewer.

You should now have completed your plan and prepared your answers. Give your plan to your teacher for feedback. Compare your answers with the online sample version – you might find some useful hints to make yours even better.

kerboodle!

3 ✏️ L'environnement

Your French friend Yannick has been asked to participate in a debate on the environment at school. He is keen to have an international perspective, and he has asked you:

1 what your local town is like
2 if there are any environmental problems
3 what you think the solutions to those problems are
4 what you do that makes environmental problems worse
5 what the main problems of the environment are in today's world
6 what we as individuals can do about it
7 if we should stop going on holiday by plane.

1 What your local town is like

■ Write about where your local town is situated and what sort of town it is.
■ Describe the town centre and the suburbs.
■ Include what you think of your local town and why.
■ Mention whether you prefer to live in town or in the country and why.

2 If there are any environmental problems

■ Describe the litter and graffiti situation and give your opinion.
■ Explain to what extent the town suffers from pollution.
■ Give details of how much traffic there is in the town and whether it is a problem.
■ Give your opinion of whether there is enough green space in the town.

3 What you think the solutions to those problems are

■ Write about what should be done about litter and graffiti.
■ Say what can be done to improve the traffic situation.
■ Say what can be done to reduce pollution.
■ Say what can be done to improve the town for pedestrians.

AQA Examiner's tips

Start with *Ma ville …*
Use *se trouve / est située dans le* (county), *dans le* (compass direction) *de l'* (country) (for Wales, you would say *du pays de Galles*).
To say what sort of town it is, use adjectives such as *industrielle, propre,* etc. You can qualify them with *assez* and *très*.
Use *je pense que … parce que …* to give your opinion and justify it.

AQA Examiner's tips

Now, start your plan. Write a maximum of six words. Here are some suggested words for the first section: *où, industries, centre, banlieue, opinion, préférence*.
Remember to use words that you know the meaning of in your plan. If one of the words you use is new to you, make a point of learning it.

AQA Examiner's tips

Vary the ways in which you give your opinion. This time, use *À mon avis, c'est …*
Use *la circulation* for 'traffic'.
In your plan, use words that generate other ideas or words, e.g. *sale* leads you to say what is dirty (e.g. the pavement) and what makes it dirty (e.g. litter).

AQA Examiner's tips

Use *On devrait* + verb in the infinitive to say what we should do.
Use *Pour réduire la pollution, il faut …* to say what can be done to reduce industrial or traffic pollution.
If it is appropriate to do so, use verbs in your plan. Make sure you write them in the infinitive or as the past participle.

4 **What you do that makes environmental problems worse**
- Say whether you occasionally drop litter.
- Say whether you always cycle or walk to your destination and what the benefits of doing so are.
- Mention what you recycle and how you do it.
- Say whether you sometimes travel by plane and say why (or why not).

> **AQA Examiner's tips**
>
> Use *laisser tomber* for 'to drop'. Change the ending of the first verb only, e.g. *Je laisse tomber …*
>
> Use *Je vais* + destination + *à pied / à vélo* to say that you walk or cycle to a place.
>
> Remember you can also use visuals as part of your plan. These are permitted for both speaking and writing.

5 **What the main problems of the environment are in today's world**
- Mention climate change and give an example of its effects.
- Say how the weather has changed, comparing it to what it used to be.
- Write about pollution and give an example of its effects.
- Write about the need to look at renewable sources of energy.

> **AQA Examiner's tips**
>
> Use *le changement climatique* for 'climate change'. Use the imperfect tense to say what the weather used to be like. See grammar section page 182.
>
> In your plan, use grammatical markers, e.g. *avant,* to remind yourself that you will be writing in the past tense at that point.

6 **What we as individuals can do about it**
- Write about cycling, walking and public transport.
- Write about recycling and saving energy.
- Write about new technology, e.g. electric or solar-powered cars.
- Mention what else you are going to do to protect the environment.

> **AQA Examiner's tips**
>
> Use *on peut … / on doit … / il est possible de … +* infinitive. Extend your answers to the first two bullet points by saying what you, as an individual, do and have done in the past to be environmentally friendly. Use the future tense or *je vais* + infinitive to start the last point.
>
> In your plan, use cognates and near cognates if you can, e.g. *transport, énergie, nouvelle technologie, protection.* You can be sure of knowing what these words mean!

7 **If we should stop going on holiday by plane**
- Say if you sometimes go on holiday by plane, where and how often.
- Say whether you agree that flying should be more expensive and why.
- Include how often you holiday in Britain, where you go and how you travel.
- Describe the effects of flying on the environment.

> **AQA Examiner's tips**
>
> In French, words that express frequency, e.g. *quelquefois, souvent, rarement,* are placed immediately after the verb in the present tense.
>
> You could expand the first and third sections by referring to a holiday you have had.
>
> Remember to check the total number of words you have used in your plan. It should be 40 or fewer.

You should now have completed your plan and prepared your answers. Give your plan to your teacher for feedback. Compare your answers with the online sample version – you might find some useful hints to make yours even better.

3

Résumé

1 Choose the correct phrase to complete this sentence:

Tout le monde se souhaite une bonne année …

a pour mon anniversaire.

b à la Saint-Valentin.

c à Noël.

d le jour de l'an.

2 Choose the correct phrase to complete this sentence:

Un immeuble se compose de beaucoup …

a de maisons.

b d'appartements.

c de pièces.

d de meubles.

3 Choose the correct phrase to complete this sentence:

Dans les banlieues des grandes villes, il manque …

a d'espaces verts.

b d'habitants.

c de pollution.

d d'embouteillages.

4 Choose the correct form of the verb to fill the gap.

Il faut réduire le niveau de pollution dans le monde avant que le changement climatique _____ permanent.

a fasse   b soit

c aille   d est

5 Choose the correct phrase to complete this sentence:

Pour économiser l'énergie, …

a j'éteins la lumière quand je quitte une pièce.

b je recycle mes déchets.

c j'utilise des sacs en coton.

d je prends une douche plutôt qu'un bain.

6 Choose the correct form of the verb to fill the gap:

Il faut que tout le monde _____ régulièrement au centre de recyclage.

a va   b fasse

c aller   d aille

4 Work and education

School / college and future plans

What school / college is like

Pressures and problems

Current and future jobs

Looking for and getting a job

Advantages and disadvantages of different jobs

4.1 Comment est ton collège?
- Position of object pronouns
- Working out answers

4.2 Des écoles différentes
- Relative pronouns
- Making complex sentences

4.3 Problèmes scolaires
- The pluperfect tense
- Covering all content

4.4 Améliorer la vie scolaire
- *On pourrait / on devrait*
- Adding detail using different tenses

4.5 Stages et petits jobs
- Present participle
- Distinguishing *-ant* and *-ement*

4.6 Je cherche un emploi
- Using *vous* (polite form)
- Masculine and feminine forms of jobs

4.7 La vie commence
- Interrogative forms
- Include a range of tenses

4.8 Le monde du travail
- *Venir de* and *après avoir / être*
- Checking grammar

School buildings, rooms and equipment

1a 📖📖🎧 Look at the plan of the ground floor of a school and decide which four of the statements below are true.

Grammaire

After a negative, use *de* (*d'* before a vowel) instead of *un*, *une* or *des*.

Il n'y a pas de cantine.

Il n'y a pas d'élèves.

See grammar section page 172.

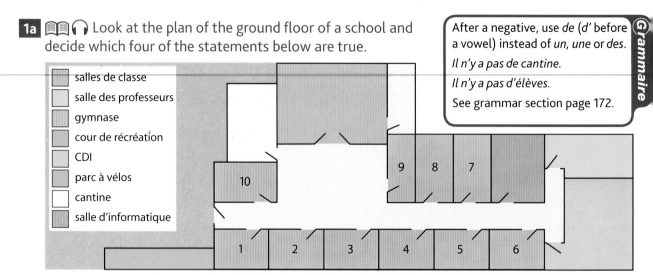

- salles de classe
- salle des professeurs
- gymnase
- cour de récréation
- CDI
- parc à vélos
- cantine
- salle d'informatique

1 Il n'y a pas de gymnase.
2 On peut manger à l'école.
3 Il y a une cour de récréation.

4 On peut venir au collège à vélo.
5 Il y a vingt salles de classe au rez-de-chaussée.
6 Il y a une salle d'informatique.

1b ✏️ Adapt the statements from activity 1a to describe your school.

2a 📖📖🎧 Copy and complete the speech bubble. Use the vocabulary list to help you.

Dans mon collège, il y a un _____ et un tableau _____ _____ dans toutes les _____ de classe. Pour manger, il y a une _____ avec des _____ et des chaises. Au CDI, on peut lire des livres et faire des recherches; il y a aussi une _____ pour _____ des photocopies. Mon endroit préféré, c'est la cour de _____ où on s'amuse et on bavarde.

Vocabulaire

bavarder	to chat
la cantine	dining hall
le CDI (centre de documentation et d'information)	library
la cour de récréation	playground
le dictionnaire (bilingue)	(bilingual) dictionary
le gymnase	gym
le laboratoire	laboratory
le livre	book
l'ordinateur (m)	computer
le parc à vélos	bicycle park
la photocopieuse	photocopying machine
la salle d'informatique	ICT room
la salle des profs	staff room
le tableau blanc interactif	interactive whiteboard

2b 💬 Work in pairs. Partner A chooses one of the places on the plan from activity 1a. Partner B asks yes/no questions to find out which one it is. Then swap over.

Il y a des élèves?

Oui.

Il y a un tableau blanc interactif?

School subjects; jobs

1a 📖🎧 Decide if the following statements are positive (P), negative (N) or a mixture of both (P/N)?

1 Le dessin, je trouve ça super!
2 Je déteste l'EPS car le prof n'est pas sympa.
3 J'aime bien l'espagnol. À mon avis, c'est facile.
4 Je n'aime pas la géographie car c'est barbant.
5 J'adore les maths, mais je trouve que c'est difficile.
6 Je n'aime pas du tout les sciences car c'est trop difficile.
7 La prof d'histoire est marrante, mais je suis nulle en histoire.
8 Ma matière préférée, c'est l'anglais parce que le prof est génial!

1b 💬 Work in pairs and discuss your school subjects.

> Tu aimes les maths?

> Oui, j'aime bien les maths parce que c'est intéressant et la prof est super. Par contre, je déteste la physique car je suis nul(le).

2a 📖🎧 Which three of these sentences make sense and which five are ridiculous?

1 Je voudrais être danseur car j'aime l'EPS.
2 Je voudrais être danseuse car j'aime le français.
3 Je voudrais être chanteuse car j'aime la musique.
4 Je voudrais être journaliste car j'adore le français.
5 Je voudrais être chanteur car je déteste la musique.
6 Je voudrais être comptable car je déteste les maths.
7 Je voudrais être prof d'espagnol car j'adore les sciences.
8 Je voudrais être hôtesse de l'air car je suis nulle en langues.

2b ✏️ Write a caption to match each picture on the right using sentences as in activity 2a.

2c 💬 Work in pairs. Partner A makes up one statement as in activity 2a. Partner B repeats it and says whether it makes sense or is ridiculous.

> Je voudrais être comptable car j'adore l'espagnol.

> Tu voudrais être comptable car tu adores l'espagnol … OK! / C'est ridicule!

Vocabulaire

l'anglais (m)	English
la biologie	biology
la chimie	chemistry
le dessin	art
l'EPS (f)	PE
l'espagnol (m)	Spanish
le français	French
la géographie	geography
l'informatique (f)	ICT
l'instruction civique (f)	citizenship
l'instruction religieuse (f)	RE
les maths (f) (mathématiques)	maths
la physique	physics
les sciences (f)	science
la technologie	DT

Grammaire *page 172*

When talking about school subjects you like and dislike, you need to use the definite article (*le, la, l', les*) before the noun.

J'aime l'histoire et la géographie, mais je déteste les sciences.
– I like history and geography, but I hate science.

Grammaire *page 172*

You do not use the indefinite article (*un, une, des*) to introduce names of jobs in French.

Mon père est plombier.
– My father is a plumber.

Refer to the list of jobs on page 144 to help you with activities 2a–c.

Comment est ton collège?

Objectifs

What school / college is like

Position of object pronouns

Working out answers

1 **V** Find the French for these English expressions. Scan the text below and look in the vocabulary list on page 144.

1. to teach
2. to pass (an exam)
3. an IT room
4. to show
5. someone who eats lunch at school
6. year 9
7. a meeting
8. funny
9. headteacher

Collège Charlemagne

Directeur: M. Alphonse Moreau

A Notre école

Le collège Charlemagne est un établissement moderne avec six cent cinquante garçons et filles de onze à seize ans et cinquante-cinq professeurs. Il est situé au centre-ville. Il y a quarante salles de classe dont douze équipées d'un tableau blanc interactif. Le collège possède aussi un CDI moderne avec une bibliothèque et de grandes salles d'informatique. Nous en avons trois, chacune équipée de trente ordinateurs. Les demi-pensionnaires peuvent déjeuner dans l'une ou l'autre des deux cantines.

B Nos élèves

Émilie Letort, élève de quatrième

Je suis élève ici depuis presque trois ans et je trouve que c'est un collège génial du point de vue équipement. Moi, ce que j'aime le plus, c'est le théâtre où on peut répéter des pièces de théâtre ou faire de la musique. Les professeurs sont tous très gentils et ils font leur meilleur possible pour aider les élèves. Mon professeur principal m'enseigne le français.

Je travaille bien dans l'ensemble parce que j'aime être ici. J'étudie toutes sortes de matières mais celle qui me plaît le plus est l'anglais. L'année dernière, j'ai passé une dizaine de jours en Angleterre en voyage scolaire et on s'est tous bien amusés.

Cette année, on m'a demandé de représenter ma classe au Conseil des élèves, et ça, c'est une grosse responsabilité mais je suis contente de participer aux réunions du Conseil.

2a Read Section A and decide which three statements are true.

1. Forty classrooms have interactive whiteboards.
2. There's a library.
3. There is one canteen.
4. There are three ICT rooms.
5. It is a mixed school.

2b Read Section B and answer the questions in English.

1. Approximately how old is Émilie?
2. What facilities are there for pupils who enjoy drama?
3. Why does Émilie see her form tutor often?
4. What does Émilie tell us about school visits?
5. What position of responsibility does she have this year?

3 🎧 🌐 Listen to Sections A and B and correct the six statements that are wrong.

🎧 You may need to work out the answers from information that is provided, as they may not be given directly in the interviews. For example, we are not told that Florian got on well with his teachers. We can, however, deduce that as he tells us that they were nice, helpful and gave interesting lessons.

Stratégie

A 1 La salle que Stéphanie a préférée est le CDI.
2 Quand un des professeurs a parlé anglais, elle a trouvé ça drôle.
3 Elle espère étudier une langue vivante.
4 L'année prochaine, elle sera en cinquième.
5 Elle a beaucoup aimé sa visite.

B 6 Florian préfère son lycée à son ancien collège.
7 Il n'a pas échoué à ses examens.
8 Les professeurs étaient gentils mais quelquefois, les cours étaient ennuyeux.
9 Il n'est pas allé à l'étranger avec son collège.
10 Il représentait son école en tant que capitaine de l'équipe de foot.

4 🄶 Work with a partner. Partner A asks the question and Partner B answers using direct and indirect object pronouns. Note that the last two have two pronouns.

Tu aimes le collège?

Oui, je l'aime.

1 Tu trouves cet exercice difficile?
Non, _____.

2 Tu comprends le chinois?
Non, _____.

3 Tu as écrit à tes copains français?
Oui, _____.

4 Tu es allé(e) à la piscine hier?
Oui, _____.

5 Tu donneras tes devoirs à ton prof demain?
Oui, _____.

6 Tu as parlé à ton prof principal de tes difficultés en maths?
Oui, _____.

Position of direct and indirect object pronouns

These come immediately before the verb or the auxiliary verb (*avoir* or *être*).

If both direct and indirect object pronouns occur in one sentence, the direct pronoun always comes first.

Je donne le livre à la fille. ➡ *Je le lui donne.*

When two indirect object pronouns occur in the same sentence, the *y* or *en* comes second.

Tu as parlé à ton ami au sujet de ton problème? ➡ *Tu lui en as parlé?*

Also learn about demonstrative adjectives (words for 'this' and 'that').   *See page 142* ➡

Grammaire   page 177

Stuck for ideas? Try adapting sentences from the text on page 132 to express what you want to say.

Astuce

5 ✏️ Work in a group to design a website advertising an imaginary French secondary school (*collège*).

- Student A describes the buildings and facilities.
- Student B is a current student and talks about the school, giving plenty of opinions.
- Student C is still at primary school and writes about their hopes for when they are at the *collège*.
- Student D is at the *lycée* and is looking back at their *collège* days, describing good and bad memories.

Mon collège / lycée s'appelle …	
Dans mon collège / lycée, il y a / nous avons	(900) élèves et (50) profs.
Ce collège / lycée est	bien / mal équipé.
Je trouve que le collège / lycée est ennuyeux / intéressant.	
Les professeurs sont stricts / barbants / paresseux.	
Nous avons	(30) salles de classes / ordinateurs / laboratoires.
Quand j'étais au collège / lycée,	j'ai fait … / joué … / appris …
Quand je serai au collège / lycée,	je vais … / j'espère … / je ferai … / j'apprendrai …

kerboodle!

Des écoles différentes

L'école: c'est mieux en France ou en Grande-Bretagne?

Il y a bien sûr des différences entre les collèges français et leurs équivalents britanniques.

En France, la journée scolaire commence plus tôt qu'en Grande-Bretagne (à huit heures) et peut continuer jusqu'à dix-sept heures. La pause-déjeuner est plus longue en France et peut durer deux heures, ce qui explique que pas mal d'élèves rentrent chez eux à midi. Il y a donc moins de demi-pensionnaires français.

Les vacances sont plus longues en France. Les élèves ont une semaine fin octobre, deux semaines à Noël, deux semaines en avril et deux mois en été.

Comme la pause-déjeuner est longue, il y a toutes sortes d'activités sportives et artistiques organisées pour occuper les élèves. Cependant, après les cours, il n'y en a pas. Tout le monde rentre chez soi.

Dans la plupart des écoles secondaires britanniques, les élèves portent un uniforme scolaire, ce qui n'est pas le cas en France. Les directeurs d'école sont contre l'idée d'imposer aux familles des dépenses inutiles. L'éducation est gratuite et c'est un principe important dans la société française.

En France, si on n'a pas fait assez de progrès, on redouble l'année, c'est-à-dire qu'on refait exactement la même chose l'année scolaire suivante. Les élèves détestent ça parce que leurs copains sont alors dans une autre classe. De plus,

ceux qui redoublent sont dans une classe avec de plus jeunes élèves et trouvent ça un peu humiliant. Refaire le même programme scolaire est aussi plutôt ennuyeux. En Grande Bretagne, personne ne redouble.

1a 📖📖🎧 Read the text and put these headings into the order in which the topics are mentioned.

1 Holidays
2 The repetition of a school year
3 The length of the school day
4 School uniform
5 Going home for lunch
6 Extra-curricular activities

1b 📖📖🎧 Read the text again and answer these questions in English.

1 In which country is the school day longer? What about the holidays?
2 Why do many pupils go home for lunch in France?
3 Why don't pupils wear a school uniform in France?
4 Identify two things that French pupils dislike about repeating a school year.

2a 🎧 Listen to Section A, in which Mani Mustafa talks about his school in Sénégal, and decide which three statements are correct.

1 There weren't enough books.
2 The classes were small.
3 He didn't fail his exams.
4 He didn't have to repeat a year.
5 He didn't like his teachers.

2b 🎧 Listen to Section B and choose the three statements which are true according to Mani.

1 Having good teachers was more important than having good equipment.
2 At primary school he used to eat in the canteen.
3 As a secondary school pupil, he was a boarder.
4 The school rules were quite different from the rules in France.
5 He is going to raise funds for the school in Sénégal.

3 🄶 Select the correct word to complete each sentence.

1 J'ai écrit une rédaction que / qui / où s'appelait «Les collèges écossais».
2 La rédaction que / qui / où j'ai écrite était excellente.
3 Je suis allé à un cours que / qui / où était nul.
4 L'uniforme que / qui / où je porte est super.
5 Je suis allé à la cantine, que / qui / où j'ai mangé.
6 Le repas que / qui / où j'ai mangé était délicieux.

4 🗩 🌐 In pairs, compare your school to a typical French school. Student A is an interviewer from the French school and Student B talks about life in your own school and makes comparisons.

Here are some suggested questions, but you may like to add others:

■ Qu'est-ce que tu portes pour aller au collège?
■ À quelle heure est-ce que tu es arrivé(e) au collège ce matin?
■ La pause-déjeuner dure combien de temps?
■ À quelle heure est-ce que tu vas quitter le collège cet après-midi?
■ Il y a des choses qui t'énervent dans le règlement scolaire?
■ Et il y a des choses que tu trouves justes dans le règlement?

Ⓖrammaire *page 178*

Relative pronouns *qui*, *que* and *où*

qui means 'who', 'which' or 'that'. It is usually followed by a verb.

J'ai un prof d'anglais qui s'appelle Mr Smith.

que (qu') means 'which' or 'that'. It is usually followed by a person or a thing.

C'est une matière que j'aime bien.

où means 'where'.

Le café où on va d'habitude est près de chez moi.

Don't mix it up with *ou* with no accent (same pronunciation), which means 'or'.

Also learn how to recognise the relative pronoun *dont*.

See page 142 ➡

Ⓢtratégie

🗩 You can make sentences longer and more complex by using words such as *qui* (who – see grammar activity), *quand* (when) and *si* (if), e.g. *Je fais mes devoirs quand j'ai beaucoup de temps.*

En France / En Grande-Bretagne / Au Sénégal, il y a … heures de cours par jour / semaine.	
Il y a un uniforme scolaire. / Il n'y a pas d'uniforme scolaire.	
Il y a des activités	après les cours / pendant la pause-déjeuner.
Il y a plus / moins de vacances.	
La journée scolaire commence / finit à …	
Je crois que … / Je pense que … / À mon avis, …	
Il y a un règlement, par exemple on doit … / il est interdit de …	
Hier au collège, j'ai … et demain je vais …	

Qu'est-ce que tu portes pour aller au collège?

Je dois porter un uniforme scolaire que je déteste.

4.3 Problèmes scolaires

1 **V** Put each expression into the correct category: facilities, discipline or testing.

1 incivilités
2 punir
3 installations technologiques
4 examens
5 contrôles
6 bâtiments anciens

Les collèges: une catastrophe?

A Tout le monde parle de la situation dans les collèges en France. On dit qu'il y a quelques écoles dans les banlieues des grandes villes où on attaque les professeurs, on voit des graffitis partout, il y a des problèmes de vandalisme, de sécurité et de violence. Mais est-ce que tout ça est vrai?

M. Alphonse Moreau, directeur du collège Charlemagne, donne son avis:

«Bien sûr, comme dans tous les pays européens, il existe des difficultés dans notre collège. Il y a toujours quelques élèves qui empêchent les autres de travailler en refusant de se taire pendant les cours. On ne leur permet pas de continuer comme ça et on les punit. La majorité de nos élèves sont travailleurs et disciplinés.»

B Nous avons parlé à Sandrine Letellier, élève de troisième d'un grand collège de banlieue:

«Il y a six mois, j'ai eu des examens et aussi des contrôles. Je m'y étais bien préparée mais c'était quand même difficile. J'avais décidé de travailler dur plutôt que de m'amuser, mais certains professeurs n'étaient pas assez sévères et il y a eu des problèmes de discipline, ce qui fait qu'il n'était pas facile d'entendre ce que le prof essayait d'expliquer.

On dit qu'il y a des élèves qui sont indisciplinés, et c'est vrai. Moi, j'avais des soucis parce que j'ai été victime d'un acte de violence. Récemment, sans aucune raison, une autre élève m'a frappée dans la cour. Mais quand je l'ai dit au prof, l'élève a menti et c'est moi qu'on a punie. Ce n'est pas juste.»

2a Read Section A and choose the three correct statements according to the text.

1 Il y a toutes sortes de problèmes dans la majorité des écoles françaises.
2 Il y a des problèmes au collège Charlemagne.
3 Il y a des élèves qui parlent en classe et dérangent les autres.
4 Les élèves qui dérangent les autres ne sont pas punis.
5 La plupart des élèves du collège Charlemagne travaillent bien.

2b Read Section B and choose the three correct statements.

1 Sandrine worked hard for her tests.
2 Some teachers were too strict.
3 She was attacked in the playground.
4 The pupil bullying her was punished.
5 Sandrine was not happy with the outcome.

3a 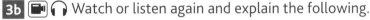 Watch or listen to both sections of the interview and put the issues into the order in which they are mentioned.

1 Problem with a parent about homework
2 Problem with a teacher about homework
3 School facilities being too old-fashioned
4 Pupils wearing cool clothes
5 Wearing jewellery and make-up

3b 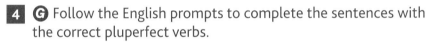 Watch or listen again and explain the following.

1 What Pascal is concerned about
2 His attitude on the matter
3 What worries Laurent
4 Sanja's problem
5 What she had to do
6 What happened to Fatima
7 The consequence the next day
8 Marc's views on school rules

4 **G** Follow the English prompts to complete the sentences with the correct pluperfect verbs.

1 J'_____ _____ mes devoirs sans problème, mais j'ai eu une mauvaise note. (had done)
2 Je suis allé au CDI, où j'_____ _____ un livre la semaine dernière. (had looked for)
3 Comme il _____ _____ son dictionnaire, il est allé en acheter un autre. (had lost)
4 On est arrivé trop tard à l'arrêt de bus: le bus _____ _____. (had left)
5 Mehmet _____ _____ une calculatrice, puis il l'a perdue. (had bought)
6 Je croyais que j'_____ _____ tous mes devoirs, mais en fait, j'_____ _____ ceux de français. (had finished) (had forgotten)

> ## Grammaire — page 182
>
> ### The pluperfect tense
>
> The pluperfect indicates one step further back than the perfect tense, i.e. what **had** happened before something else happened.
>
> It is formed like the perfect tense, but instead of using the auxiliaries in the present tense, you use them in the imperfect.
>
> ***avoir* verbs:**
>
> | perfect | pluperfect |
> |---|---|
> | *j'ai cherché* | *j'avais cherché* |
>
> ***être* verbs:**
>
> | perfect | pluperfect |
> |---|---|
> | *je suis allé(e)* | *j'étais allé(e)* |
>
> Also learn about using *il y a*, meaning 'ago'.   *See page 142* ➡

5 ✏ 🔍 Write a short article about school pressures and problems.

Mention:

- the teachers and lessons
- homework and exams
- problems with buildings and equipment
- clothes and fashion
- a specific problem you have had which has been solved (using the pluperfect).

> ## Stratégie
>
> ✏ When you are given a writing task like this one, there are normally bullet points to guide you. Make sure you include all the information and that everything you write is relevant to the task.

Il y a / n'y a pas beaucoup de problèmes.	
Il y a des problèmes de	vandalisme / sécurité et violence.
Il y a trop de	devoirs / contrôles.
À mon avis, certains professeurs sont	trop sévères / barbants.
Les bâtiments sont vieux.	
Beaucoup d'élèves portent des vêtements chic et chers.	

Il y a deux mois / ans,	j'ai eu / on a eu des problèmes de …	mais après, j'ai décidé de… / on a fait …
On m'a puni(e)	parce que je n'avais pas fait mes devoirs.	

> ## Astuce
>
> Don't forget to give reasons (using *parce que*) and include opinions (*je suis pour / contre l'uniforme*).

kerboodle!

4.4 Améliorer la vie scolaire

At the last meeting of the student council at the Collège Charlemagne, students discussed how to make the school a better place. Here is an extract from the minutes of the meeting.

Le Conseil des élèves

Le Conseil des élèves est arrivé aux conclusions suivantes lors de sa dernière réunion:

A Afin d'aider les élèves à faire leurs devoirs dans de bonnes conditions de travail, on devrait avoir une salle de classe réservée à cela, ouverte pendant une heure en fin de journée, après les cours. Cette classe aurait un professeur qui serait là pour faciliter la tâche de ceux qui trouvent leurs devoirs difficiles à faire.

B La pause-déjeuner est trop longue pour la majorité des élèves. Il devrait y avoir un cours supplémentaire pour aider les élèves qui ont des difficultés dans certaines matières. L'école offrirait une matière différente chaque jour de la semaine.

C L'école devrait employer des professeurs de langues qui ne sont pas enseignées dans notre collège actuellement, par exemple des professeurs de russe et de chinois. Les cours ne seraient pas obligatoires. Les élèves que ça intéresse pourraient y assister et donc avoir la possibilité d'apprendre d'autres langues.

D Notre collège devrait devenir partenaire d'une école du Tiers-Monde. Le côté éducatif pour nos élèves est évident. Nos élèves pourraient également aider cette école en lui envoyant des livres et d'autres choses dont elle a besoin. Le collège pourrait aussi, par exemple, organiser une fête payante à laquelle les parents d'élèves seraient invités. On pourrait envoyer l'argent à l'école partenaire.

E Récemment, un groupe de nos élèves a fait un échange scolaire avec une école anglaise. Ils ont remarqué des différences importantes entre nos écoles, par exemple leur uniforme scolaire, l'absence de redoublement, la durée courte de leur pause-déjeuner et aussi de leurs retenues. On devrait discuter de certaines de ces différences avec le directeur et lui recommander des changements qui contribueraient à améliorer la vie scolaire ici à Charlemagne.

1a 📖 🎧 Read the meeting minutes and match the five resolutions (A–E) with these headings.

1 Using another school's ideas
2 Extra optional subjects
3 Pairing up with a school in a developing country
4 Extra tuition
5 A homework room

1b 📖 🎧 Read the minutes again and answer the questions in English.

1 Why would there be a teacher in the homework room?
2 How would the extra tuition be organised?
3 What extra opportunities would there be for pupils keen on languages?
4 In what **two** ways would students help their partner school?
5 What are the **four** differences between British and French schools that were noted during the last exchange visit?

2 🎧 Listen to the students discussing with their teacher what could be done to make their school better. Complete each statement with the correct person: K (Kemal), M (Marine), F (Frédérique) or B (Bruno).

> *Qu'est ce qu'on pourrait faire pour améliorer le collège?*

A
1 xxxxx thinks there is too much assessment.
2 xxxxx would prefer to see fewer books in schools.
3 xxxxx would like to be able to email completed homework to the teachers.
4 xxxxx would like students to be more involved in discussing their progress.

B
5 xxxxx suggests showing real school life on the website.
6 xxxxx suggests asking students to improve the website.
7 xxxxx thinks that students should each have their own laptop.
8 xxxxx thinks that examples of students' work should be displayed on the website.

3a **G** Write out *devoir* (to have to / must) in the conditional, in the same way as *pouvoir* is set out in the grammar box.

3b **G** Complete the sentences with the correct conditional form of *pouvoir* or *devoir*.

1 On _____ travailler dans le CDI. (could)
2 On _____ faire nos devoirs. (should)
3 Sascha _____ acheter un appareil numérique. (should)
4 Laure _____ acheter un ordinateur. (could)
5 Les profs _____ être plus stricts. (could)
6 Ils _____ préparer leurs cours. (should)

Grammaire *pages 183, 185*

On pourrait / on devrait

Je pourrais (I could) and *on devrait* (you / we / they ought to) are examples of modal verbs in the conditional. They are always used with the infinitive of another verb.

Don't forget that the conditional is formed from a future stem and imperfect endings.

pouvoir – to be able to / can

je pourrais	*nous pourrions*
tu pourrais	*vous pourriez*
il / elle pourrait	*ils / elles pourraient*

Also revise a range of question words. *See page 143* ➡️

4 💬 🌐 In groups, discuss how your school could be improved.

- Start by suggesting a problem or situation that could be improved.
- Give one possible way of improving it.
- Give another possible way of improving it.
- Say which is the best solution and why.

> Qu'est-ce qu'on pourrait faire pour améliorer la vie scolaire?

> On pourrait aider les élèves à faire leurs devoirs plus facilement.

Qu'est-ce qu'on pourrait faire pour améliorer la vie scolaire?	On pourrait …
	On devrait …
Quelle est la solution?	On devrait / pourrait … parce que …
Il y a d'autres possibilités?	Les élèves devraient / pourraient …
Quelle est la meilleure solution des deux? Pourquoi?	Je pense que la première / la deuxième solution est meilleure parce que …

Stratégie

💬 If you want to do well in the controlled coursework, you need to offer extra information and use different tenses.

Give examples of situations you have been involved in using *par exemple* and the perfect tense.

Suggest different possibilities using *peut-être* (perhaps) and the conditional.

Give your opinion using *à mon avis* or *je pense / trouve que* and justify it using *car* or *parce que* and the present tense.

Astuce

To find possible problems to discuss, look at the student council minutes on page 138 and also the article on page 136.

cent trente-neuf **139**

School / college and future plans

L'école des parents en Centrafrique

A Il est 7h20, le soleil est déjà bien haut dans le ciel. Achille, en maillot de foot et short aux couleurs de son équipe préférée, s'amuse avec ses camarades en attendant le signal pour entrer en classe. Ils viennent ainsi très tôt tous les jours pour suivre la classe avant qu'il ne fasse trop chaud. À 12 ans, Achille est en cinquième et il travaille avec les plus grands.

B Il y a deux ans, Achille vivait dans un village à quelques kilomètres d'ici et il allait à l'école du village. Un jour, les soldats sont arrivés, le village a été attaqué, les maisons brûlées. Toute la famille a dû partir et a vécu quelques mois au milieu de la brousse, dans des conditions très difficiles. Maintenant, son père a construit une nouvelle maison.

C L'école est à environ 800 mètres de la maison d'Achille. Cette école (seulement temporaire), ce sont les parents qui l'ont construite rapidement pour leurs enfants, et ce sont eux encore qui font la classe avec le minimum d'équipement. On veut donner une idée de normalité et de protection aux enfants. «Cette école est très différente de celle du village. Là-bas il y avait des cahiers, des crayons, des professeurs. Ici, on n'a rien», dit Achille.

D La directrice de l'école décrit les conditions ici:

«Nous avons plus de cent enfants. Nous essayons de faire la classe mais, comme vous voyez, dans des conditions qui sont très difficiles. Il ne nous reste presque rien du bâtiment, et nous n'avons pas assez de professeurs. Si vous demandez aux enfants, ils vont dire qu'ils veulent des livres, des cahiers, des tables, des bancs et un professeur.

E Sans l'aide d'AaE (Attention aux Enfants), notre travail serait impossible. On nous a donné des livres, et on va payer la construction d'un bâtiment permanent. AaE a aussi pris en charge la formation de six parents – des parents qui peuvent nous aider à travailler avec les enfants en classe. Ça, c'est le plus important. Dans six mois, il y aura une école où les enfants pourront vraiment avancer dans leurs études, on aura peut-être même l'électricité et un ordinateur!»

1a 📖🎧 Skim the whole article and choose the correct heading for each paragraph.

1 A village under attack
2 The difficulties of running the school
3 An early morning start
4 International aid
5 Achille's school – a convenient solution for the time being

1b 📖🎧 Read the article in more detail and correct the mistakes in these sentences.

1 Achille has lessons with younger children.
2 Achille's old house was destroyed in a bush fire.
3 Achille is happy with the new facilities.
4 The headteacher refuses to run classes without enough staff.
5 The priority is to train parents to help build the school.
6 The head expects few improvements over the next six months.

2a 🎧 Blandine has recently arrived from France to stay with her Canadian friend Cécile. Listen to Section A, where they compare their schools. Choose the correct ending to each sentence.

In Canada …

1 the school is
   a bigger.
   b smaller.
   c about the same size.
2 teachers, in general, are
   a nicer.
   b worse.
   c about the same.
3 the music teacher is
   a better.
   b worse.
   c about the same.
4 the range of subjects studied is
   a very different.
   b mostly the same.
   c exactly the same.
5 their priorities, when choosing their secondary school, were
   a exactly the same.
   b the same in some ways.
   c completely different.

2b 🎧 Listen to Section B. Which of the following has Cécile planned for Blandine to see or do while in Canada? Write a ✓ or ✗ for each activity.

1 American football
2 Two different forms of ice hockey
3 Ice skating
4 Stay in a tent in the forest
5 Stay in a lodge by a lake
6 Canoeing
7 Learn to play a musical instrument
8 Sing in a concert

> **Grammaire** page 182
>
> The pluperfect tense is used twice in the conversation: at the end of Section A, and near the beginning of Section B. Can you pick out both examples, and say exactly what they mean?
>
> For more help with the pluperfect tense, see page 137.

> **AQA** *Examiner's tip*
>
> In activity 2b, you will hear all the activities mentioned in the conversation, but you need to pay careful attention: are they mentioned because they are part of the plans, or for some other reason? Do not fall into the trap of assuming that if you hear the word, it is bound to be among the correct answers.

> **Vocabulaire**
>
> | | |
> |---|---|
> | *améliorer* | to improve |
> | *la brousse* | bush / bushes |
> | *brûler* | to burn |
> | *le dortoir* | dormitory |
> | *la municipalité* | local council |
> | *prêter* | to lend |

(G) School / college and future plans

Demonstrative adjectives; relative pronoun *dont*; *il y a* and *pendant*

1 Complete the following sentences with *ce, cet, cette* or *ces*.

1 _____ élèves préparent le bac.
2 _____ matière est assez facile.
3 Je vais acheter _____ ordinateur.
4 Il y a 1200 élèves dans _____ lycée.
5 _____ examen n'est pas très difficile.
6 Je peux utiliser _____ calculatrice?
7 _____ professeurs m'ont encouragé.
8 Dans _____ collège, les élèves sont travailleurs.

2 Translate the following sentences into English.

1 J'étudie les matières dont j'ai besoin.
2 Elle aime les élèves dont elle s'occupe.
3 Tu connais la fille dont je suis amoureux?
4 Il déteste le garçon dont la mère est prof de maths.
5 Ils vont passer les examens dont je t'ai parlé.
6 Il y a quelques résultats dont elle est fière.

3 Translate the English in brackets into French to complete the sentences.

1 J'ai passé mon bac _____.
   (a long time ago)
2 Ils ont étudié la géographie _____.
   (for four years)
3 Le prof de maths l'a puni _____.
   (three days ago)
4 Tu as commencé l'espagnol _____?
   (six months ago)
5 Il a acheté ce dictionnaire _____.
   (a week ago)
6 Elle est restée dans la salle des professeurs
   _____. (for five minutes)

Demonstrative adjectives — *Grammaire* page 174

The French for 'this' or 'that' is:

■ *ce* before a masculine noun: *ce professeur* – this teacher

■ *cet* before a masculine noun starting with a vowel or a silent *h*: *cet étudiant* – this student

■ *cette* before a feminine noun: *cette université* – this university.

The French for 'these' or 'those' is *ces*: *ces stylos* – those pens.

Relative pronoun *dont* — *Grammaire* page 178

Dont is used to link phrases together. It is usually needed when the verb in the second phrase is constructed with *de*, e.g. *avoir besoin de*, or *s'occuper de* or *être fier de*. *Dont* can be translated by 'that', but in English the word 'that' is often left out.

la note dont je suis fier – the grade (that) I am proud of

le prof dont j'ai besoin – the teacher (that) I need

Il y a* and *pendant — *Grammaire* page 188

Although *il y a* normally means 'there is' or 'there are', it is translated as 'ago' when it is followed by a phrase expressing a period of time. Note the word order: *il y a* comes before the time expression, whereas 'ago' comes after it.

Il a commencé l'espagnol il y a trois ans.
– He started Spanish three years ago.

Il y a refers to the time when the action took place, but *pendant* refers to how long it lasted.

Il a étudié l'espagnol pendant deux ans.
– He studied Spanish for two years.

Revision of question words; the pluperfect tense

4 Select the correct word from the list to complete each question.

1 _____ livre choisit-il?
2 _____ matière préfères-tu?
3 _____ étudiez-vous le français?
4 _____ d'élèves y a-t-il dans ta classe?
5 _____ est la salle d'informatique?
6 _____ vas-tu passer l'examen?
7 _____ va réussir?
8 _____ tu vas faire ce soir?

Qui

Qu'est-ce que

Quel

Où

Quand

Combien

Quelle

Pourquoi

5 Complete the story using verbs from the list below in the pluperfect tense.

La journée avait mal commencé! J'_____ _____ à l'école à vélo …

parce que j'étais encore au lit quand le car de ramassage _____ _____ !

La prof de maths m'avait punie parce que j'_____ _____ mon livre.

Mon chat _____ _____ mes devoirs d'anglais!

Mes parents _____ _____ … une fois de plus.

Je _____ _____ très déprimée!

aller   arriver   se coucher   se disputer   manger   oublier

---

Grammaire · page 186

Revision of question words

Make sure you know the following words and use them to introduce questions.

combien?	how much / how many?
où?	where?
pourquoi?	why?
quand?	when?
qu'est-ce que?	what?
qui?	who?
quel?	which / what?

Remember that *quel* agrees with the noun it goes with.

masculine singular: *quel livre?* – which book?

feminine singular: *quelle matière?* – which subject?

masculine plural: *quels stylos?* – which pens?

feminine plural: *quelles affaires?* – which things?

Grammaire · page 182

The pluperfect tense

When using the pluperfect tense, remember to use the imperfect of *avoir* (with most verbs) or *être* (with verbs like *aller, venir* and *arriver* and with reflexive verbs).

Il avait oublié son devoir de géo et il était arrivé en retard.
– He had forgotten his geography homework and he had arrived late.

When using the pluperfect with *être*, make the past participle agree with the subject.

Elle était sortie parce que ses parents s'étaient disputés.
– She had gone out because her parents had argued.

School / college and future plans

Les métiers ➡ *page 131*

l'	*agriculteur / agricultrice*	farmer
le/la	*boucher / bouchère*	butcher
le/la	*boulanger / boulangère*	baker
le/la	*caissier / caissière*	cashier
le/la	*chanteur / chanteuse*	singer
le/la	*comptable*	accountant
le/la	*cuisinier / cuisinière*	cook
le/la	*danseur / danseuse*	dancer
l'	*électricien(ne)*	electrician
l'	*hôtesse de l'air (f)*	air stewardess
l'	*ingénieur (m)*	engineer
le/la	*mécanicien(ne)*	mechanic
le/la	*musicien(ne)*	musician
le/la	*plombier / plombière*	plumber
le/la	*professeur*	teacher
le/la	*programmeur / programmeuse*	programmer
le/la	*secrétaire*	secretary
le/la	*serveur / serveuse*	waiter / waitress
le/la	*technicien(ne)*	technician
le/la	*vendeur / vendeuse*	sales assistant
le/la	*vétérinaire*	vet

Comment est ton collège? ➡ *pages 132–133*

	ancien(ne)	former
	apprendre (appris)	to learn
le	*conseil*	council / advice
le	*cours*	lesson
le / la	*demi-pensionnaire*	day boarder (someone who has lunch at school)
le / la	*directeur / directrice*	headteacher
	discipliné(e)	disciplined / punished
l'	*élève (m / f)*	pupil

	enseigner	to teach
	expliquer	to explain
le	*lycée*	high school (for students aged 16–18)
	montrer	to show
la	*réunion*	meeting
	réussir (réussi)	to pass (an exam) / to succeed
	rigolo(-te)	fun / funny
le	*voyage scolaire*	school trip

Des écoles différentes ➡ *pages 134–135*

	bien équipé(e)	well equipped / with good facilities
le	*car de ramassage*	school bus
la	*confiance en soi*	self-confidence
	doué(e)	gifted / clever
	échouer à	to fail
	interdit(e)	forbidden
la	*langue vivante*	modern language
la	*pause-déjeuner*	lunch hour
	redoubler	to repeat a school year
la	*règle*	rule
le	*règlement*	rules
	retenir (retenu)	to keep
la	*retenue*	detention
	scolaire	school / to do with school
	travailleur(-se)	hardworking

1 **V** Match each expression on the left with one on the right.

1	échouer	a	l'allemand
2	les langues vivantes	b	fort(e)
3	le car de ramassage	c	ce qu'il faut faire
4	la cantine	d	les demi-pensionnaires
5	doué(e)	e	redoubler
6	le règlement	f	le transport

Problèmes scolaires ➡ *pages 136–137*

le	*contrôle*	test
les	*devoirs (m)*	homework
	empêcher	to prevent / to get in the way of
l'	*ennui (m)*	worry / boredom
s'	*ennuyer*	to get bored / to be bored
	frapper	to hit
l'	*incivilité (f)*	rude behaviour
	mentir (menti)	to lie (tell an untruth)
se	*moquer de*	to make fun of
	permettre (permis)	to allow
	punir (puni)	to punish
la	*récréation*	break (in school day)
le	*souci*	worry / problem
la	*troisième*	French equivalent of year 10
la	*victime*	victim

Améliorer la vie scolaire ➡ *pages 138–139*

	améliorer	to improve
l'	*appareil (m)*	camera / machine
	assister à	to be present at / to take part in
	chinois(e)	Chinese
	démodé(e)	out of date
	obligatoire	compulsory
l'	*ordinateur portable (m)*	laptop
la	*peinture*	painting
le	*redoublement*	repeating a school year
	renouveler	to renew / to update
le	*Tiers-Monde*	the developing world

2 **V** Link each expression to a more general word. Note that there is one extra general word that you will not need.

1	un appareil	a	les arts
2	le chinois	b	la musique
3	enregistrer	c	la photographie
4	la peinture	d	les pays pauvres
5	le Tiers-Monde	e	les voyages scolaires
		f	les langues vivantes

Poser des questions

combien?	how many?
comment?	how?
où?	where?
pourquoi?	why?
quand?	when?
que	that / what
quel/quelle	which
qu'est-ce que c'est?	what is it?
qui?	who?
quoi?	what?

kerboodle!

4.5 Stages et petits jobs

Objectifs

Student jobs and work experience

Present participle

Distinguishing -ant and -ement

Les jeunes Français aiment gagner de l'argent!

Bien qu'il y ait des jeunes qui ont un travail à temps partiel pendant les vacances ou même pendant l'année scolaire, ce n'est pourtant pas la majorité. De nos jours, on ne trouve pas un travail facilement. Ceux qui ont un petit boulot travaillent à la caisse des supermarchés ou dans un restaurant, un café ou un hôtel. Le job le plus populaire, c'est de faire du baby-sitting.

Quand on leur demande pourquoi ils ont un travail en plus de leurs études, plus de quatre-vingts pour cent des jeunes disent qu'ils veulent avoir plus d'argent de poche et donc la possibilité de sortir le soir ou de s'acheter les dernières baskets par exemple.

Cependant, le ministre de l'Éducation n'est pas d'accord. Il a publié un communiqué officiel en exprimant ce que pensent beaucoup de parents d'élèves:

«Je comprends bien que les jeunes d'aujourd'hui veuillent gagner de l'argent. On vit dans une société de consommation où les adolescents pensent qu'il est essentiel d'avoir les mêmes vêtements et jeux

Le job le plus populaire est le baby-sitting

vidéo que leurs amis. Mais en travaillant le soir et le week-end, leur travail scolaire va certainement en souffrir parce que les élèves seront fatigués et n'auront pas assez de temps pour faire leurs devoirs. On retrouvera cette fatigue le lendemain en cours. Ces élèves feraient bien de se rappeler qu'on ne fait son éducation qu'une fois et que leur avenir en dépend.

La recommandation gouvernementale est de ne pas travailler pendant le trimestre scolaire. Les grandes vacances sont suffisamment longues dans notre pays et les élèves qui souhaitent gagner de l'argent devraient s'en satisfaire. Je demande donc aux parents d'élèves d'encourager ces jeunes à se concentrer sur leurs activités scolaires. C'est ce qui compte le plus à leur âge.»

1a Decide whether, according to the text, the sentences are true (T), false (F) or not mentioned (?).

1 Most young people have a part-time job.
2 80% of young people who have a job do babysitting.
3 The usual reason for wanting to work is to earn more pocket money.
4 The Minister of Education understands the reasons why young people want to work.
5 He recommends that young people should not work at all.
6 He thinks that young people should only work as preparation for their chosen career.

Stratégie

Don't confuse words ending in -ant and -ement.

Those ending in -ant are present participles (see grammar section page 184).

Those ending in -ement are adverbs (like English words ending in '-ly').

There are two examples of each in the article. Re-read it and find them.

1b Read the article again and answer the questions in English.

1 How do young people spend their pocket money? Note two ways that are mentioned.
2 According to the minister, when young people work, in what way does their school work suffer?
3 How does the minister then stress the importance of education?
4 What is the government's recommendation with regard to young people working?

2 🎧 Listen to Sections A and B and answer the questions in English.

A 1　Did **Émilie** like the following aspects of her work experience?

　　a　the work experience as a whole

　　b　using her maths

　　c　making the coffee

　　d　interacting with her colleagues

　2　In what way did her colleagues show their appreciation of her work?

　3　What did her boss suggest in recognition of her good work?

　4　Why is she pleased about this?

B 5　Where did **Nicolas** do his work experience?

　6　What were the two drawbacks?

　7　What did his job consist of?

　8　What positive comment about his work experience does he make at the end?

3 🅖 Fill in each blank using *en* + the present participle of a verb from the list.

1　J'ai cherché du travail _____ dans le journal.

2　J'ai gagné 20 euros _____ dans un magasin.

3　Laurent s'est blessé _____ au travail.

4　J'ai gagné de l'expérience _____ un stage.

5　Je suis arrivée au bureau de bonne heure _____ l'autobus.

　　prendre　　travailler　　aller　　regarder　　faire

> ### Present participle
>
> The French present participle ends in *-ant* ('-ing' in English). Take the *nous* form of the present tense, remove *-ons* and replace it with *-ant*.
>
> Use *en* + present participle when two actions happen together.
>
> *Il fait ses devoirs en écoutant de la musique.*
> – He does his homework while listening to music.
>
> *En travaillant le soir, je gagne de l'argent.*
> – By working in the evening, I earn money.
>
> Also learn about object pronouns with negatives.
> *See page 156* ➡️
>
> 🅖 **Grammaire** *page 184*

4 🗨️ Prepare a spoken presentation about your work experience.

Include:

■　where you worked and what you did

■　how long you worked and when you started and finished

■　what you thought of your work experience and why

■　how your working day compared to a school day

■　whether this is a job that you would like to do later.

> **Astuce**
>
> If you don't want to talk about your own work experience, feel free to make it up. Remember that in the speaking test it is the quality of your French that counts, not whether you're telling the truth!

J'ai travaillé	dans un magasin / bureau / centre sportif.
J'ai	servi des clients / travaillé à la caisse.
Il a fallu que	je fasse le café / aille à la poste.
Ça m'a plu	parce que …
C'était ennuyeux	
Je trouve que le travail était	barbant / dur / intéressant / fatigant / amusant / mal payé.
C'était plus / moins intéressant	qu'une journée au collège parce que …
Ce genre de travail	m'intéresse / ne m'intéresse pas pour l'avenir parce que …

OFFRES D'EMPLOI

Si vous désirez un emploi dans une entreprise de logiciels, ceci est pour vous.
SOFTIQUE, 292 rue Bellevue, Troyes, cherche analyste-programmeur/programmeuse qualifié(e). Salaire à discuter. Minimum de deux ans d'expérience souhaitable. Envoyez-nous votre CV.

École maternelle SAINT-JACQUES, 24 rue des Pins, Belley. On cherche une personne pour travailler avec des enfants de 2 à 5 ans. Lundi à vendredi, tous les matins de 8h à 12h30. Formation: CAP (certificat d'aptitude professionnelle) minimum.
Pour poser votre candidature à ce poste, écrivez-nous.

Vous êtes au chômage? Supermarché OMNIMARCHÉ cherche 3 vendeurs / vendeuses pour travailler tous les après-midi de 4 à 6 heures (lun.– ven.). Salaire à négocier. Âge: sans importance. Expérience préférable. Présentez-vous au chef du personnel.

> Au niveau qualifications, pas de problème. J'ai fait une formation et j'ai réussi mon certificat d'aptitude professionnelle l'année dernière. Le seul problème, c'est que je n'ai pas d'expérience. Ce serait mon premier travail. Dans leur petite annonce, ils ne disent pas que l'expérience est essentielle. Donc, il n'y a pas de raison que je ne pose pas ma candidature. Je vais leur écrire, on verra bien.

Mohamed

> En ce moment, je travaille le samedi dans un petit magasin mais ce que je cherche, c'est un travail qu'il est possible de faire après l'école. Je ne veux pas finir trop tard sinon je n'aurai pas le temps de faire mes devoirs le soir. Je vais y aller cet après-midi pour voir ce qu'ils disent à propos du salaire.

Marine

> J'ai fait des études d'informatique mais maintenant j'ai changé d'idée. Ce qui me plaît, c'est l'enseignement. J'aimerais bien faire la classe aux élèves du primaire. Malheureusement, je n'ai pas fait de formation professionnelle pour ça. Tout de même, ce serait une bonne idée de contacter l'école, on ne sait jamais.

Robert

> La formation professionnelle que j'ai faite est exactement ce qu'ils demandent et mes deux dernières années de travail me donnent assez d'expérience pour poser ma candidature à ce poste. Je vais leur écrire tout de suite. J'espère qu'ils vont m'inviter à passer un entretien.

Fatima

1a 📖🎧🌐 Read the job adverts and then what the four potential applicants are thinking. Who is best suited to each job?

1 Softique
2 Saint-Jacques
3 Omnimarché

1b 📖🎧🌐 Answer the questions in English.

1 Why is Robert unsuitable for the Softique position?
2 Why is he unsuitable for the teaching assistant position?
3 Who is the youngest applicant?
4 Which two people are working now?
5 Which two people have had training for a job?

2 🎧 Listen to Marine and Fatima's job interviews, and select the correct answers.

A 1 Marine has worked for the last six weeks / months / years.

    2 She likes / dislikes / hates her present job.

    3 She wants to work at weekends / on Friday evenings / Monday to Friday.

    4 She will earn 7 euros / 8 euros / 80 euros an hour.

    5 She can start work on Monday / next month / today.

B 6 Fatima has a degree in maths / physics / IT.

    7 She studied a further year / two years / three years to get her masters degree.

    8 She never / regularly / occasionally works on a Saturday.

    9 She wants to give her current employer enough time to offer her a better salary / find a replacement / write her a reference.

    10 The job offer is subject to good references / agreeing about the salary / a position becoming available.

> ### Using *vous* (polite form)
> Use *tu* for friends, family and children. Use *vous* for adults, strangers and more than one person.
>
> The *vous* form of a verb in the present tense usually ends in -*ez*.
>
> Use *Monsieur, Madame* or *Mademoiselle* and the surname for someone you would address as *vous*.
>
> *S'il vous plaît* is the formal equivalent of *s'il te plaît*. *Votre / vos* are the formal equivalents of *ton / ta / tes*.
>
> Also revise demonstrative pronouns such as *celui* and *celle*.
> *See page 156* ➡
>
> **Grammaire** *page 176*

3 🄖 Work in pairs. Partner A asks the first question. Partner B makes up an answer and asks the question back, but using the *vous* form. Partner A gives a different answer. Swap over for each question.

    1 Tu cherches un emploi?

    2 Quelle formation as-tu?

    3 As-tu de l'expérience?

    4 Es-tu au chômage?

    5 Quel est ton nom de famille?

    6 Peux-tu venir passer un entretien?

> Tu cherches un emploi?

> Oui, je voudrais travailler dans un magasin. Vous cherchez un emploi?

> Oui, je voudrais travailler pendant les vacances scolaires.

4 🗨 Hold a telephone conversation about one of the job adverts. Partner A is the employer and asks the questions and notes down Partner B's answers. Compare notes at the end. Then swap roles and use different details.

Ask and answer questions about the following:

- the type of job being applied for
- name and age, including spelling
- qualifications and experience
- availability (hours and days)
- arranging the interview date.

> **Astuce**
> Look at activity 3 to get help with forming the questions. Use ideas from the thought bubbles on page 148 to help you talk about your (made-up) qualifications and experience.

> Bonjour, monsieur. Je téléphone à propos de l'emploi de vendeuse dans votre supermarché.

> Oui, vous vous appelez comment?

Ce qui m'intéresse, c'est le poste de	vendeuse / programmeur.
J'ai	un certificat d'aptitude professionnelle (CAP) / une licence / un master.
J'ai déjà travaillé	dans l'informatique / un bureau / une école primaire.
Je pourrais commencer	immédiatement / demain / dans six semaines.
Pouvez-vous venir passer un entretien	mardi / mercredi à dix / onze heures?

L'avenir des jeunes. Qui fait quoi?

Maëlle espère trouver un métier dans le monde du théâtre, peut-être comme actrice. Elle pense que si on travaille avec le public, la vie n'est jamais monotone ou ennuyeuse. «Comme actrice on peut voyager et gagner beaucoup d'argent si on a du succès» dit-elle, mais la réalité est que la plupart des actrices sont au chômage.

Rajid a seize ans et s'est toujours intéressé à tous les aspects du droit. Il espère faire une carrière d'avocat. Les études universitaires durent quatre ans et sont suivies de dix-huit mois de formation professionnelle. À la fin de chaque année, il y a des examens difficiles auxquels, malheureusement, beaucoup de candidats échouent. Si on réussit, on passe dans l'année supérieure, sinon on doit refaire l'année que l'on n'a pas réussi. Ceux qui arrivent au bout deviennent avocat et reçoivent un très bon salaire. C'est l'ambition de Rajid. Il ne veut pas être homme au foyer ou avoir un travail qui ne l'intéresse pas.

Anjelica trouve qu'aller à l'université coûte trop cher. Elle a toujours aimé le plein air et son rêve est de devenir jardinière paysagiste. Bien qu'elle puisse faire un bac professionnel ou un bac techno, la formation professionnelle en apprentissage est la meilleure solution. Comme elle aimerait être indépendante le plus vite possible, elle pense à l'apprentissage qui lui permettra de se former en même temps que de gagner un peu d'argent. Anjelica, comme tout le monde, voudrait faire quelque chose qui lui plaît, donc, être femme de ménage ou femme au foyer, ça ne l'intéresse pas.

1a 📖🎧🌐 Read the first two paragraphs and decide who the statements are about. Write M (Maëlle) or R (Rajid) depending on who is being referred to.

1 xxxxx doesn't want a boring life.

2 xxxxx intends to study for four years.

3 xxxxx wants to have an interesting job.

4 xxxxx is unlikely to be working all the time.

5 xxxxx is a 'people person'.

1b 📖🎧🌐 Read about Anjelica and decide whether the statements are true (T), false (F) or not mentioned in the text (?).

1 Anjelica doesn't intend to go to university.

2 Her dream is to be a gardener in a different country.

3 She will do an apprenticeship as she can earn money while learning on the job.

4 She would like to find a job in a public park or garden.

5 If she fails to be a gardener, she will be a housewife.

> **Stratégie**
>
> 📖 To get a high grade, you need to show that you can recognise modal verbs and a range of tenses (future, present, perfect, imperfect, conditional).
>
> Modal verbs (*devoir, pouvoir, vouloir*) are commonly used. They are often followed by another verb in the infinitive. Find at least one example of each modal verb in the article.

2a 🎧 Listen to Section A. Who might say each of the sentences below? Nicolas (N), Mehmet (M) or Émilie (E)?

1   Je voudrais travailler dans un autre pays.
2   J'aimerais travailler dans le monde de la médecine.
3   Je vais quitter l'école à seize ans.
4   Je vais continuer mes études après le bac.
5   Je n'ai pas encore décidé ce que je veux faire plus tard.
6   J'aimerais travailler en France.

2b 🎧 Listen to Section B and answer the questions in English.

1   How does Jérémie justify his choice of career?
2   What two ambitions does Charlotte have?
3   What two things does Nadia have to do to become a journalist?
4   After their studies / training, who is the most likely to find the job they want?

> ### Interrogative forms
>
> Question words such as *qui?* (who?), *combien?* (how many?), *où?* (where?), *pourquoi?* (why?), *quand?* (when?), and *quel / quels / quelle / quelles?* (which?) can be used with various tenses.
>
> The question word is followed by the verb or the auxiliary, so remember to invert the verb and the pronoun.
>
> *Quand commences-tu à travailler?*
>
> *Quand as-tu commencé à travailler?*
>
> Also learn about comparative and superlative adverbs.
>
> *See pages 156 and 157* ➡
>
> **Grammaire** *page 186*

3 🄶 Write the jumbled questions in the correct order. Start each one with a question word from the list. Make sure you use the correct form of *quel*.

1   _____ passé as les vacances tu ?
2   _____ film commence le ?
3   _____ vous choisi avez métier ?
4   _____ études tu faire aimerais ?
5   _____ as gagné tu ?
6   _____ d'aller lycée as choisi tu au ?

Quand	Où
Combien	Quel
Pourquoi	Quelles

4 🗨 Discuss with your partner your plans for the future. Some sample answers are given below. Work out what the questions should be, then use them with your partner, adapting the sample answers to your own (or an imaginary) situation.

- J'ai l'intention de devenir professeur de langues.
- Parce que j'aimerais travailler avec des adolescents et je suis doué(e) en langues.
- Oui, je dois y faire des études pendant trois ans parce que je vais faire une licence.
- Je voudrais étudier l'anglais parce que j'aime beaucoup cette langue.

> **Astuce**
> Choose from the following when forming your questions:
> *Quel(s) / quelle(s) … ?*
> *Pourquoi … ?*
> *Est-ce que … ?*
> *Qu'est-ce que … ?*

> Qu'est-ce que tu veux faire comme métier?

> J'aimerais devenir professeur de langues.

Je voudrais / J'aimerais	devenir	vétérinaire / infirmière / avocat.
J'aimerais / Je voudrais / J'ai l'intention de	travailler	à l'étranger / en plein air.
		avec des enfants / des adolescents / des animaux / le public.
		dans l'informatique / le journalisme.
Je voudrais / Je ne veux pas		aller à l'université (y aller) / faire des études parce que …
Je voudrais	étudier les sciences / faire un apprentissage / faire une formation professionnelle parce que …	

4.8 Le monde du travail

Métiers: les avantages et les inconvénients

A Nathalie Chevet a commencé sa carrière de mannequin à un très jeune âge. À huit ans elle dansait déjà en public comme pom-pom girl avant le début des matchs de basket à Lyon, où elle a grandi. Actuellement, sa place est plutôt sur les podiums des plus grandes maisons de mode parisiennes. Mais ce métier a tout de même ses inconvénients. On peut être photographié à n'importe quel moment. Il faut aussi faire attention à ce qu'on mange de manière à rester mince. En plus, c'est un métier extrêmement fatigant. «Mais les avantages sont plus importants», explique-t-elle. «Après avoir voyagé partout dans le monde et rencontré des vedettes de film et de musique, je suis devenue une célébrité et on me voit souvent à la télé. Je dois aussi dire que ce n'est quand même pas mal payé.»

B Cédric Timplet vient de déménager à Bruxelles où il travaille pour l'Union européenne. Il avait déjà décidé de devenir interprète quand il était adolescent. En effet, après avoir passé un an en Allemagne, les langues étrangères sont petit à petit devenues ses matières préférées. Pour devenir interprète, il faut faire de longues études: trois ans d'université pour obtenir une licence de langues et deux ans d'école d'interprète. C'est un métier toutefois qui offre beaucoup d'avantages. Pour commencer, c'est assez bien payé et on est souvent en contact avec le public. De temps en temps, on a l'occasion de voyager et comme Cédric habite près de son bureau, il peut y aller à pied. Mais il y a aussi des inconvénients. On doit vraiment se concentrer sur ce qu'on fait et avoir suffisamment de confiance en soi pour faire une traduction simultanée. Les journées de travail sont quelquefois longues et on doit souvent se lever de très bonne heure.

1a 📖 🎧 Read Section A and select the three statements which are true.

1 Nathalie used to be a cheerleader.
2 She doesn't mind the paparazzi.
3 She needs to watch her diet.
4 She doesn't get tired.
5 She gets to meet film stars.
6 She has to stay in Paris.

1b 📖 🎧 Read Section B. List three advantages and three disadvantages of Cédric's job.

les avantages   les inconvénients

2a 🎧 Listen to Section A. Note an advantage and a disadvantage of each person's job: Élodie's father and Monsieur Collin.

2b 🎧 Listen to Section B and read the statements. Decide whether they apply to Daniel's mother (D), Malika (M) or to both of them (D+M).

1 She has just started her job.
2 She has / had a boring job.
3 Her salary is / was not good.
4 She regrets not having been given responsibilities.
5 She works / worked for a charity.
6 She gets / got on well with her colleagues.

3a 🅖 Follow the prompts in English to complete the sentences.

1 Je _____ _____ faire mon stage. (have just)
2 Je _____ _____ rentrer d'Afrique. (have just)
3 Mon père _____ _____ téléphoner. (has just)

3b 🅖 Make each pair of sentences into one sentence by linking them with *après avoir* or *après être*.

Exemple: Elle a téléphoné à son patron. Elle a perdu son emploi. ➡
          Après avoir téléphoné à son patron, elle a perdu son emploi.

1 Elle est devenue danseuse. Elle est souvent passée à la télé.
2 Il a appris l'allemand. Il est devenu interprète.
3 Il est allé en Namibie. Il a pratiqué la médecine.
4 Il a quitté son emploi d'ouvrier d'usine. Il est allé travailler dans un supermarché.

> ## Grammaire
> ### *Venir de* and *après avoir / être*
>
> ■ *Venir de* + infinitive, in the present tense, means 'to have just done something'.
> *Je viens de finir mon travail.*
> – I have just finished my work.
>
> ■ Use *après avoir / être* + past participle for perfect tense sentences where you want to give the order of events.
> *Après avoir fini le travail, il est allé à la maison.*
> Don't forget the agreement with *être*.
> *Après être rentrée du travail, elle a regardé la télé.*
> Also learn about no article before words for jobs.
> *See page 157* ➡
>
> *pages 180, 187*

4 ✏ 🔊 Describe the jobs of two members of your family or of other adults you know.

Mention:

■ the kind of job
■ where they work
■ one advantage and one disadvantage
■ what they think of their jobs
■ something that happened recently at their workplace.

> ## Stratégie
> ✏ Before handing in written work, always check your grammar carefully.
> Have you remembered plural endings on nouns and adjectives?
> Do your verbs have the correct endings?
> If a past participle ends in -é, have you remembered the accent?
> If you have used an *être* verb in the perfect tense, does the past participle agree?

Mon père / ma mère est	employé(e) de banque / professeur.
Il / Elle travaille	dans un hôpital / un lycée / un supermarché.
	comme médecin / secrétaire / ouvrier / ouvrière.
L'avantage, c'est que / qu'	c'est … / il y a … / on peut … / il faut …
L'inconvénient, c'est que / qu'	on doit … / il / elle n'aime pas … / ce n'est pas …
Il / Elle pense / trouve que son travail est	très / assez / plutôt … parce que …
La semaine dernière, au travail	on a dû … / il a fallu … / il y a eu ….
Je rêve de / d'	devenir … / être …
Mon travail idéal serait de / d'	

> ## Astuce
> When you want to talk about the pros and cons of jobs, if you don't know the French for certain terms, make up information using language that you do know.

kerboodle!

Current and future jobs

Un four marocain ouvert à tous!

Nadège Gahinet, une étudiante française de Rouen, passe une année sabbatique au Maroc. Un jour, elle a visité une boulangerie marocaine. Voilà sa description de la visite:

A «J'étais à Assilah, une petite ville historique. Un dimanche matin, j'ai vu un groupe de femmes. Chaque personne portait une grande assiette sur la tête. Elles portaient leurs morceaux de pâte à pain chez le boulanger. Elles sont entrées dans le petit bâtiment, le boulanger a mis la pâte dans un grand four. Il m'a invitée à passer quelques heures avec lui.

Il a continué son travail. Un peu plus tard les clientes sont revenues chercher leur pain. Beaucoup des clientes ont aussi acheté des gâteaux traditionnels préparés par la femme du boulanger.

J'ai comparé son système avec la boulangerie de mon père en France. Mon père utilise des machines pour préparer la pâte. Le pain aussi est différent. On ne voit pas de baguettes françaises au Maroc, mais un pain rond et plat.»

B Ibrahim, le boulanger, m'a expliqué la tradition du four communal.

«Il y a longtemps, il y avait seulement un four pour tout le village. Chaque matin, on commençait avec le pain, et après, comme le four était toujours chaud, on apportait des plats de viande ou de poisson. Maintenant, je n'accepte que le pain et seulement le week-end.

De nos jours, beaucoup de familles préfèrent acheter du pain et des gâteaux, comme en France. Mais le week-end, quand les gens ne travaillent pas, il y a des familles qui continuent à préparer le pain selon la tradition, mais seulement celles qui ne préfèrent pas rester au lit! Pour les autres, on prépare du pain et on le leur vend.

Je fais tout à la main. C'est très fatigant car je dois aussi chauffer le four. Ce qui n'est pas typique, c'est que ma femme travaille avec moi, et elle fait de bonnes pâtisseries. Les gâteaux sont importants pour attirer les clients, surtout les touristes, qui sont plus nombreux maintenant.»

1a 📖🎧 Read Section A. Which five of the pictures could illustrate the scene at the Moroccan bakery?

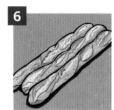

> ### AQA Examiner's tip
> All the pictures are in some way connected to the article. The trick is to sort out the ones that are a perfect fit from those that do not quite fit. For example, look out for negatives and references to other places – clues such as these will help you work out whether the item shown applies to the Moroccan bakery or not.

1b 📖🎧 Read Section B. Which of the following statements apply to the bakery before (B), now (N) or both (B + N)?

1 It's Wednesday, and I am taking my bread dough to cook in the village oven.

2 It's Saturday, and I am taking my bread dough to cook in the village oven.

3 It's Saturday, and I'm taking my beef dish to cook in the village oven.

4 I have to heat the oven early in the mornings.

5 I make cakes while my husband cooks the bread.

6 We are here on holiday, and want to try the cakes.

2a 🎧 Listen to Section A of an interview with Youenn, who has just finished his gap year in Mauritania, West Africa. Choose the correct ending for each sentence in English.

1 Youenn took a break from his studies in ICT / maths / accountancy.

2 In Mauritania, he was able to use his skills in the classroom and in the school office / post office / sports centre.

3 He was usually woken by the other people in his house / noise from the café / noise of dogs barking.

4 They worked hard to make lessons more interesting in music / art / maths.

5 He escaped the heat at lunchtime by staying indoors / sitting in the garden / going to the beach.

6 In the afternoon, he found it quite easy to work until three o'clock / install the new computer system / explain the new system to the staff.

2b 🎧 Listen to Section B. Which of the following statements are true?

1 They have enough computers in the school in Mauritania.

2 The children appreciate the most basic equipment.

3 The children lack energy.

4 There is overcrowding in many homes.

5 Youenn would like to spend more time in the desert.

6 He would like to work with homeless children.

7 He wants to pursue his career in France.

8 He has changed his ambition for the future since going to Mauritania.

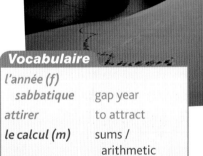

Vocabulaire

l'année (f) sabbatique	gap year
attirer	to attract
le calcul (m)	sums / arithmetic
manquer	to miss
le Maroc	Morocco
la pâte (à pain)	(bread) dough
tel(le)	such

Grammaire

Youenn's account of his time in Mauritania is mainly in the past tense: a mixture of the imperfect to describe his routine, and the perfect when he describes particular occasions. You will also find examples of verbs used in the present and future tenses, as well as other structures such as *en* + present participle. You will need to be able to cope with this variety of tenses at Higher level. Listen again to the last question and Youenn's reply. How many different verb forms can you pick out?

(G) Current and future jobs

Object pronouns with negatives; demonstrative pronouns *celui* and *celle*; comparative adverbs

1 Change the following into negative sentences, then translate them into English.

1 Ils lui disent la vérité.
2 Je leur donne les certificats.
3 Le jardinier nous demande de l'aider.
4 La secrétaire vous permet de téléphoner.
5 On te demande la permission.
6 Le patron les paye bien.

2 Use the correct phrases from the list to fill in the gaps. You will need to use one of them twice. Then translate the sentences into English.

Exemple: Je vais lui envoyer une carte de vœux. Celle-ci ou celle-là?
(I am going to send him a greetings card. This one or that one?)

1 Tu veux quels timbres? _____?
2 Tu préfères quel stage? _____?
3 Il va parler à deux caissières: _____.
4 Tu appelles quel numéro? _____?
5 On choisit quelles boîtes? _____?
6 Il y a deux candidats pour l'entretien: _____.

> Celui-ci ou celui-là   celui-ci et celui-là
> celle-ci et celle-là   Ceux-ci ou ceux-là
> Celles-ci ou celles-là

3 Follow the English prompts and use the adverb given to complete the sentences.

1 Ma mère finit le travail _____ mon père. (later than, *tard*)
2 Le vétérinaire le voit _____ avant. (as often as, *souvent*)
3 Je joue au football _____ que toi. (as well as, *bien*)
4 Il travaille _____ Amina, sa collègue. (less fast than, *vite*)
5 Le médecin parle _____ l'infirmière. (louder than, *fort*)
6 Ce comptable réussit _____ les autres. (better than, *mieux*)

Object pronouns with negatives
Grammaire page 186

Think carefully about the word order when using negatives with verbs that take an object pronoun.

In the present tense, the word order is:

subject + *ne* + pronoun + verb + *pas*

Il ne me regarde pas.
– He is not looking at me.

Je ne lui parle pas.
– I am not speaking to him / her.

Demonstrative pronouns *celui* and *celle*
Grammaire page 178

The French words for 'this one' and 'that one' and 'these' and 'those' vary according to gender and number.

this one	masculine	*celui-ci*
	feminine	*celle-ci*
that one	masculine	*celui-là*
	feminine	*celle-là*
these	masculine	*ceux-ci*
	feminine	*celles-ci*
those	masculine	*ceux-là*
	feminine	*celles-là*

Comparative adverbs
Grammaire page 175

Comparisons can be made using adverbs, as with adjectives.

Tu parles plus lentement que moi.
– You speak more slowly than me.

Je travaille moins vite que le chef.
– I work less fast than (don't work as fast as) the boss.

Elle parle aussi bien que sa sœur.
– She speaks as well as her sister.

Note that the French for better (as an adverb) is *mieux*.

Il chante mieux que son frère.
– He sings better than his brother.

Superlative adverbs; use of definite and indefinite articles

4 Find the French for the following phrases in the email.

1 the best paid   3 loudest   5 best
2 most often   4 fastest

> Dans ma famille, tout le monde chante, mais c'est ma mère qui chante le mieux! Mon père et ma sœur sont plombiers tous les deux. C'est ma sœur qui travaille le plus vite et c'est elle qu'on appelle le plus souvent. Pourtant, c'est mon père qui est le mieux payé. C'est bizarre! C'est peut-être parce que c'est lui qui crie le plus fort …

5 Match the captions and the pictures. Then decide which nouns need an article (*un, une, le, la* or *les*) and which ones don't. Complete the captions with the missing word if necessary.

1 C'est _____ jardinier qui cultive de bons légumes.
2 Je vais appeler _____ plombier pour qu'il répare la douche.
3 Il adore _____ animaux et il a trouvé un stage chez _____ vétérinaire.
4 Ma mère adorait _____ maths au lycée, maintenant elle est _____ comptable.
5 Ma grand-mère aimait beaucoup _____ dessin et elle est devenue _____ architecte.
6 _____ mode m'intéresse et je rêve d'être _____ mannequin!

Grammaire page 175

Superlative adverbs

Superlatives can be expressed with adverbs as well as with adjectives.

Qui parle le plus lentement? – Who speaks slowest / most slowly?

C'est moi qui travaille le moins vite. – I'm the one who works least fast.

Note than the French for best (as an adverb) is *le mieux*.

Qui chante le mieux? – Who sings best?

Grammaire page 172

Use of definite and indefinite articles

Remember not to use the indefinite article (*un, une*) when stating what someone's job is in French.

Ma sœur est architecte.
– My sister is an architect.

It is needed in all other cases.

C'est un très bon professeur.
– He is a very good teacher.

However, use the definite article (*le, la, les*) when talking about likes and dislikes, even though it is not needed in English.

J'aime les sciences et j'adore les animaux. – I like science and I love animals.

Current and future jobs

Stages et petits jobs ➡ *pages 146–147*

l'	*avenir (m)*	the future
le	*boulot*	work
la	*caisse*	cash register / till
	compter	to count
	exprimer	to express
	fatigué(e)	tired
le	*genre*	type
le / la	*patron / patronne*	boss
	plaire (plu)	to please
le	*plaisir*	pleasure / enjoyment
	pourtant	however
se	*rappeler*	to remember
	souffrir (souffert)	to suffer
	souhaiter	to wish
à	*temps partiel*	part-time

Je cherche un emploi ➡ *pages 148–149*

l'	*annonce (f)*	advert
l'	*entreprise (f)*	business / firm
l'	*entreprise (f) de logiciels*	software business
l'	*entretien (m)*	interview
la	*formation professionnelle*	professional training
	gagner	to earn
la	*licence*	degree
l'	*offre (f) d'emploi*	job advert / job offer
la	*petite annonce*	small advert / classified advert
	poser sa candidature	to apply
le	*poste*	job / post
	prévenir (prévenu)	to inform
	remplacer	to replace
	suivant(e)	following

1 Ⓥ Solve these anagrams to find French words to do with work and future plans, then match them with their English translations. Try to work them out before checking in the vocabulary list.

1	not par		a	accountant
2	blu too		b	work
3	blame copt		c	future
4	vain er		d	to wish
5	i shout era		e	boss
6	for u firs		f	to suffer

2 Ⓥ Complete the sentences by selecting words from the list.

1 Faire une demande d'emploi, c'est _____ .
2 Une _____ demande trois ou quatre ans d'études universitaires.
3 Quand on cherche un emploi, on lit _____ dans le journal.
4 Comme j'adore les ordinateurs, je pense faire des études d' _____ .
5 On m'a invité à venir passer un _____ .

entretien   les petites annonces   licence

informatique   poser sa candidature

La vie commence ➡ *pages 150–151*

l'	ado (m / f)	adolescent / young person
l'	avocat (m) / avocate (f)	lawyer
l'	apprentissage (m)	apprenticeship
au	bout de	at the end of
le	chômage	unemployment
le	droit	law
la	femme au foyer	housewife
la	femme de ménage	cleaning lady
l'	homme au foyer (m)	house husband
l'	infirmier (m) / infirmière (f)	nurse
le / la	jardinier / jardinière (paysagiste)	(landscape) gardener
en avoir	marre de	to be fed up of
le	métier	job / line of work
	rater	to fail
la	société	company / business

3 Ⓥ Match the sentence beginnings (1–6) and endings (a–f).

1 J'ai réussi
2 Comme le droit m'intéresse, je veux devenir
3 Je reste chez moi. Je suis
4 Je nettoie la maison des autres. Je suis
5 L'année prochaine, j'irai au
6 À l'hôpital, il y a beaucoup d'

a femme de ménage.
b ma licence.
c avocat.
d lycée.
e infirmières.
f homme au foyer.

Le monde du travail ➡ *pages 152–153*

l'	association (f) caritative	charity / charitable organisation
l'	avenir (m)	future
	bien payé	well paid

le	boulot	work (informal)
le	candidat	candidate
le/la	collègue	colleague
la	confiance	confidence
	décider	to decide
	déménager	to move house
l'	emploi (m)	employment
l'	employé(e) (m / f)	employee
	enrichissant(e)	rewarding
l'	entreprise (f)	company
l'	interprète (m / f)	interpreter
le	mannequin	fashion model (male or female)
l'	ouvrier (m) / ouvrière (f)	worker
le	patron	boss/manager
la	pom-pom girl	cheerleader
	répondre	to reply
le	rêve	dream
le	salaire	salary
l'	usine (f)	factory
la	vedette	star (male or female)

4 Ⓥ Make sentences by matching each job with what that person does.

1 Un interprète
2 Un employé
3 Une vedette
4 Un ouvrier
5 Un mannequin
6 Un médecin

a travaille pour un patron.
b est célèbre dans le monde de la musique, du cinéma, etc.
c fait de la traduction orale.
d travaille par exemple dans une usine.
e s'occupe des malades.
f porte des vêtements de couturiers, comme Jean-Paul Gaultier.

4 ⬭ Au travail

You are talking to your French friend Aurore about part-time jobs, work experience, future careers and your free time. Your teacher will play the part of your friend and will ask you:

1 what part-time job you do and when
2 further details about your part-time job
3 details about your work experience
4 the possibilities for when you leave school
5 what career you envisage for yourself
6 what you do with your leisure time
7 !

! Remember you will have to respond to something that you have not yet prepared.

1 **What part-time job you do and when**
- Say what job you do and give details of your activities.
- Say how long you have had your job for, how long you intend to keep it for and why.
- Mention your hours of work and say whether they are convenient.
- Say which days you work and say whether you would prefer other times.

2 **Further details about your part-time job**
- Say where you work and how far it is from home and school.
- Say how you get to work and how long it takes using different means of transport.
- Say how much you earn and what you think of your wages.
- Say what you think of the job and give reasons for your opinion.

3 **Details about your work experience**
- Say when it took place and how long it lasted.
- Say what work you did, including three different tasks.
- Say what you enjoyed doing and comment on the value of work experience in general.
- Say whether you preferred a day of work experience to a typical day at school and ask Aurore if she has done work experience herself.

AQA Examiner's tips

If you don't have a part-time job, be creative and make one up!

Start with *Je travaille …*

For the second bullet point, use the present tense with *depuis* for the first part and a phrase that refers to a future event for the second part, e.g. *Je fais ce travail depuis … et je vais continuer à …*

Use *je voudrais / j'aimerais commencer à … / finir à …* to say what working hours you would prefer.

AQA Examiner's tips

Now, start your plan. Write a maximum of six words for each section of the task. Here are some suggested words for the first section: *activités, depuis, heures (opinion), jours – préférences.*

Using brackets on your plan allows you to associate two ideas, for instance *heures* and *opinion*, therefore making it clear that it is your opinion of the hours of work that you intend to give.

AQA Examiner's tips

Use *le trajet dure …* to say how long it takes to travel.

Vary the ways in which you give your opinion, e.g. *je pense que … / je trouve que … / à mon avis, c'est …*

If the purpose of your plan is to help you with vocabulary, use *gagner*. If, however, you are likely to forget what the word means, think of another word which is more immediately understandable, e.g. *salaire*.

AQA Examiner's tips

Most of this section refers to something that happened in the past. See grammar section pages 181–182. Use *plus / moins / aussi … que …* to make comparisons, e.g. *plus utile que …*

4 The possibilities for when you leave school

- Say that you can take up an apprenticeship and give an example.
- Say that you can continue at school, then go to university, mentioning costs.
- Say that you can go straight into a job, giving an advantage and a disadvantage of doing that.
- Talk about what you intend to do and give reasons.

Use *faire un apprentissage* for 'to take up an apprenticeship'.

Use *on peut / tu peux / il est possible de ...* to say that 'you can'.

Add a maximum of six words to your plan. You may have to revise what is on your plan after you have completed the task and studied the online response to the task, which is there to help you improve your work.

5 What career you envisage for yourself

- Say what career you envisage for yourself and what you will have to do to achieve it.
- Say what the advantages of that career are.
- Say what the disadvantages are.
- Say what career you will do if that proves impossible.

Use *je dois* + infinitive to say what you have to do.

Use the present tense to say what the advantages and disadvantages are, e.g. *C'est assez bien payé*.

How good is your plan? Can you recall what is in the bullet points by looking only at your plan?

6 What you do with your leisure time

- Say how much leisure time you have now and how the rest of your time is accounted for.
- Say what you do when you stay at home on weekdays and say what you did last weekend.
- Say what you do when you go out on weekdays and say what you will do next weekend.
- Say what you think you will do with your free time when you have a career.

There are references to past, present and future in this section; the clues are 'now', 'last', 'next' and 'will'. Take care and check the relevant pages in the grammar section as necessary.

Use *Quand j'aurai commencé ma carrière ...* to introduce the last point.

Use grammatical markers on your plan to help you, e.g. *maintenant, dernier, prochain*.

7 ! At this point you may be asked:

- if you are prepared to move to another area and, if so, what you would gain and lose
- about holidays – where you normally go, what you will do this year and if it will be different when you have a career
- whether when you have a career, you will settle down, get married and have children
- what you think of the idea of a gap year, what you would do, where you would go and how you would fund it.

Choose the two options which you think are the most likely, and for each of these, note down three different ideas. In your plan, write three words that illustrate each of the two most likely options. For the third option you might choose: *s'installer, mariage, enfants*. Learn these two options using your reminder words. If you decide on the last one, the term to use for gap year is *année sabbatique*.

You should now have completed your plan and prepared your answers. Give your plan to your teacher for feedback. Compare your answers with the online sample version – you might find some useful hints to make yours even better.

4 ✏ Mon collège

Your French friend Myriam has asked you to write an article in French for her school magazine entitled *La vie scolaire en Grande-Bretagne, c'est comment?* You could include:

1 the facilities in your school
2 your school routine
3 your subjects and teachers
4 your friends
5 extra-curricular activities
6 your school uniform
7 your ambitions for the future.

1 The facilities in your school

- Introduce your school (name, location, what you think of it).
- Mention the size of the school, comparing it to the primary school you went to.
- Say a little about its organisation (mixed or single sex, age range, options in year 10).
- Mention the buildings and their purposes, what the facilities are and what you think of them.

2 Your school routine

- Include when you arrive, what you do then, when lessons start, the number of lessons.
- Mention at what time morning break is, how long it lasts and what you do at break.
- Describe what you eat, where you eat and what else you do at lunchtime.
- Mention at what time school finishes, how you get back home, how long it takes and how much homework you get.

3 Your subjects and teachers

- Write about compulsory subjects and options and say what you think of your school's options system.
- Say which subject is your favourite and why.
- Say which subject is your least favourite and why. Say what you would prefer to study.
- Describe your favourite teacher, saying why you like him / her.

4 Your friends

- Mention who your friends at school are and why you are friends with them.
- Describe your best friend (physically and also their character).
- Write about when and where you meet and what you like talking about.
- Mention what you did with him / her yesterday and what you thought of it.

If your best friend is a girl, make sure that you make the adjectives you use to describe her feminine, e.g. *intelligente.*

Use *se retrouver* to say that you meet.

Using names in your plan, e.g. your best friend's name, is sometimes the most economical way of summarising what you want to write.

5 Extra-curricular activities

- Write about the extra-curricular activities that are on offer and when they take place.
- Write about an activity that you are involved in, who runs it, where, when and if it is well attended.
- Describe the last time you went.
- Say which activity (not currently on offer) you would like to do and say why.

Use *avoir lieu* or *se passer* to say where or when something takes place, e.g. *Ça a lieu … / ça se passe …*

Use *Je fais partie d'un club de …* to say what you are involved in.

A good way to remind yourself when you should be referring to past and future events is to use time clues such as *hier* and *demain*.

6 Your school uniform

- Describe what you wear at school, and say what you think of it and why.
- Describe what you wear when not at school and say why.
- Give your opinion of the school rules regarding what pupils can and cannot wear.
- French students do not wear a school uniform. Say whether you think British schools should have the same policy.

Use *on a le droit de … / on n'a pas le droit de …* to introduce what you are allowed / not allowed to wear.

Use *on devrait* + infinitive to say whether British schools should have uniforms or not.

The content of the task gives an extra clue, i.e. your school uniform. It is unnecessary to repeat those words in French in your plan.

7 Your ambitions for the future

- Mention whether you intend to continue with your education in September, giving details.
- Mention whether you intend to go to university and why / why not.
- Say what job you would like to do in the future and give reasons for your choice.
- Say in which town / area you would like to work in the future and say why.

Remind yourself of the various ways of referring to a future event, e.g. *je vais, j'espère, j'aimerais, je voudrais, j'ai l'intention de,* and the future tense itself. See grammar section pages 182–183.

All the phrases above can be made negative by placing *ne … pas* around the verb. Take care! *J'ai l'intention de …* becomes *Je n'ai pas l'intention de …*

Remember to check the total number of words you have used in your plan. It should be 40 or fewer.

You should now have completed your plan and prepared your answers. Give your plan to your teacher for feedback. Compare your answers with the online sample version – you might find some useful hints to make yours even better.

4

Résumé

1 Voilà quatre aspects d'un collège britannique. Lequel n'existe pas dans les collèges français?

a les devoirs   c l'uniforme

b le règlement   d les matières

2 Qu'est-ce qu'il ne faut pas faire au collège?

a travailler dur   c finir ses devoirs

b arriver à l'heure   d manquer les cours sans raison valable

3 Choose the correct ending for this sentence:

Les élèves qui bavardent tout le temps en classe …

a sont disciplinés et travailleurs.

b réussissent toujours leurs examens.

c empêchent les autres d'apprendre.

d montrent un bon exemple aux autres.

4 Choose the correct ending for this sentence:

Je voudrais être institutrice. J'aime beaucoup …

a les enfants   c les étudiants

b les ados   d les institutions

5 Find the question that goes with this answer:

Oui, j'ai l'intention de poser ma candidature.

a Pouvez-vous venir passer un entretien?

b Vous voulez poser votre candidature pour quel poste?

c Avez-vous l'intention de poser votre candidature?

d Avez-vous l'intention de poser des questions?

6 Choose the correct form of the verb to fill the gap:

Je _____ faire mon stage.

a viens de   c ai juste

b venir de   d ai viens de

Le sais-tu?

Pendant les trois années que les adolescents français passent au lycée pour préparer le bac, ils doivent apprendre à organiser au mieux leur nouvelle liberté. Par exemple, pendant les heures de permanence ou à l'heure du déjeuner, les élèves ont souvent la possibilité de sortir du lycée. Ils peuvent aller au café ou en ville avec les copains. Ces moments de relaxation sont importants!

Le sais-tu?

90% des entreprises françaises considèrent que l'apprentissage est le mode de formation le plus apte à développer l'autonomie chez les jeunes. Pendant un mois typique, le jeune passe trois semaines en entreprise et une semaine en CFA (centre de formation d'apprentis). 80% des apprentis trouvent rapidement un emploi à la fin de leur formation et, pour beaucoup d'entre eux, dans l'entreprise qui les a formés.

Frequently asked questions: Speaking

This general guidance is in the form of answers to 'frequently asked questions' (FAQs).

1 How many tasks do I have to complete for the Speaking part of my GCSE French?

There are two Speaking tasks, both of a similar kind. Your teacher will ask you the questions and listen to your answers. One of your tasks will be recorded as it may have to be submitted to the AQA Examination Board. Each task lasts between four and six minutes. The Speaking test counts for 30 per cent of the whole GCSE French – so, each of the two speaking tasks is worth 15 per cent.

2 When do the tasks have to be done?

There is no specified time for the completion of the tasks. When your teacher thinks that you have been taught the language you need and feels that you are ready, you will be given the task to prepare. It could be a task designed by the AQA Examination Board or a task designed by French teachers in your school. Your teacher will decide how long you are allowed to prepare for the task (it cannot be more than six hours).

3 Who will mark my work?

Your teacher will mark your work. A Moderator (i.e. an examiner) will sample the work of your school and check that it has been marked correctly. A Team Leader will check the work of the Moderator. The Principal Moderator will check the work of the Team Leader. The Chief Examiner will check the work of the Principal Moderator. This complicated but secure system ensures that candidates are given the correct mark.

4 What am I allowed to write on my plan?

You are allowed to write a maximum of 40 words on your plan. These words can be in French or English. Choose them carefully so that your plan works well as an *aide-mémoire*. Remember that you are not allowed to use conjugated verbs (i.e. verbs with an ending other than the infinitive or the past participle) on your plan. Codes, letters or initialled words, e.g. *j … s … a …* standing for *je suis allé*, are not allowed. There is no limit to the number of visuals you can use, and you can mix visuals and words if you wish.

5 What help is allowed from the moment I am given the task to prepare?

Your teacher is allowed to discuss the task in English with you, including the kind of language you may need and how to use your preparatory work. You can have access to a dictionary, your French books and internet resources. This is the stage when you will prepare your plan using the Task Planning Form. You will then give this form to your teacher, who will give you feedback on how you have met the requirements of the task. When you actually perform the task, you will only have access to your plan and your teacher's comments (i.e. the Task Planning Form).

6 How can I prepare for the unpredictable element (the exclamation mark)?

Ask yourself: What question would logically follow the questions I have already answered? Practise guessing what the unpredictable bullet point might be about. You are likely to come up with two or three possibilities. Prepare answers to cover those possibilities. Practise your possible responses. When you are asked the question, focus on the meaning of the question itself to make sure you understand it and then give it your full answer.

7 How best can I practise for the test?

Treat each bullet point as a mini task. Practise your answer to one bullet point at a time. Say the answer aloud that is represented by one word on your plan. Repeat the process for each word on your plan. Next, try to account for two words, then for three words, etc. Time your answer for one whole bullet point. Repeat the process for each bullet point. Practise saying things aloud. Record yourself if possible.

8 Does it matter if my verbs are wrong as long as I can be understood?

Communication can break down because of poor grammatical accuracy. If that happens, you will lose marks in Communication and also in Accuracy. If you give the correct message but grammatical accuracy is poor, you will only lose marks in Accuracy. Communication is of primary importance, of course, but the quality of that communication matters too and is enhanced by grammatical accuracy.

Frequently asked questions: Speaking

9 How do I make sure I get the best possible marks for my answers?

You will score well in the Speaking test if:

- you say a lot that is relevant to the question
- you have a good range of vocabulary
- you can include complex structures
- you can refer to present, past and future events
- your French accent is good
- you can speak fluently
- you can show initiative
- you can speak with grammatical accuracy.

10 How will my mark be affected if my French accent is not very good?

You will receive a mark for Pronunciation. However, as long as your spoken French is understandable, your Communication mark will not suffer.

11 What will I gain by giving long answers?

Consider the task as an opportunity for you to show off what you can do in French. Offer long answers whenever possible, develop the points you are trying to make, give your opinion and justify that opinion as appropriate, etc. As a general rule, the more French you speak, the more credit you will be given (provided that what you say is relevant and understandable).

12 What does speaking with fluency mean?

Fluency is your ability to speak without hesitation. Try and speak with fluency but not too fast. If you are likely to be nervous when performing the task, practise it and practise it again. Time your whole response. Make a point of slowing down if you feel that you are speaking too fast. Practise with your plan in front of you so that you know what you are going to say next and, therefore, do not hesitate when delivering your contribution to the dialogue.

13 What does showing initiative mean?

Showing initiative does not mean that you suddenly ask your teacher, 'What about you, where did you go on holiday?' (although you could do that!). You are generally expected to answer questions. For instance, if you are asked the question *Tu aimes le foot?*, you should first answer it directly and then try to develop your answer, e.g. *Oui, j'aime le foot. J'y joue trois fois par semaine avec mes copains.*

Showing initiative means that you take the conversation elsewhere, but in a way that is connected to your answer and still relevant to the original question, e.g. *J'aime aussi jouer au basket. En fait, c'est mon sport préféré.* You were not asked about basketball, but you decided to add it to your response. It is relevant, linked to what you were asked and follows your developed answer quite naturally. That is showing initiative. Use it to extend your answers and, therefore, to show off extra knowledge of French.

14 Why is it important to refer to present, past and future events?

If you are aiming at a grade C, you will need to use a variety of structures, and you may include different time frames and make reference to past and future events in your spoken language. To achieve grade A, you will be expected to use a variety of verb tenses.

15 How many bullet points are there in each task?

There are typically between five and eight bullet points. One of the bullet points will be the unpredictable element and will appear on your task as an exclamation mark. All bullet points will be written in English.

16 Will I be asked questions which are not written in the task?

That is possible. Although you will have prepared the task thoroughly and will have a lot to say, your teacher may want you to expand or give further details on particular points you have made. You must listen to your teacher's questions attentively, as you will have to understand his/her questions in order to answer them.

Frequently asked questions: Writing

This general guidance is in the form of answers to 'frequently asked questions' (FAQs).

1 How many Writing tasks do I have to complete and what proportion of my French GCSE is the Writing test?

You have to complete two Writing tasks. The tasks can be those provided by the AQA Examination Board. Alternatively, your French teachers have the option of devising their own tasks if they wish. As in the Speaking test, the two tasks count for 30 per cent of your grade (15 per cent for each Writing task).

2 How much time do I have to complete the final version of a task?

You will be given 60 minutes to complete the final version of a task. It will be done under the direct supervision of your teacher. You will not be allowed to interact with others.

3 What resources will I be able to use on the day?

You can have access to a dictionary. You will also have the task itself, your plan and your teacher's feedback on your plan. These will be on the AQA Task Planning Form. That is all. You cannot use your exercise book, textbook or any drafts you may have written to help you practise.

4 What am I allowed to write on my plan?

Much the same as you are allowed in your plan for Speaking – a maximum of 40 words and no conjugated verbs or codes. You also have the option of using visuals instead of or as well as words on your Task Planning Form. Your teacher will comment on your plan, using the AQA Task Planning Form. Make sure you take that information on board before you write the final version.

5 How many words am I expected to write for each task?

Students aiming at grades G–D should produce 200–350 words across the two tasks (i.e. 100–175 words per task).

Students aiming at grades C–A* should produce 400–600 words across the two tasks (i.e. 200–300 words per task).

6 Can I write a draft?

You may produce a draft, but this is for your use only. Your teacher cannot comment on it and you cannot have access to any draft when you write the final version.

7 What do I have to do to gain the best possible mark?

You will score well if:

- you communicate a lot of relevant information clearly
- you can explain ideas and points of view
- you have a good range of vocabulary
- you can include complex structures
- you can write long sentences
- you can refer to past, present and future events
- you can write with grammatical accuracy
- you organise your ideas well.

You will have noticed that there are similarities between the ways Writing and Speaking are assessed. As most of the points above are discussed in the FAQs for Speaking, you are advised to read the answers to these again, before you embark on your first task.

8 When will I do the tasks?

When your teacher has taught you the necessary language for you to complete a task, you will be given the task to prepare. You may be asked to do a plan using the Task Planning Form. You will get some feedback on your plan from your teacher at that point, covering how you have met the requirements of the task. You will produce the final version after that, under the direct supervision of your teacher.

9 Who will mark my work?

An AQA Examiner will mark your work. A Team Leader will check the work of the Examiner. The Principal Examiner will check the work of the Team Leader. The Chief Examiner will check the work of the Principal Examiner. This is a complicated but secure system to ensure that candidates are given the correct mark for their work.

On fait du camping

■ Cross-context task

You are camping in France. You meet Jessica who asks you for details about:

1 yourself
2 your holidays
3 your family
4 your last holiday
5 your free time
6 your friends
7 !

! Remember you will have to respond to something that you have not yet prepared.

1 Yourself

- Give your name, your age and your birthday and say how you celebrated it last year.
- Say where you live in Britain and what you think of it.
- Say whether it is your first visit to France.
- Say how long you have been learning French for and how well you speak it.

2 Your holidays

- Say that you are on holiday with your family and say what you think of it so far.
- Say what you think of the campsite and its facilities.
- Say where you normally go on holiday and what accommodation you have.
- Say where you would like to go next year and why.

3 Your family

- Talk about your brothers and sisters and say who you get on with and why.
- Say what your parents are like and what they do for a living.
- Say whether your family is important to you and why.
- Say whether you like going on holiday with your family and why.

4 Your last holiday

- Say where you went and what it was like.
- Say who you went with and whether you got on well with them.
- Say what you did.
- Say what you enjoyed and did not enjoy.

5 Your free time

- Say how much free time you have at home and what you do with it.
- Say where you go when you go out and what you did last weekend.
- Say whether you prefer weekdays or weekends and why.
- Ask Jessica what she likes doing with her free time.

6 Your friends

- Say who your friends are and why you are friends with them.
- Say who your best friend is and how well you get on.
- Say what you do together and how often you see each other.
- Say whether you have a boyfriend / girlfriend and describe him / her.

7 ! At this point, you may be asked:

- whether you prefer going on holiday in France or in Britain and why
- whether you would like to be friends with Jessica for the rest of the holiday
- to talk about your dream holiday
- whether holidays are important to you and why.

Compare your answers with the online sample version – you might find some useful hints to make yours even better.

À propos de moi!

■ Cross-context task

You have been asked to send a letter introducing yourself to Ahmed, a pupil in a French school. You could include information about:

1 yourself
2 your house
3 your local town
4 your school
5 your daily routine
6 what you do to stay healthy
7 your work experience.

1 Yourself
- Give your name, your age and what year group you are in.
- Give a physical description of yourself and say whom you look like.
- Describe your personal qualities.
- Describe what you like and don't like doing.

2 Your house
- Mention whether you live in a house or a flat and where it is situated.
- Include whether you like your house / flat and why.
- Say whether you share a room and what you think of the arrangement.
- Describe what your ideal house / flat would be like.

3 Your local town
- Give details of where your local town is situated and what sort of town it is.
- Describe what the town centre is like.
- Include what there is for young people to do and what you think of the facilities.
- Say whether traffic is a problem in your local town.

4 Your school
- Describe how big your school is, where it is and how you get there.
- Say how many subjects you study, which one is your favourite and why.
- Give your opinion of your school uniform.
- Say whether you like your school and why.

5 Your daily routine
- Describe what you do before breakfast.
- Give details of what you have for breakfast and whether it is a healthy option.
- Say where and when you do your homework and how long it takes to complete it.
- Mention what you do in the evening and what time you go to bed.

6 What you do to stay healthy
- Say whether you play a sport and, if so, where and how frequently.
- Describe what you did last week to keep fit.
- Give details of what you eat and drink that is healthy.
- Mention how you could improve your fitness.

7 Your work experience
- Give details of where you did your work experience and how you travelled to get there.
- Say when it was and what the working hours were.
- Describe what you did and say whether you got on well with your supervisor.
- Give your opinion of your work experience and ask Ahmed to write back to you.

Now compare your first draft with the online sample version – you might find some useful hints to make yours even better.

(G) Grammaire

▉ Contents

Glossary of terms   171

A Nouns   171
Masculine and feminine nouns
Singular and plural forms

B Articles   172
Definite articles: *le, la, les*
Indefinite articles: *un, une, des, de*
Partitive articles: *du, de la, de l', des*

C Adjectives   173
Feminine and masculine, singular and
  plural adjectives
The position of adjectives
Adjectives of nationality
Comparative and superlative adjectives
Demonstrative adjectives: *ce, cet,*
  cette, ces
Indefinite adjectives
Possessive adjectives, one 'owner'
Possessive adjectives, several 'owners'
Interrogative adjectives: *quel, quelle,*
  quels, quelles

D Adverbs   175
Comparative and superlative adverbs
Adverbs of time, frequency, place, etc.

E Pronouns   176
Subject pronouns: *je, tu, il, elle, on,*
  nous, vous, ils, elles
Direct object pronouns: *me, te,*
  le, la, nous, vous, les
Indirect object pronouns: *me, te, lui,*
  nous, vous, leur
Indirect object pronouns: *en, y*
Order of object pronouns
Emphatic pronouns
Possessive pronouns
Relative pronouns: *qui, que, qu', dont*

Demonstrative pronouns: *ce, cela,*
  ça, celui-ci, etc.
Indefinite pronouns: *quelqu'un, quelque*
  chose, tout, etc.

F Verbs   179
The infinitive
The present tense
Reflexive verbs
The perfect tense
The imperfect tense
The pluperfect tense
The immediate future
The future tense
The imperative
The conditional
The subjunctive
The passive
en + present participle
Useful verbs
Modal verbs: *devoir, pouvoir, vouloir*
Impersonal verbs: *il neige, il pleut, il faut*

G Negatives   186

H Questions   186

I Prepositions   187
à, au, à l', à la
de
en, au / aux
More prepositions
Expressions of time

J Conjunctions   189

K Numbers, dates and time   190
Ordinal numbers: *premier, deuxième*, etc.
Days and dates
Time

▉ Verb tables   192

■ Glossary of terms

Adjectives   *les adjectifs*

Words that describe somebody or something:
petit   small   *timide*   shy

Adverbs   *les adverbes*

Words that complement (add meaning to) verbs, adjectives or other adverbs:
très   very   *lentement*   slowly

Articles   *les articles*

Short words used before nouns:
un / une   a, an   *des*   some, any
le / la / les   the

The infinitive   *l'infinitif*

The verb form given in the dictionary:
aller   to go   *avoir*   to have

A   Nouns

Masculine and feminine nouns

All French nouns are either masculine or feminine.

In the singular, masculine nouns are introduced with *le, l'* or *un*:

le père	**the** father
*l'*hôtel	**the** hotel
un livre	**a** book

Feminine nouns are introduced with *la, l'* or *une*:

la mère	**the** mother
*l'*eau	**the** water
une table	**a** table

Some nouns have two different forms, masculine and feminine:

un copain	a male friend
une copine	a female friend
un coiffeur	a male hairdresser
une coiffeuse	a female hairdresser
un facteur	a postman
une factrice	a postwoman

Some nouns stay the same for masculine and feminine:

le prof	the male teacher
la prof	the female teacher
un enfant	a male child
une enfant	a female child

There are patterns to help you remember the correct gender of a noun.

■ All words ending in *-isme* are masculine:
   l'alcoolisme, l'alpinisme, le racisme

Nouns   *les noms*

Words that identify a person, a place or a thing:
mère   mother   *maison*   house

Prepositions   *les prépositions*

Words used in front of nouns to give information about when, how, where, etc.:

à	at	*avec*	with
de	of, from	*en*	in

Pronouns   *les pronoms*

Short words used to replace nouns:

je	I	*tu*	you
il	he	*elle*	she
moi	me	*toi*	you

Verbs   *les verbes*

Words used to express an action or a state:
*je **parle**   I **speak**   *il **est**   he **is**

■ Words ending in *-tion* are usually feminine:
   la climatisation, la manifestation, la récréation, la station

There are many other patterns, e.g. nouns ending in *-age, -eau, -ment* (masculine); *-ie, -ière, -ité* (feminine). Look out for patterns when you are learning vocabulary, but make a note of exceptions.

Singular and plural forms

As in English, French nouns can be either singular (one) or plural (more than one).

Most plural nouns end in *-s*. Unlike English, the added *-s* is usually not pronounced.

   un chat, deux chats   one cat, two cats

As in English, there are some exceptions.

■ With most nouns ending in *-al*, you change the ending to *-aux* in the plural:

un animal,	an animal,
des animaux	animals

■ With many nouns ending in *-au* or *-eu*, you add an *-x*:

un gâteau, des gâteaux	a cake, cakes
un jeu, des jeux	a game, games

■ Words already ending in *-s*, or in *-x* or *-z*, do not change:

le bras, les bras	arm, arms
le nez, les nez	nose, noses

■ A few nouns change completely:

un œil, des yeux	an eye, eyes

B Articles

Definite articles: *le, la, les* – the

The word for 'the' depends on whether the noun it goes with is masculine (m), feminine (f), singular or plural.

m singular	f singular	m + f plural
le	la	les

le grand-père   **the** grandfather
la grand-mère   **the** grandmother
les grands-parents   **the** grandparents

When a singular noun starts with a vowel or a silent *h*, *le* and *la* are shortened to *l'*:

*l'*ami   **the** friend
*l'*histoire   **the** story

In French, you often need to use *le*, *la* and *les* even when we wouldn't say 'the' in English:

- When talking about likes and dislikes:
  *J'adore **le** poulet.*   I love chicken.
  *Elle déteste **les** maths.* She hates maths.

- When referring to abstract things:
  ***La** musique est très*   Music is very
  importante.   important.

Indefinite articles: *un, une, des, de* – a, an, some

Like the words for 'the' (*le / la / les*), the words for 'a/an' and 'some' depend on whether the noun they go with is masculine or feminine, singular or plural.

m singular	f singular	m + f plural
un	une	des

un vélo   **a** bike
une moto   **a** motorbike
une orange   **an** orange
des voitures   (**some**) cars

When talking about jobs, *un* and *une* are not used in French where 'a' or 'an' is used in English.

Il est professeur.   He is **a** teacher.

In negative constructions, *de* replaces *un*, *une* or *des* after *pas*:

*J'ai un frère. – Je n'ai **pas de** frère*.*
       I don't have **any** brothers.

*Il y a une piscine. – Il n'y a **pas de** piscine.*
       There is **no** swimming pool.

*J'ai des sœurs. – Je n'ai **pas de** sœur*.*
       I don't have **any** sisters.

* Note that in French you use a singular noun after a negative construction, unlike English.

Change *de* to *d'* in front of a vowel or a silent *h*:

*Je n'ai pas **d'**animal.*   I don't have **any** pets.

Partitive articles: *du, de la, de l', des* – some, any

masculine	feminine	words beginning with a vowel or silent h	plural
de + le = du	de + la = de la	de + l' = de l'	de + les = des

du café   (**some**) coffee
de la limonade   (**some**) lemonade
*de l'*aspirine   (**some**) aspirin
des chocolats   (**some**) chocolates

- ***du*** always replaces *de + le*
- ***des*** always replaces *de + les*

Use *du, de la, de l', des* to mean 'some' or 'any':

*Je voudrais **du** poulet.*   I'd like **some** chicken.

*Elle prend **de la** limonade.*   She's having (**some**) lemonade.

*Elle boit **de l'**eau.*   She's drinking (**some**) water.

*Avez-vous **des** croissants?*   Do you have **any** croissants?

Also use *du, de la, de l', des* to talk about activities someone is doing or musical instruments someone is playing:

*Je fais **du** judo.*   I do judo.
*Elle joue **de la** guitare.*   She is playing the guitar.
*Il fait **de l'**équitation.*   He goes horse riding.
*Ils font **des** excursions.*   They go on trips.

After a negative, *de* or *d'* replaces these forms:

*Je ne fais pas **de** judo.*   I don't do judo.

C Adjectives

Feminine and masculine, singular and plural adjectives

In French, adjectives have different endings depending on whether they describe masculine, feminine, singular or plural nouns.

▪ The masculine singular form has no extra ending:
Mon frère est petit.   My brother is small.

▪ Add -e if the noun is feminine singular:
Ma sœur est petite.   My sister is small.

▪ Add -s to the masculine singular form if the noun is masculine plural:
Mes frères sont petits.   My brothers are small.

▪ Add -s to the feminine singular form if the noun is feminine plural:
Mes sœurs sont petites.   My sisters are small.

▪ When an adjective describes a group of masculine and feminine people or things, it has to be the masculine plural form:
Mes parents sont grands.   My parents are tall.

There are many exceptions in the feminine forms.

▪ With adjectives that already end in -e, don't add another -e in the feminine:
un vélo rouge   a red bike
une moto rouge   a red motorbike

▪ But with adjectives that end in -é, do add another -e in the feminine:
mon film préféré   my favourite film
ma chanson préférée   my favourite song

▪ With some adjectives, you double the final consonant before the -e in the feminine:
Il est italien.   He is Italian.
Elle est italienne.   She is Italian.

▪ Adjective endings -eux and -eur change to -euse in the feminine:
un garçon paresseux ➡ *une fille paresseuse*
a lazy boy   a lazy girl
un garçon travailleur ➡ *une fille travailleuse*
a hard-working boy   a hard-working girl

▪ The adjective ending -eau changes to -elle in the feminine:
un nouveau vélo   a new bike
une nouvelle voiture   a new car

▪ The adjective ending -if changes to -ive in the feminine:

un copain sportif   a sporty (boy)friend
une copine sportive   a sporty (girl)friend

▪ The feminine of blanc is blanche:
Elle porte une robe blanche.
She is wearing a white dress.

▪ The feminine of frais is fraîche:
Je voudrais une boisson fraîche.
I would like a cool drink.

▪ The feminine of gentil is gentille:
Ma grand-mère est gentille.
My grandmother is kind.

▪ The feminine of sympa is sympa:
Ma mère est sympa.   My mother is nice.

There are also some exceptions in the plural forms.

▪ Adjective endings -al and -eau change to -aux or -eaux in the masculine plural:
J'ai des poissons tropicaux.
I have got some tropical fish.
J'ai des nouveaux livres.
I have got some new books.

▪ With adjectives that end in -s or -x, don't add an -s in the plural:
Mes frères sont paresseux.   My brothers are lazy.
Les nuages sont gris.   The clouds are grey.

Some adjectives, such as *marron* and *super*, do not change at all in the feminine or plural:
Elle porte des bottes marron.
She's wearing brown boots.

The position of adjectives

Most adjectives follow the noun they describe:
un prof sympa   a nice teacher
une copine intelligente   an intelligent friend
des idées intéressantes   interesting ideas

However, a few adjectives, such as *petit, grand, bon, mauvais, joli, beau, jeune* and *vieux*, usually come in front of the noun:
un petit garçon   a small boy
une jolie ville   a pretty town

A few adjectives that come in front of the noun have a special masculine form before a vowel or a silent *h*:
un bel endroit   a beautiful place
un vieil homme   an old man
un nouvel ami   a new friend

Adjectives of nationality

Adjectives of nationality do not begin with a capital letter:

Nicolas est français.   Nicolas is French.
Laura est galloise.   Laura is Welsh.

Like other adjectives, feminine adjectives of nationality have an *-e* at the end, unless there is one there already:

Sophie est française.   Sophie is French.
Juliette est suisse.   Juliette is Swiss.

Comparative and superlative adjectives

To make comparisons, use:

- *plus ... que*   more ... than / ...er than
  *La Loire est **plus** longue **que** la Tamise.*
  The Loire is **longer than** the Thames.

- *moins ... que*   less ... than
  *Les vélos sont **moins** rapides **que** les trains.*
  Bicycles are **less** fast **than** trains.

- *aussi ... que*   as ... as
  *Les tomates sont **aussi** chères **que** les pêches.*
  Tomatoes are **as** expensive **as** peaches.

For superlatives (the most ...), use:

- *le / la / les plus ...*   the most ... / the ...est
  *C'est la chambre **la plus** chère.*
  It is **the most** expensive room.
  *C'est **le plus** petit vélo.*
  It is **the smallest** bicycle.

- *le / la / les moins ...*   the least ...
  *C'est le film **le moins** intéressant.*
  It is **the least** interesting film.

The adjectives *bon* and *mauvais* have irregular comparatives and superlatives:

*Ce CD est **meilleur** que l'autre.*
This CD is **better** than the other one.

*Elle est la **meilleure**!*
She's the **best**!

*Je suis **pire** que ma sœur.*
I am **worse** than my sister.

*Mon frère est **le pire**.*
My brother is **the worst**.

Demonstrative adjectives: *ce, cet, cette, ces* – this, that, these, those

The French for 'this' or 'that' is *ce, cet* or *cette* and for 'these' or 'those' is *ces*.

masculine	feminine	masculine and feminine plural
ce	cette	ces

***ce** magasin*	**this / that** shop
***cette** chemise*	**this / that** shirt
***ces** baskets*	**these / those** trainers

But *ce* changes to *cet* when the noun after it begins with a vowel or a silent *h*:

***cet** ami*	**this / that** friend
***cet** hôtel*	**this / that** hotel

Indefinite adjectives

The most common indefinite adjectives are:

autre(s)	other
certain(e)(s)	certain / some
chaque	each
même(s)	same
plusieurs	several
quelque(s)	some
tout / toute / tous / toutes	all

Chaque is always singular and *plusieurs* is always plural:

*Il y a une télévision dans **chaque chambre**.*
There is a television in **each room**.

*Il a **plusieurs voitures**.*
He has **several cars**.

Possessive adjectives, one 'owner'

mon / ma / mes	my
ton / ta / tes	your
son / sa / ses	his / her / its

There are three different ways of saying 'my' in French, as it depends on whether the noun is masculine or feminine, singular or plural. It is the same for 'your' and 'his' / 'her' / 'its'.

masculine singular	feminine singular	masculine and feminine plural
mon, ton, son	ma, ta, sa	mes, tes, ces

mon père	**my** father
ma mère	**my** mother
ton* père	**your** father
ta* mère	**your** mother
son pied	**his / her / its** foot
sa porte	**his / her / its** door
mes parents	**my** parents
tes* parents	**your** parents
ses fenêtres	**his / her / its** windows

* to someone you normally say *tu* to

French doesn't have three different words for 'his', 'her' and 'its'. The word changes according to whether the noun it is used with is masculine, feminine, singular or plural.

Possessive adjectives, several 'owners'

notre / nos	our
votre / vos	your
leur / leurs	their

masculine and feminine singular	masculine and feminine plural
notre, votre, leur	*nos, vos, leurs*

notre père	**our** father
notre mère	**our** mother
votre* père	**your** father
votre* mère	**your** mother
leur frère	**their** brother
leur sœur	**their** sister
nos parents	**our** parents
vos* copains	**your** friends
leurs profs	**their** teachers

* to several people **or** to someone you normally say *vous* to

Interrogative adjectives: *quel, quelle, quels, quelles*

Quel (meaning 'which' or 'what') agrees with the noun it refers to.

m singular	f singular	m plural	f plural
quel	*quelle*	*quels*	*quelles*

C'est **quel** *dessin?*
Which drawing is it?

Quelle *heure est-il?*
What time is it?

Quelles *sont tes matières préférées?*
What are your favourite subjects?

D Adverbs

Adverbs are used with a verb, an adjective or another adverb to express how, when, where or to what extent something happens.

Many French adverbs are formed by adding *-ment* (the equivalent of '-ly' in English) to the feminine form of the adjective.

m adjective	f adjective	adverb
doux	*douce*	*doucement* – gently
final	*finale*	*finalement* – finally
heureux	*heureuse*	*heureusement* – fortunately
probable	*probable*	*probablement* – probably

There are several exceptions, which are not formed from the feminine form of the adjective, including these:

m adjective		adverb
vrai	-	*vraiment* – really
évident	-	*évidemment* – obviously

Many common adverbs are completely irregular:

bien	well	*Elle joue* **bien**.	She plays well.
mal	badly	*Il mange* **mal**.	He eats badly.
vite	fast	*Tu parles* **vite**.	You speak fast.

Comparative and superlative adverbs

As with adjectives, you can make comparisons using *plus, moins* and *aussi … que*:

Tu parles **plus** *lentement* **que** *moi.*
You speak **more** slowly **than** me.

Je mange **moins** *vite* **que** *ma sœur.*
I eat **less** quickly **than** my sister.

Elle joue **aussi** *bien que Paul.*
She plays **as** well **as** Paul.

The comparative of the adverb *bien* is an exception:

Elle joue **mieux** *que Paul.*
She plays **better** than Paul.

You can also use adverbs as superlatives:

Il joue **le mieux**.
He plays **the best**.

Il a fini son travail **le plus vite**.
He finished his work **the fastest**.

Adverbs of time, frequency, place, etc.

Adverbs of time include:

aujourd'hui	today
demain	tomorrow
hier	yesterday
après-demain	the day after tomorrow
avant-hier	the day before yesterday
déjà	already

Adverbs of frequency include:

quelquefois	sometimes
souvent	often
toujours	always

Adverbs of place include:

dedans	inside
dehors	outside
ici	here
là-bas	(over) there
loin	far
partout	everywhere

Adverbs of intensity and quantity (qualifying words) include:

assez	enough
trop	too (much)
beaucoup	a lot
un peu	a little
très	very

Adverbs of sequence include:

d'abord	firstly
après	afterwards
ensuite	next
enfin	finally
puis	then

E Pronouns

Subject pronouns: *je, tu, il, elle, on, nous, vous, ils, elles*

Subject pronouns usually come before the verb and express who or what performs the action.

singular	plural
je – I	*nous* – we
tu – you	*vous* – you
il – he / it	*ils* – they (m)
elle – she / it	*elles* – they (f)
on – we / you / they	

Je parle français.	I speak French.
Tu as quel âge?	How old are **you**?
Il s'appelle Théo.	**He** is called Théo.
Elle s'appelle Aïcha.	**She** is called Aïcha.
On se retrouve où?	Where shall **we** meet?
Nous habitons en ville.	**We** live in town.
Vous avez une chambre?	Do **you** have a room?
Ils s'appellent Do et Mi.	**They** are called Do and Mi.
Elles sont marrantes.	**They** are fun.

Je is shortened to *j'* if the word that follows begins with a silent *h* or a vowel:

J'aime les pommes.	I like apples.
J'habite en Écosse.	I live in Scotland.

There are two French words for 'you': *tu* and *vous*.

- Use *tu* when talking to someone (one person) of your own age or someone in your family.

- Use *vous* when talking to an adult not in your family (e.g. your teacher). The following phrases are useful to remember:

Avez-vous … ?	Have **you** got … ?
Voulez-vous … ?	Do **you** want … ?
Voudriez-vous … ?	Would **you** like … ?

- Also use *vous* when talking to more than one person – whatever their age and whether you know them well or not.

Il and *elle* can both also mean 'it', depending on the gender of the noun they replace.

L'hôtel est bien? – Oui, il est très confortable.
Is the hotel good? – Yes, **it** is very comfortable.

Je déteste ma chambre: elle est trop petite.
I hate my bedroom: **it** is too small.

On can mean 'we', 'you' or 'they', depending on the context:

> **On** *s'entend bien.*
> **We** get on well.

> *Comment dit-***on** *«pencil» en français?*
> How do **you** say 'pencil' in French?

> **On** *parle français au Canada.*
> **They** speak French in Canada.

There are two French words for 'they': *ils* and *elles*.

- Use *ils* when all the people / things you are talking about are male, or it is a mixed group of males and females:

  J'ai un frère et une sœur, **ils** *s'appellent Nicolas et Aurélie.*

  I have a brother and a sister; **they** are called Nicolas and Aurélie.

- Use *elles* when all the people / things you are talking about are female:

  J'ai deux copines espagnoles, **elles** *habitent à Madrid.*

  I have two Spanish friends; **they** live in Madrid.

Direct object pronouns: *me, te, le, la, nous, vous, les*

Direct object pronouns replace a noun that is not the subject of the verb.

singular	plural
me / m' – me	*nous* – us
te / t' – you	*vous* – you
le / l' – him / it (m)	*les* – them
la / l' – her / it (f)	

Direct object pronouns come in front of the verb, unlike in English:

> *Je* **le** *prends.*   I'll take **it**.
> *Je peux* **vous** *aider?*   Can I help **you**?

Le and *la* are shortened to *l'* in front of a vowel or a silent *h*:

> *Mon petit frère a deux ans. Je* **l'***adore!*
> My little brother is two. I love **him**!

Indirect object pronouns: *me, te, lui, nous, vous, leur*

Indirect object pronouns are used to replace a noun that would be introduced with the preposition *à*.

singular	plural
me / m' – (to) me	*nous* – (to) us
te / t' – (to) you	*vous* – (to) you
lui – (to) him / her / it	*leur* – (to) them

> *Je donne du café à mon père.*
> ➡ *Je* **lui** *donne du café.*
>   I give **him** some coffee.
> *Je parle à ma mère.*
> ➡ *Je* **lui** *parle.*   I speak to **her**.
> *J'écris à mes grands-parents.*
> ➡ *Je* **leur** *écris.*   I write to **them**.

Beware! Some French verbs are followed by a preposition when their English equivalents are not:

> *Je téléphone* **à** *mon père.*   I ring my father.
> *Je* **lui** *téléphone.*   I ring **him**.

Indirect object pronouns: *en* – of it / them; *y* – there

Use *en* to avoid repeating a noun that is introduced with *du, de la, de l'* or *des*:

> *Tu as des chiens?*   Have you got any dogs?
> *Oui, j'***en** *ai trois.*   Yes, I've got three (**of them**).
> *Tu manges de la viande?*   Do you eat meat?
> *Oui, j'***en** *mange.*   Yes, I do.

Y usually means 'there'. You can use *y* to avoid repeating the name of a place:

> *Tu vas à Paris?*   Are you going to Paris?
> *Oui, j'***y** *vais demain.*   Yes, I'm going **there** tomorrow.

Order of object pronouns

When two object pronouns are used together in the same sentence, follow this sequence:

me te se nous vous		le la l' les		leur lui		y en
	come before		come before		come before	

> *Je* **te les** *donne maintenant.*
> I'm giving **them** to **you** now.

> *Il* **nous en** *a parlé.*
> He has talked to **us** about **it**.

Emphatic pronouns: *moi, toi, lui, elle, nous, vous, eux, elles*

These are also called disjunctive pronouns. Use them:

■ for emphasis:

Moi, j'adore les fraises.	I love strawberries.
Toi, tu as quel âge?	How old are **you**?

after *c'est*:

*C'est **moi**.*	It's **me**.

■ after a preposition:

*avec **moi***	with **me**
*avec **nous***	with **us**
*pour **toi***	for **you**
*pour **vous***	for **you**
*chez **lui***	at **his** house
*chez **eux***	at **their** house
*à côté d'**elle***	next to **her**
*à côté d'**elles***	next to **them**

■ after a comparative:
*Elle est plus sympa que **toi**.*
She is nicer than **you**.

■ with *à*, to express possession:
*Il est **à toi**, ce CD?*
Does this CD **belong to you?**

Possessive pronouns

m singular	f singular	m plural	f plural	
le mien	*la mienne*	*les miens*	*les miennes*	mine
le tien	*la tienne*	*les tiens*	*les tiennes*	yours
le sien	*la sienne*	*les siens*	*les siennes*	his / hers / its
le nôtre	*la nôtre*	*les nôtres*	*les nôtres*	ours
le vôtre	*la vôtre*	*les vôtres*	*les vôtres*	yours
le leur	*la leur*	*les leurs*	*les leurs*	theirs

*C'est **le mien** ou **le tien**?*   Is it **mine** or **yours**?

Relative pronouns: *qui, que, qu', dont*

Relative pronouns are used to link phrases together.

Use *qui* as the subject of the relative clause. It can refer to people and things, and means 'who', 'that' or 'which':

*le copain **qui** habite à Lyon*
the friend **who** lives in Lyon

*le livre **qui** est sur la chaise*
the book **that** is on the table

Use *que* (*qu'* before a vowel or a silent *h*) as the object of the relative clause. It means 'whom' or 'that':

*le copain **que** j'ai vu*
the friend (**that / whom**) I saw

*le livre **qu'**il a acheté*   the book (**that**) he bought

■ Remember that *que* is not optional. Although it is often not translated in English, you cannot leave it out in French.

■ If you cannot decide between *qui* and *que*, remember that *qui* is subject and *que* is object. If the relative clause already has a subject, then the pronoun you need must be *que*.
*J'ai trouvé un job **qui** me va.*
I have found a job **that** suits me.
– The subject of *va* is *qui*.

*C'est une couleur **que** je déteste.*
It's a colour (**that**) I hate.
– The subject of *déteste* is *je*, and *que* is object.

You will need to understand sentences containing the word *dont*. It is usually translated as 'whose' or 'of which'.

*J'ai un ami **dont** le père est espagnol.*
I have a friend **whose** father is Spanish.

*J'ai cinq robes **dont** trois sont rouges.*
I've got five dresses **of which** three are red.

Demonstrative pronouns: *ce, cela, ça, celui-ci*, etc.

Ce (shortened to *c'* before a vowel) means 'it', 'that' or 'those' and is usually followed with a form of *être*:

Ce sont mes parents.	**Those** are my parents.
C'est facile.	**It's** easy.

Cela means 'that' and is often shortened to *ça*:

Cela m'étonne.	**That** surprises me.
*Tu aimes **ça**?*	Do you like **that**?

Ça is also used in various phrases:

Ça va?	Are you OK?
Ça ne fait rien.	It doesn't matter.
*C'est **ça**.*	That's right.

Celui (masculine), *celle* (feminine), *ceux* (masculine plural) and *celles* (feminine plural) are used with *-ci* or *-là* for emphasis or contrast, meaning 'this one', 'that one', 'these ones' or 'those ones':

*Tu veux **celui-ci** ou **celui-là**?*
Do you want **this one** or **that one**?

*J'hésite entre **celles-ci** et **celles-là**.*
I'm hesitating between **these** and **those**.

Indefinite pronouns: *quelqu'un, quelque chose, tout, tout le monde* and *personne*

The French for 'someone' is *quelqu'un*:

*Il y a **quelqu'un** à la maison.*
There's **someone** at home.

The French for 'something' is *quelque chose*:

*Vous avez perdu **quelque chose**?*
Have you lost **something**?

The French for 'all' is *tout / toute / tous / toutes*:

*C'est **tout**.*	That's **all**.
*Je les aime **tous**.*	I love them **all**.

The French for 'everybody' is *tout le monde*:

Tout le monde *aime le chocolat.*

Everybody likes chocolate.

The French for 'nobody' is *personne*. In a sentence, it is followed by *ne* in front a verb or *n'* before a vowel, and it doesn't need *pas*:

Personne ne *veut danser.*

Nobody wants to dance.

F Verbs

French verbs have different endings depending on who is doing the action and whether the action takes place in the past, the present or the future. The verb tables on pages 192–196 set out the patterns of endings for several useful verbs.

When using a name or a singular noun instead of a pronoun, use the same form of the verb as for *il / elle*:

*Martin **parle** espagnol.*   Martin **speaks** Spanish.

When using two names or a plural noun, use the same form of the verb as for *ils / elles*:

*Thomas et Lola **jouent** au basket.*
Thomas and Lola **are playing** basketball.

*Mes frères **écoutent** de la musique.*
My brothers **are listening** to music.

The infinitive

The infinitive is the form of the verb you find in a dictionary, e.g. *jouer, finir, être*. It never changes.

When two verbs follow each other, the second one is always in the infinitive.

▪ All verbs of liking, disliking and preferring (such as *aimer, adorer, préférer, détester*) are followed by the infinitive:
*J'aime **jouer** de la guitare.*
I like **playing** the guitar.

*Je préfère **écouter** des CD.*
I prefer **listening** to CDs.

*J'adore **être** au bord de la mer.*
I love **being** by the sea.

▪ Modal verbs *vouloir, pouvoir* and *devoir* and the verb *savoir* are also followed by the infinitive:
*Tu veux **aller** au cinéma?*
Do you want **to go** to the cinema?

*On peut **faire** du shopping.*
You can **go** shopping.

*Je dois **faire** mes devoirs.*
I must **do** my homework.

*Je sais **conduire**.*
I know how **to drive**.

▪ Verbs expressing a future wish or intention are followed by the infinitive:
*J'espère **partir** en vacances.*
I hope **to go** on holiday.
*Je voudrais **aller** en Italie.*
I'd like **to go** to Italy.

The infinitive is used after *avant de* to mean 'before doing something':

*Je me lave les mains avant de **manger**.*
I wash my hands before **eating**.

Some verbs always need *à* between them and the infinitive:

*aider quelqu'un **à***	to help someone **to**
*apprendre **à***	to learn **to**
*arriver **à***	to manage **to**
*commencer **à***	to start **to**
*continuer **à***	to continue **to**
*s'intéresser **à***	to be interested **in**
*inviter quelqu'un **à***	to invite someone **to**
*réussir **à***	to succeed **in**

*Il **apprend à** nager.*   He is **learning to** swim.

Some verbs always need *de* between them and the infinitive:

*arrêter **de***	to stop
*décider **de***	to decide **to**
*essayer **de***	to try **to**
*être obligé(e) **de***	to be forced **to**
*oublier **de***	to forget **to**
*refuser **de***	to refuse **to**

*J'ai **oublié de** fermer la porte.*
I **forgot to** close the door.

Faire + infinitive

Faire + infinitive is used to say that someone is having something done:

> *Je **fais réparer** ma voiture.*
> I **have** my car **repaired**.

> *Il **se fait couper** les cheveux.*
> He **is having** his hair **cut**.

> *Ils **font construire** une maison.*
> They **are having** a house **built.**

The perfect infinitive: *après avoir / être* + past participle

The perfect infinitive is the infinitive of *avoir* or *être* (depending on which one the verb normally uses to form the perfect tense), plus the past participle of the verb. It is used after *après* to mean 'after doing something':

> *Après avoir regardé l'heure, il est parti.*
> **After looking** at the time, he left.

> *Il a lu le livre **après être allé** là-bas.*
> He read the book **after going** there.

> *Elle a mangé **après s'être levée**.*
> She ate **after getting up**.

The present tense

Use the present tense to describe:

- something that is taking place now:
  > *J'écoute un CD.*
  > I **am listening** to a CD.

- something that happens regularly:
  > *J'ai maths le lundi.*
  > I **have** maths on Mondays.

Present tense verb endings change depending on who is doing the action:

> *Je parle à ma grand-mère.*
> **I speak** to my grandmother.

> *Nous lavons la voiture.*
> **We wash** the car.

Most verbs follow a regular pattern.

Regular -er verbs

To form the present tense of *-er* verbs, remove the *-er* from the infinitive to form the stem, e.g. *parl* from *parler*. Then add the endings shown below.

parler – to speak / to talk	
*je parl***e**	*nous parl***ons**
*tu parl***es**	*vous parl***ez**
*il / elle / on parl***e**	*ils / elles parl***ent**

Some other regular *-er* verbs:

adorer	to love	*habiter*	to live
aimer	to like	*jouer*	to play
détester	to hate	*regarder*	to watch
écouter	to listen	*rester*	to stay

Regular -ir verbs:

To form the present tense of *-ir* verbs, remove the *-ir* from the infinitive to form the stem, e.g. *fin* from *finir*. Then add the endings shown below.

finir – to finish	
*je fin***is**	*nous fin***issons**
*tu fin***is**	*vous fin***issez**
*il / elle / on fin***it**	*ils / elles fin***issent**

Other regular *-ir* verbs:

choisir	to choose
remplir	to fill

Regular -re verbs:

To form the present tense of *-re* verbs, remove the *-re* from the infinitive to form the stem, e.g. *attend* from *attendre*. Then add the endings shown below.

attendre – to wait	
*j'attend***s**	*nous attend***ons**
*tu attend***s**	*vous attend***ez**
il / elle / on attend	*ils / elles attend***ent**

Other regular *-re* verbs:

descendre	to go down
répondre	to reply
vendre	to sell

Irregular verbs

Some verbs are irregular and do not follow these patterns. Turn to pages 193–196 for details of the most common ones.

Reflexive verbs

Reflexive verbs have an extra pronoun in front of the verb:

me	je **me** réveille	I wake up
te	tu **te** lèves	you get up
se	il / elle **s'**appelle	he / she is called
	on **s'**amuse bien	we have a good time
nous	nous **nous** lavons	we get washed
vous	vous **vous** couchez	you go to bed
se	ils / elles **s'**excusent	they apologise

Note that *me, te* and *se* are shortened to *m', t'* and *s'* in front of a vowel or a silent *h*.

Common reflexive verbs are:

s'amuser	to have fun
s'habiller	to get dressed
s'appeler	to be called
se laver	to have a wash
s'asseoir	to sit down
se lever	to get up
se coucher	to go to bed
se passer	to happen
s'ennuyer	to be bored
se promener	to go for a walk
s'excuser	to apologise
se réveiller	to wake up

The perfect tense

Use the perfect tense to talk about what somebody did or has done.

> *Il **a mangé** un sandwich.*
> He **ate** a sandwich. / He **has eaten** a sandwich.

To make the perfect tense of most verbs, use the present tense of *avoir* + past participle:

parler – to speak / to talk	
j'**ai parlé**	nous **avons parlé**
tu **as parlé**	vous **avez parlé**
il / elle / on **a parlé**	ils / elles **ont parlé**

Some verbs use the present tense of *être* instead of *avoir*:

aller – to go	
je **suis allé(e)**	nous **sommes allé(e)s**
tu **es allé(e)**	vous **êtes allé(e)(s)**
il **est allé**	ils **sont allés**
elle **est allée**	elles **sont allées**
on **est allé(e)(s)**	

Verbs that use *être* to form the perfect tense include:

aller	to go	*rentrer*	to come back
arriver	to arrive	*rester*	to stay
descendre	to go down	*retourner*	
entrer	to enter		to return /
monter	to go up		to go back
mourir	to die	*sortir*	to go out
naître	to be born	*tomber*	to fall
partir	to leave	*venir*	to come

All reflexive verbs use *être* to form the perfect tense. Don't forget the extra pronoun that comes before the part of *être*:

se lever – to get up	
je **me suis levé(e)**	nous **nous sommes levé(e)s**
tu **t'es levé(e)**	vous **vous êtes levé(e)(s)**
il **s'est levé**	ils **se sont levés**
elle **s'est levée**	elles **se sont levées**
on **s'est levé(e)(s)**	

When using *être*:

- add *-e* to the past participle if the subject is female:
  *Elle est parti**e** en Écosse.*
  She went off to Scotland.

- add *-s* to the past participle if the subject is masculine plural:
  *Ils sont arrivé**s** en retard.*   They arrived late.

- add *-es* to the past participle if the subject is feminine plural:
  *Elles sont arrivé**es** en retard.*   They arrived late.

When making a negative statement in the perfect tense, *ne* comes before *avoir / être* and *pas* comes after it:

> *Je **n'**ai **pas** mangé.*   I **haven't** eaten.
> *Elle **n'**est **pas** sortie.*   She **didn't** go out.

Past participles

The past participle of *-er* verbs ends in *-é*:

*aller – all**é***	gone
*donner – donn**é***	given
*parler – parl**é***	spoken

The past participle of regular *-ir* verbs ends in *-i*:

*choisir – chois**i***	chosen
*finir – fin**i***	finished

The past participle of regular *-re* verbs ends in *-u*:

*attendre – attend**u***	waited
*vendre – vend**u***	sold

Many common verbs have an irregular past participle:

avoir – **eu**	had
boire – **bu**	drunk
devoir – **dû**	had to
dire – **dit**	said
écrire – **écrit**	written
être – **été**	been
faire – **fait**	done / made
lire – **lu**	read
mettre – **mis**	put
pouvoir – **pu**	been able to
prendre – **pris**	taken
venir – **venu**	come
voir – **vu**	seen
vouloir – **voulu**	wanted

The imperfect tense

Use the imperfect tense:

- to describe what something or someone was like in the past:

  *Il y **avait** une grande piscine.*
  There **was** a big pool.

  C'était délicieux.
  It **was** delicious.

  J'étais triste.
  I **was** sad.

- to say what was happening at a certain time in the past:

  *Je **regardais** la télé quand il a téléphoné.*
  I **was watching** TV when he rang.

- to describe something that used to happen regularly in the past:

  *Je **prenais** le bus tous les matins.*
  I **used to catch** the bus every morning.

- after *si* to make a suggestion:

  *Si on **allait** au cinéma?*
  Shall we **go** to the cinema?

To form the imperfect tense, take the *nous* form of the verb in the present tense, remove -*ons* to form the stem, then add the correct endings:

finir – to finish

(present tense: *nous finissons*)

je finiss**ais**	nous finiss**ions**
tu finiss**ais**	vous finiss**iez**
il / elle / on finiss**ait**	ils / elles finiss**aient**

The verb *être* is the only exception. The endings are as above, but they are added to the stem *ét*-:

être – to be

j'ét**ais**	nous ét**ions**
tu ét**ais**	vous ét**iez**
il / elle / on ét**ait**	ils / elles ét**aient**

Perfect or imperfect?

To help you decide between the perfect and the imperfect, remember that:

- the perfect tense usually describes single events in the past:

  *Hier, je **me suis levée** à six heures.*
  Yesterday, I **got up** at six.

- the imperfect describes what used to happen:

  *Je **me levais** à huit heures.*
  I **used to get up** at eight.

The pluperfect tense

This tense is used to refer to something further back in the past than the perfect or the imperfect, to say what someone had done or had been doing. You use the imperfect of *avoir* or *être*, plus a past participle:

J'avais parlé.
I **had spoken**.

*Il **était parti**.*
He **had left**.

*Vous **vous étiez habillés**.*
You **had got dressed**.

*Je savais qu'il **était allé** en Égypte.*
I knew that he **had gone** to Egypt.

The immediate future

Use the present tense of *aller* followed by an infinitive to say what you are going to do or what is going to happen:

je **vais pleurer**	I am going to cry
nous **allons manger**	we are going to eat
tu **vas partir**	you are going to leave
vous **allez boire**	you are going to drink
elle **va chanter**	she is going to sing
ils **vont dormir**	they are going to sleep

*Je **vais continuer** mes études.*
I'm **going to continue** studying.

*Il **va neiger**.*   It's **going to snow**.

The future tense

The future tense expresses what will happen or will be happening in the future:

*Qu'est-ce que vous **ferez** après l'école?*
What **will you do** after school?

*Vous **travaillerez** dans l'informatique?*
Will you work in computing?

It is used for predictions such as weather forecasts:

*Il **fera** beau / froid / chaud.*
It **will be** fine / cold / hot.

*Le temps **sera** pluvieux / nuageux.*
The weather **will be** rainy / cloudy.

*Il **neigera**.*	It **will snow**.
*Il **pleuvra**.*	It **will rain**.
*Il **gèlera**.*	It **will freeze**.

To form the future tense, add the correct ending to the infinitive of the verb:

parler – to speak / to talk	
je parler**ai**	nous parler**ons**
tu parler**as**	vous parler**ez**
il / elle / on parler**a**	ils / elles parler**ont**

With some verbs, you add the same set of endings to an irregular stem instead of the infinitive:

*aller – j'**ir**ai*	*pouvoir – je **pourr**ai*
*avoir – j'**aur**ai*	*savoir – je **saur**ai*
*être – je **ser**ai*	*venir – je **viendr**ai*
*faire – il **fer**ai*	*voir – je **verr**ai*
*falloir – il **faudr**a*	*vouloir – je **voudr**ai*

The imperative

Use the imperative to give advice or instructions.

Use the *tu* form with a person your own age or a person you know very well:

Continue *tout droit.*	**Go** straight on.
Prends *la première rue.*	**Take** the first street.
Tourne *à gauche.*	**Turn** left.

Use the *vous* form with a person you don't know very well or to more than one person:

Continuez *tout droit.*	**Go** straight on.
Prenez *la première rue.*	**Take** the first street.
Tournez *à gauche.*	**Turn** left.

The imperative is the same as the *tu* or the *vous* form of the present tense, but without using a word for 'you' first. In the case of *-er* verbs, you miss off the *-s* of the *tu* form (unless the verb is followed by *y* or *en*):

Va *au lit!*	**Go** to bed!
Achète *des pommes.*	**Buy** some apples.
Vas-*y!*	**Go** on!
Achètes-*en un kilo.*	**Buy** a kilo (of them).

Note that all *vous* form imperatives end in *-ez* except for faire:

Faites *vos devoirs!*	**Do** your homework!

Reflexive verbs in the imperative are hyphenated with their reflexive pronouns:

Lève-toi.	Stand up.
Asseyez-vous.	Sit down.

The conditional

You use the conditional in French when 'would' is used in English:

*Je **voudrais** te voir.*
I **would like** to see you.

*Si j'**étais** riche, j'**achèterais** un piano.*
If I **were** rich, I **would buy** a piano.

The conditional has the same stem as the future tense and the same endings as the imperfect:

	future	imperfect	conditional
aimer	j'aimer**ai**	j'aim**ais**	j'aimer**ais**
aller	j'ir**ai**	j'all**ais**	j'ir**ais**

parler – to talk / to speak	
je parler**ais**	nous parler**ions**
tu parler**ais**	vous parler**iez**
il / elle / on parler**ait**	ils / elles parler**aient**

The subjunctive

The following expressions are followed by a form of the verb called the subjunctive:

avant que	before
bien que	although
à condition que	provided that
il faut que	we / you / one must / it is necessary that

The most commonly used of these phrases is *il faut que*.

The subjunctive form is usually the same, or similar, to the present tense, so it is easy to recognise.

*Il faut que vous **parliez** avec le patron.*
You must **speak** to the owner.

Some exceptions are *faire, aller, avoir* and *être* – these are different, and you need to be able to recognise them.

*Il faut qu'on **fasse** des économies d'eau.*
We must **save** water.

*Bien qu'il **ait** 25 ans, il habite toujours chez ses parents.*
Although he **is** 25, he still lives with his parents.

*Avant qu'elle **aille** à l'université, nous allons passer une semaine en Espagne.*
Before she **goes** to university, we're going to spend a week in Spain.

*Mon père m'a promis un nouveau vélo, à condition que mes résultats **soient** bons.*
My father has promised me a new bicycle, on condition that my results **are** good.

parler (regular -er verb)	faire	aller
je parle	je fasse	j'aille
tu parles	tu fasses	tu ailles
il / elle / on parle	il / elle / on fasse	il / elle / on aille
nous parlions	nous fassions	nous allions
vous parliez	vous fassiez	vous alliez
ils / elles parlent	ils / elles fassent	ils / elles aillent

avoir	être
j'aie	je sois
tu aies	tu sois
il / elle / on ait	il / elle / on soit
nous ayons	nous soyons
vous ayez	vous soyez
ils / elles aient	ils / elles soient

The passive

The passive is used to say what is done to someone or something. It is formed from a part of *être* and a past participle. The past participle must agree with the noun:

active form: *Il lave la pomme.*
He washes the apple.

passive form: *La pomme **est lavée**.*
The apple **is washed**.

The passive can be used in different tenses:

present: *Les lits **sont faits**.*
The beds **are made**.

imperfect: *Les murs **étaient peints**.*
The walls **were painted**.

perfect: *J'ai **été invité**.*
I've **been invited**.

future: *La maison **sera vendue**.*
The house **will be sold**.

The passive is used less often in French than in English, as most sentences can be turned round:

■ either by using *on*:
On parle *français au Québec.*
French **is spoken** in Quebec.

■ or by using a reflexive verb:
*Les tickets **se vendent** par carnets de 10.*
Tickets **are sold** in books of 10.

en + *present participle*

The English present participle ends in '-ing', and the French present participle ends in *-ant*. Take the *nous* form of the present tense, remove *-ons* and replace it with *–ant*:

arriver ➡ *arrivons* ➡ *arrivant*

En + present participle can be used when two actions happen together:

*Il fait ses devoirs **en chantant**.*
He does his homework **while singing**.

***En travaillant** le soir, je gagne de l'argent.*
By working in the evening, I earn money.

Useful verbs

avoir – to have

Use *avoir* to say how old someone is:

*J'**ai** 15 ans.*   I **am** 15 years old.

Use *avoir mal* to talk about a pain or an ache:

*J'**ai mal** à la tête.*   I **have** a headache.

Use *avoir envie* to talk about feeling like or wanting to do something:

*J'**ai envie** de courir.*   I **feel like** running.

Use *en avoir marre* to talk about being fed up with something:

*J'**en ai marre** des examens.*
I'm **fed up** with the exams.

Some more useful expressions with *avoir*:

avoir chaud	to be hot
avoir faim	to be hungry
avoir froid	to be cold
avoir mal au cœur	to feel sick
avoir peur	to be afraid
avoir raison	to be right
avoir soif	to be thirsty
avoir tort	to be wrong

il y a – there is, there are

Il y a *une banque.*	**There is** a bank.
Il y a *beaucoup de cafés.*	**There are** lots of cafés.
Il n'y a pas de *piscine.*	**There isn't** a swimming pool.

faire – to do

This verb can mean 'to do', 'to make' or 'to go':

faire *du judo*	**to do** judo
faire *la vaisselle*	**to do** the washing up
faire *le lit*	**to make** the bed
faire *de la natation*	**to go** swimming

This verb is also used with *il* to talk about the weather:

Il **fait** *beau.*	The weather is nice.
Il **fait** *mauvais.*	The weather is bad.

jouer à and *jouer de* – to play

To talk about playing games, use *jouer + au / à la / à l / aux*:

Je **joue au** *basket.*   I play basketball.

To talk about playing a musical instrument, use *jouer + du / de la / de l' / des*:

Je **joue des** *percussions.*
I play percussion instruments.

se trouver – to be found, *être situé(e)* – to be situated

These verbs can be used in place of *être* to talk about where things are located:

La gare **se trouve** *au centre-ville.*

The station can be found in the town centre.

Make sure that *situé* agrees with the gender of the subject.

La ville **est située** *au bord de la mer.*

The town is situated by the sea.

Modal verbs: *devoir, pouvoir, vouloir*

Modal verbs are usually followed by an infinitive.

Use *devoir* (to have to) + infinitive to say what you must / mustn't do:

Je **dois porter** *un uniforme.*
I **have to wear** a uniform.

On **ne doit pas jeter** *de papiers par terre.*
You **mustn't drop** litter on the floor.

Use *pouvoir* (to be able to) + infinitive to say what you can / can't do:

On **peut faire** *des randonnées.*
You **can go** hiking.

Elle **ne peut pas sortir** *pendant la semaine.*
She **can't go out** during the week.

Use *vouloir* (to want to) + infinitive to say what you want and don't want to do. Adding *bien* changes the meaning:

Je **veux partir**.	I **want to leave**.
Je **veux bien partir**.	I **am quite happy to leave**.

The conditional of *vouloir, je voudrais,* means 'I would like':

Je **voudrais** *partir en vacances.*
I **would like** to go on holiday.

Note that *j'aimerais,* the conditional form of *aimer,* means the same as *je voudrais*:

*J'***aimerais** *faire de la planche à voile.*
I **would like** to go windsurfing.

Impersonal verbs: *il neige, il pleut, il faut*

These verbs are only used with *il*:

Il neige.	It's snowing.
Il pleut.	It's raining.

Il faut can have different meanings depending on the context:

Il **faut** *boire beaucoup d'eau.*
You must drink a lot of water.

Il **ne faut pas** *fumer.*
You mustn't smoke.

Il **me faut** *un kilo de tomates.*
I need a kilo of tomatoes.

Il **faut** *trois heures pour aller là-bas.*
It takes three hours to get there.

G Negatives

To make a sentence negative, you normally put *ne* before the verb and *pas* after it:

Je parle espagnol. ➡ *Je **ne** parle **pas** espagnol.*
I **don't** speak Spanish.

Shorten *ne* to *n'* if the word that follows begins with *h* or a vowel:

C'est difficile. ➡ *Ce **n'**est **pas** difficile.*
It's **not** difficult.

In negative sentences, use *de* instead of *un*, *une* or *des*:

Il y a un cinéma. ➡ *Il **n'**y a **pas de** cinéma.*
There is **no** cinema.

J'ai des frères. ➡ *Je **n'**ai **pas de** frère.*
I **don't** have **any** brothers.

Other common negative phrases:

ne ... plus – no more	*Il n'y a **plus de** savon.* There is **no more** soap.
ne ... jamais – never	*Je **ne** fume **jamais**.* I **never** smoke.
ne ... rien – nothing / not anything	*Il **ne** fait **rien**.* He doesn't do **anything**.
ne ... personne – nobody / not anybody	*Je **ne** vois **personne**.* I don't see **anybody**.
ne ... que – only	*Je **n'**ai **qu'**une sœur.* I **only** have one sister.
ne ... ni ... ni – neither ... nor	*Il **ne** parle **ni** français **ni** espagnol.* He speaks **neither** French **nor** Spanish.

Negatives in the perfect tense

In most negative phrases in the perfect tense, the phrase goes around the part of *avoir* or *être*.

*Je **n'**ai **pas** dormi.*   I **didn't** sleep.

But the negative phrases *ne ... que* and *ne ... ni ... ni* go around *avoir / être* and also the past participle:

*Je **n'**ai mangé **que** du pain.*
I **only** ate some bread.

Direct and indirect object pronouns are included within the negative phrase:

*Je ne **l'**ai pas vu.*   I didn't see **it**.

*Il ne **me** parle plus.*   He no longer speaks to **me**.

With reflexive verbs, the *ne* goes before the reflexive pronoun (*me, te*, etc.):

*Il **ne** s'est **pas** lavé.*   He **didn't** have a wash.

H Questions

You can turn statements into questions by adding a question mark and making your voice go up at the end:

Tu joues au tennis. ➡ *Tu joues au tennis**?***
Do you play tennis?

You can also add *est-ce que ...* at the beginning of the question:

Je peux vous aider. ➡ ***Est-ce que** je peux vous aider?*
Can I help you?

In more formal situations, you can change the word order so that the verb comes first:

Vous pouvez m'aider. ➡ ***Pouvez**-vous m'aider?*
Can you help me?

In the perfect tense, the auxiliary verb comes first:

Vous avez aidé la dame. ➡ ***Avez-vous** aidé la dame?*
Did you help the lady?

Many questions start with *qu'est-ce que ...*

***Qu'est-ce que** c'est?*   **What** is it?

***Qu'est-ce qu'**il y a à manger?*
What is there to eat?

***Qu'est-ce que** vous avez comme journaux?*
What kind of papers have you got?

Other question words

combien (de)	how much / how many	*Tu as **combien de** chats?* **How many** cats have you got?
comment	how	***Comment** vas-tu?* **How** are you?
où	where	***Où** habites-tu?* **Where** do you live?
pourquoi	why	***Pourquoi** est-ce que tu n'aimes pas ça?* **Why** don't you like it?
quand	when	*Il vient **quand**?* **When** is he coming?
		***Quand** a-t-il commencé?* **When** did he start?

quel / quelle / quels / quelles	which / what	*Ça commence à* **quelle** *heure?* **What** time does it start?
que / qu'	what	*Que veux-tu?* **What** do you want?
qui	who	*C'est **qui**?* **Who** is it?
quoi	what	*Elle fait **quoi**?* **What** is she doing?

▌ Prepositions

à, au, à l', à la, aux

À can mean:

in	*J'habite à Nice.*	I live **in** Nice.
at	*Je me lève à sept heures.*	I get up **at** seven.
to	*Je vais à l'école.*	I go **to** school.

Some special expressions with *à*:

à pied	**on** foot
à vélo	**by** bike
à gauche	**on** the left
à droite	**on** the right
aller à la pêche.	to go fishing.

à + le / la / les:

masculine	feminine	nouns which start with a vowel or silent *h*	plural
à + le = au	*à + la = à la*	*à + l' = à l'*	*à + les = aux*

au théâtre	**at / to the** theatre
à la piscine	**at / to the** pool
à l'hôtel	**at / to the** hotel
aux États-Unis	**in / to the** USA

Use *au, à la, à l', aux* to talk about flavours and fillings:

*un sandwich **au jambon***	a **ham** sandwich
*une glace **à la vanille***	a **vanilla** ice cream
*un gâteau **à l'orange***	an **orange** cake

Use with *avoir mal* to talk about a part of the body that hurts:

| *J'ai mal à l'oreille.* | I've got ear ache. |
| *Il a mal aux genoux.* | His knees hurt. |

de

De is shortened to *d'* before a vowel or a silent *h*.

De can mean 'of':

> *la mère **de** ma copine* (the mother of my friend)
> my friend's mother

> *le prof **d'**histoire* (the teacher of history)
> the history teacher

Note that the word order can be different from English:

> *un jus **d'**orange*
> an orange juice

> *un match **de** foot*
> a football match

> *la maison **de** mes grands-parents*
> my grandparents' house

De can also mean 'from':

> *Elle vient **d'**Écosse.*
> She comes **from** Scotland.

De is sometimes part of an expression:

près de	near
*Il habite **près de** Lyon.*	He lives **near** Lyon.
de ... à ...	from ... to ...
de neuf heures à cinq heures	**from** nine **to** five

De is used for expressing contents and quantities. Some examples are:

beaucoup de	a lot of
une boîte de	a jar / tin of
une bouteille de	a bottle of
cent grammes de	100 grammes of
un kilo de	a kilo of
un peu de	a little / a bit of
*une **bouteille** d'eau*	a **bottle of** water
*un **kilo** de poires*	a **kilo of** pears
*un **peu** de sucre*	a **little** sugar

In a different context, *venir de* can mean 'to have just …'

> *Il **vient de** retourner de vacances.*
> He **has just** returned from his holidays.

en, au / aux

En is used to introduce most names of countries. It means both 'to' and 'in':

Je vais **en** Allemagne.	I am going **to** Germany.
Il habite **en** France.	He lives **in** France.
Elle part **en** Angleterre.	She's going **to** England.

A few names of countries are masculine. These are introduced with au or aux:

Il va **au** Portugal.
He's going **to** Portugal.

Elle habite **au** pays de Galles.
She lives **in** Wales.

Nous partons **aux** États-Unis.
We're going **to** the USA.

More prepositions

à côté de	next to	**à côté de** la salle de bains **next to** the bathroom
avec	with	Je me dispute **avec** ma sœur. I argue **with** my sister.
chez	at / to someone's house	Je suis **chez** ma copine. I'm **at** my friend's house. Je vais **chez** mon copain. I'm going **to** my friend's house.
dans	in	Il est **dans** sa chambre. He is **in** his bedroom.
derrière	behind	**derrière** l'hôtel **behind** the hotel
devant	in front of	On se retrouve **devant** le théâtre? Shall we meet **in front of** the theatre?
en face de	opposite	**en face du** parking **opposite** the car park
entre	between	**entre** la salle à manger et l'ascenseur **between** the dining room and the lift
pendant	during	Qu'est-ce que tu fais **pendant** les vacances? What are you doing **during** the holidays?

près de	near	Mon chien est **près de** moi. My dog is **near** me.
pour	for	C'est super **pour** les jeunes. It's great **for** young people.
sous	under	Le chat est **sous** le lit. The cat is **under** the bed.
sur	on	Il y a des livres **sur** les étagères. There are books **on** the shelves.

Expressions of time

depuis – for / since

To say how long you've been doing something, use the present tense with depuis:

J'apprends le français **depuis** quatre ans.
I have been learning French for **four years.**

J'ai mal à la gorge **depuis** hier.
I have had a sore throat **since** yesterday.

To say how long you had been doing something, use the imperfect tense with depuis:

J'attendais **depuis** une heure.
I had been waiting **for** an hour.

pendant – for / during

To talk about a completed activity in the past and say how long it went on for, use the perfect tense and pendant:

J'ai joué au squash **pendant** deux ans.
I played squash **for** two years.

Il y a

You can use il y a with the perfect tense to mean 'ago', not to be confused with il y a meaning 'there is' or 'there are'.

Il a commencé à travailler **il y a** trois mois.
He started work three months **ago.**

J Conjunctions

Conjunctions are words used to link parts of sentences together:

alors	so	*Je suis fatiguée, **alors** je me repose.*
		I am tired, **so** I'm having a rest.
car	because / as	*J'ai faim, **car** je n'ai pas mangé à midi.*
		I'm hungry **as** I didn't eat at lunchtime.
donc	therefore	*Je pense, **donc** je suis.*
		I think, **therefore** I am.
et	and	*J'ai 15 ans **et** j'habite en France.*
		I am 15 **and** I live in France.
et puis	and then	*Je me lève **et puis** je prends mon petit déjeuner.*
		I get up **and then** I have breakfast.
mais	but	*J'ai deux frères, **mais** je n'ai pas de sœur.*
		I've got two brothers, **but** I haven't got a sister.
ou	or	*Je joue au foot **ou** je vais à la patinoire.*
		I play football **or** I go to the ice-rink.
parce que	because	*J'aime la géographie **parce que** c'est intéressant.*
		I like geography **because** it's interesting.
quand	when	*Je prends le bus **quand** il pleut.*
		I take the bus **when** it rains.

Certain linking expressions are used with particular tenses:

- *au moment où*   just as

This expression is useful for linking a perfect tense phrase with an imperfect one:

> *Je suis arrivé **au moment où** mon père préparait le déjeuner.*
> I arrived **just as** my father was preparing lunch.

- *pendant que*   while

The expression is useful for linking an imperfect tense phrase with a perfect one:

> ***Pendant que** je nageais, ma copine a joué au volley.*
> **While** I was swimming, my friend played volleyball.

- *quand*   when

+ future: when talking about future intentions in English, the present tense is used after 'when', but in French the future is needed:

> ***Quand** j'irai à Boulogne, je mangerai du poisson.*
> **When** I go to Boulogne, I will eat fish.

+ imperfect: when talking about continuing or regular events in the past, the imperfect tense is used in both French and English:

> ***Quand** j'habitais à Paris, j'allais souvent au cinema.*
> **When** I was living in Paris, I often used to go to the cinema.

- *tandis que*   while / whereas

This construction means 'whereas' when comparing an event in the past with an event in the future.

> *L'année dernière, j'ai fait de la voile, **tandis que** cette année je ferai du kayak.*
> Last year I went windsurfing, **whereas** this year I will go kayaking.

K Numbers, dates and time

1	un	16	seize
2	deux	17	dix-sept
3	trois	18	dix-huit
4	quatre	19	dix-neufe
5	cinq	20	vingt
6	six	21	vingt et un
7	sept	22	vingt-deux
8	huit	23	vingt-trois
9	neuf	24	vingt-quatre
10	dix	25	vingt-cinq
11	onze	26	vingt-six
12	douze	27	vingt-sept
13	treize	28	vingt-huit
14	quatorze	29	vingt-neuf
15	quinze	30	trente

40	quarante	100	cent
41	quarante et un	101	cent un
42	quarante-deux	102	cent deux
50	cinquante	200	deux cents
51	cinquante et un	201	deux cent un
52	cinquante-deux	202	deux cent deux
60	soixante	300	trois cents
61	soixante et un	301	trois cent un
62	soixante-deux	302	trois cent deux
70	soixante-dix	1000	mille
71	soixante et onze	1001	mille un
72	soixante-douze	1002	mille deux
80	quatre-vingts	2000	deux mille
81	quatre-vingt-un	2001	deux mille un
82	quatre-vingt-deux	2002	deux mille deux
90	quatre-vingt-dix		
91	quatre-vingt-onze		
92	quatre-vingt-douze		

80, *quatre-vingts,* loses the final *s* before another digit or to give a page number or a date:

quatre-vingt-sept	eighty-seven
page quatre-vingt	page eighty
l'an mille neuf cent quatre-vingt	the year 1980

The same applies to 200, *deux cents,* and other multiples of *cent*:

deux cent dix	two hundred and ten
page trois cent	page three hundred

Ordinal numbers: *premier, deuxième*, etc.

The French for 'first' is *premier* in the masculine and *première* in the feminine:

mon **premier** cours	my **first** lesson
mes **premières** vacances	my **first** holiday

To say 'second', 'third', etc., simply add *-ième* to the original number:

deuxième	second
troisième	third

To say 'fifth', add a *u* before *-ième*:

cinquième	fifth

To say 'ninth', change the *f* of *neuf* to a *v*:

neuvième	ninth

If the original number ends with an *-e*, drop the *-e* before adding *-ième*:

quatrième	fourth
onzième	eleventh

Days and dates

lundi	Monday
mardi	Tuesday
mercredi	Wednesday
jeudi	Thursday
vendredi	Friday
samedi	Saturday
dimanche	Sunday
janvier	January
février	February
mars	March
avril	April
mai	May
juin	June
juillet	July
août	August
septembre	September
octobre	October
novembre	November
décembre	December

Use normal numbers for dates and note that there is no word for 'on' or 'of':

*Son anniversaire est **le 27 décembre**.*
His / Her birthday is **on the 27th of December**.

The only exception is the first of the month, when you use *le premier*:

le premier *janvier*   **the first of** January

Days of the week and months don't have a capital letter in French (unless they are at the beginning of a sentence):

*Son anniversaire est en **avril**.*
His / Her birthday is in **April**.

Use *le* + *lundi*, *mardi*, etc. to mean 'on Mondays', 'on Tuesdays', etc.:

*Je ne vais pas à l'école **le dimanche**.*
I don't go to school **on Sundays**.

Use *lundi*, *mardi*, etc. without *le* to mean 'on Monday', 'on Tuesday', etc.:

*Je vais chez le dentiste **jeudi**.*
I'm going to the dentist's **on Thursday**.

Time

The 12-hour clock goes as follows:

Il est deux heures cinq.	It's five past two.
Il est deux heures dix.	It's ten past two.
*Il est deux heures **et quart**.*	It's a quarter past two.
Il est deux heures vingt.	It's twenty past two.
Il est deux heures vingt-cinq.	It's twenty-five past two.
*Il est deux heures **et demie**.*	It's half past two.
Il est trois heures moins. vingt-cinq.	It's twenty-five to three.
Il est trois heures moins vingt.	It's twenty to three.
Il est trois heures moins le quart.	It's a quarter to three.
Il est trois heures moins dix.	It's ten to three.
Il est trois heures moins cinq.	It's five to three.
Il est trois heures.	It's three o'clock.
Il est midi.	It's midday.
Il est minuit.	It's midnight.

As in English, when using the 24-hour clock, use numbers such as *quinze*, *trente*, etc. instead of *et quart*, *et demie*, etc.

*quatorze heures **quinze***	14.**15**
*seize heures **trente***	16.**30**

With the 24-hour clock, don't forget to use the word *heures* to separate the minutes from the hours:

*Il est treize **heures** vingt.*	It's 13.20.
*à douze **heures** quarante-cinq*	at 12.45

There are three ways to ask the time:

- The most correct and formal is:
  Quelle heure est-il?   What time is it?
- In more casual contexts, you can say:
  Il est quelle heure? or *Quelle heure il est?*
  What's the time?

To say when something happens, or has happened, use *à* (meaning 'at') to introduce the time:

*Je me lève **à** sept heures et demie.*
I get up **at** half past seven.

*Je suis sorti **à** quatre heures.*
I went out **at** four o'clock.

Verb tables

infinitive	present	perfect	imperfect	future
Regular -er verbs				
parler to speak	je parle tu parles il / elle / on parle nous parlons vous parlez ils / elles parlent	j'ai parlé tu as parlé il / elle / on a parlé nous avons parlé vous avez parlé ils / elles ont parlé	je parlais tu parlais il / elle / on parlait nous parlions vous parliez ils / elles parlaient	je parlerai tu parleras il / elle / on parlera nous parlerons vous parlerez ils / elles parleront
Reflexive verbs				
se laver to have a wash	je me lave tu te laves il se lave elle se lave on se lave nous nous lavons vous vous lavez ils se lavent elles se lavent	je me suis lavé(e) tu t'es lavé(e) il s'est lavé elle s'est lavée on s'est lavé(e)(s) nous nous sommes lavé(e)s vous vous êtes lavé(e)(s) ils se sont lavés elles se sont lavées	je me lavais tu te lavais il se lavait elle se lavait on se lavait nous nous lavions vous vous laviez ils se lavaient elles se lavaient	je me laverai tu te laveras il se lavera elle se lavera on se lavera nous nous laverons vous vous laverez ils se laveront elles se laveront
Regular -ir verbs				
finir to finish	je finis tu finis il / elle / on finit nous finissons vous finissez ils / elles finissent	j'ai fini tu as fini il / elle / on a fini nous avons fini vous avez fini ils / elles ont fini	je finissais tu finissais il / elle / on finissait nous finissions vous finissiez ils / elles finissaient	je finirai tu finiras il / elle / on finira nous finirons vous finirez ils / elles finiront
Regular -re verbs				
vendre to sell	je vends tu vends il / elle / on vend nous vendons vous vendez ils / elles vendent	j'ai vendu tu as vendu il / elle / on a vendu nous avons vendu vous avez vendu ils / elles ont vendu	je vendais tu vendais il / elle / on vendait nous vendions vous vendiez ils / elles vendaient	je vendrai tu vendras il / elle / on vendra nous vendrons vous vendrez ils / elles vendront

Irregular verbs

infinitive	present	perfect	imperfect	future
aller to go	je vais tu vas il va elle va on va nous allons vous allez ils vont elles vont	je suis allé(e) tu es allé(e) il est allé elle est allée on est allé(e)(s) nous sommes allé(e)s vous êtes allé(e)(s) ils sont allés elles sont allées	j'allais tu allais il allait elle allait on allait nous allions vous alliez ils allaient elles allaient	j'irai tu iras il ira elle ira on ira nous irons vous irez ils iront elles iront
avoir to have	j'ai tu as il / elle / on a nous avons vous avez ils / elles ont	j'ai eu tu as eu il / elle / on a eu nous avons eu vous avez eu ils / elles ont eu	j'avais tu avais il / elle / on avait nous avions vous aviez ils / elles avaient	j'aurai tu auras il / elle / on aura nous aurons vous aurez ils / elles auront
boire to drink	je bois tu bois il / elle / on boit nous buvons vous buvez ils / elles boivent	j'ai bu tu as bu il / elle / on a bu nous avons bu vous avez bu ils / elles ont bu	je buvais tu buvais il / elle / on buvait nous buvions vous buviez ils / elles buvaient	je boirai tu boiras il / elle / on boira nous boirons vous boirez ils / elles boiront
connaître to know	je connais tu connais il / elle / on connaît nous connaissons vous connaissez ils / elles connaissent	j'ai connu tu as connu il / elle / on a connu nous avons connu vous avez connu ils / elles ont connu	je connaissais tu connaissais il / elle / on connaissait nous connaissions vous connaissiez ils / elles connaissaient	je connaîtrai tu connaîtras il / elle / on connaîtra nous connaîtrons vous connaîtrez ils / elles connaîtront
croire to believe	je crois tu crois il / elle / on croit nous croyons vous croyez ils / elles croient	j'ai cru tu as cru il / elle / on a cru nous avons cru vous avez cru ils / elles ont cru	je croyais tu croyais il / elle / on croyait nous croyions vous croyiez ils / elles croyaient	je croirai tu croiras il / elle / on croira nous croirons vous croirez ils / elles croiront
devoir to have to	je dois tu dois il / elle / on doit nous devons vous devez ils / elles doivent	j'ai dû tu as dû il / elle / on a dû nous avons dû vous avez dû ils / elles ont dû	je devais tu devais il / elle / on devait nous devions vous deviez ils / elles devaient	je devrai tu devras il / elle / on devra nous devrons vous devrez ils / elles devront

infinitive	present	perfect	imperfect	future
dire to say	je dis tu dis il / elle / on dit nous disons vous dites ils / elles disent	j'ai dit tu as dit il / elle / on a dit nous avons dit vous avez dit ils / elles ont dit	je disais tu disais il / elle / on disait nous disions vous disiez ils / elles disaient	je dirai tu diras il / elle / on dira nous dirons vous direz ils / elles diront
dormir to sleep	je dors tu dors il / elle / on dort nous dormons vous dormez ils / elles dorment	j'ai dormi tu as dormi il / elle / on a dormi nous avons dormi vous avez dormi ils / elles ont dormi	je dormais tu dormais il / elle / on dormait nous dormions vous dormiez ils / elles dormaient	je dormirai tu dormiras il / elle / on dormira nous dormirons vous dormirez ils / elles dormiront
écrire to write	j'écris tu écris il / elle / on écrit nous écrivons vous écrivez ils / elles écrivent	j'ai écrit tu as écrit il / elle / on a écrit nous avons écrit vous avez écrit ils / elles ont écrit	j'écrivais tu écrivais il / elle / on écrivait nous écrivions vous écriviez ils / elles écrivaient	j'écrirai tu écriras il / elle / on écrira nous écrirons vous écrirez ils / elles écriront
être to be	je suis tu es il / elle / on est nous sommes vous êtes ils / elles sont	j'ai été tu as été il / elle / on a été nous avons été vous avez été ils / elles ont été	j'étais tu étais il / elle / on était nous étions vous étiez ils / elles étaient	je serai tu seras il / elle / on sera nous serons vous serez ils / elles seront
faire to do / to make	je fais tu fais il / elle / on fait nous faisons vous faites ils / elles font	j'ai fait tu as fait il / elle / on a fait nous avons fait vous avez fait ils / elles ont fait	je faisais tu faisais il / elle / on faisait nous faisions vous faisiez ils / elles faisaient	je ferai tu feras il / elle / on fera nous ferons vous ferez ils / elles feront
lire to read	je lis tu lis il / elle / on lit nous lisons vous lisez ils / elles lisent	j'ai lu tu as lu il / elle / on a lu nous avons lu vous avez lu ils / elles ont lu	je lisais tu lisais il / elle / on lisait nous lisions vous lisiez ils / elles lisaient	je lirai tu liras il / elle / on lira nous lirons vous lirez ils / elles liront

infinitive	present	perfect	imperfect	future
mettre to put	je mets tu mets il / elle / on met nous mettons vous mettez ils / elles mettent	j'ai mis tu as mis il / elle / on a mis nous avons mis vous avez mis ils / elles ont mis	je mettais tu mettais il / elle / on mettait nous mettions vous mettiez ils / elles mettaient	je mettrai tu mettras il / elle / on mettra nous mettrons vous mettrez ils / elles mettront
partir to leave	je pars tu pars il part elle part on part nous partons vous partez ils partent elles partent	je suis parti(e) tu es parti(e) il est parti elle est partie on est parti(e)(s) nous sommes parti(e)s vous êtes parti(e)(s) ils sont partis elles sont parties	je partais tu partais il partait elle partait on partait nous partions vous partiez ils partaient elles partaient	je partirai tu partiras il partira elle partira on partira nous partirons vous partirez ils partiront elles partiront
pouvoir to be able to	je peux tu peux il / elle / on peut nous pouvons vous pouvez ils / elles peuvent	j'ai pu tu as pu il / elle / on a pu nous avons pu vous avez pu ils / elles ont pu	je pouvais tu pouvais il / elle / on pouvait nous pouvions vous pouviez ils / elles pouvaient	je pourrai tu pourras il / elle / on pourra nous pourrons vous pourrez ils / elles pourront
prendre to take	je prends tu prends il / elle / on prend nous prenons vous prenez ils / elles prennent	j'ai pris tu as pris il / elle / on a pris nous avons pris vous avez pris ils / elles ont pris	je prenais tu prenais il / elle / on prenait nous prenions vous preniez ils / elles prenaient	je prendrai tu prendras il / elle / on prendra nous prendrons vous prendrez ils / elles prendront
recevoir to receive	je reçois tu reçois il / elle / on reçoit nous recevons vous recevez ils / elles reçoivent	j'ai reçu tu as reçu il / elle / on a reçu nous avons reçu vous avez reçu ils / elles ont reçu	je recevais tu recevais il / elle / on recevait nous recevions vous receviez ils / elles recevaient	je recevrai tu recevras il / elle / on recevra nous recevrons vous recevrez ils / elles recevront
savoir to know	je sais tu sais il / elle / on sait nous savons vous savez ils / elles savent	j'ai su tu as su il / elle / on a su nous avons su vous avez su ils / elles ont su	je savais tu savais il / elle / on savait nous savions vous saviez ils / elles savaient	je saurai tu sauras il / elle / on saura nous saurons vous saurez ils / elles sauront

infinitive	present	perfect	imperfect	future
sortir to go out	je sors tu sors il sort elle sort on sort nous sortons vous sortez ils sortent elles sortent	je suis sorti(e) tu es sorti(e) il est sorti elle est sortie on est sorti(e)(s) nous sommes sorti(e)s vous êtes sorti(e)(s) ils sont sortis elles sont sorties	je sortais tu sortais il sortait elle sortait on sortait nous sortions vous sortiez ils sortaient elles sortaient	je sortirai tu sortiras il sortira elle sortira on sortira nous sortirons vous sortirez ils sortiront elles sortiront
venir to come	je viens tu viens il vient elle vient on vient nous venons vous venez ils viennent elles viennent	je suis venu(e) tu es venu(e) il est venu elle est venue on est venu(e)(s) nous sommes venu(e)s vous êtes venu(e)(s) ils sont venus elles sont venues	je venais tu venais il venait elle venait on venait nous venions vous veniez ils venaient elles venaient	je viendrai tu viendras il viendra elle viendra on viendra nous viendrons vous viendrez ils viendront elles viendront
vivre to live	je vis tu vis il / elle / on vit nous vivons vous vivez ils / elles vivent	j'ai vécu tu as vécu il / elle / on a vécu nous avons vécu vous avez vécu ils / elles ont vécu	je vivais tu vivais il / elle / on vivait nous vivions vous viviez ils / elles vivaient	je vivrai tu vivras il / elle / on vivra nous vivrons vous vivrez ils / elles vivront
voir to see	je vois tu vois il / elle / on voit nous voyons vous voyez ils / elles voient	j'ai vu tu as vu il / elle / on a vu nous avons vu vous avez vu ils / elles ont vu	je voyais tu voyais il / elle / on voyait nous voyions vous voyiez ils / elles voyaient	je verrai tu verras il / elle / on verra nous verrons vous verrez ils / elles verront
vouloir to want	je veux tu veux il / elle / on veut nous voulons vous voulez ils / elles veulent	j'ai voulu tu as voulu il / elle / on a voulu nous avons voulu vous avez voulu ils / elles ont voulu	je voulais tu voulais il / elle / on voulait nous voulions vous vouliez ils / elles voulaient	je voudrai tu voudras il / elle / on voudra nous voudrons vous voudrez ils / elles voudront

French pronunciation

🎧 It is not hard to produce the correct sounds for a good French accent.

Remember that vowel sounds in French are not all exactly like English, and can change if they have an accent. You also need to know how some combinations of vowels sound. Vowels may have more than one sound depending on the word. Where this occurs below we have given examples.

a	chat, grand
e	sept, le, entrer
é	café
è	crème
ê	fête
i	dix
î	gîte
ie	géographie
o	dommage, poser
ô	drôle
oi	toi
u	tu
au or eau	beau
eu	deux
ou	rouge
œu	sœur
ui	puis

Vowels followed by *n* have a nasal sound, e.g. *sans, gens, fin, bon, train, bien.*

🎧 Then there are some patterns of letters which make these sounds:

ç or ce or ci (soft c)	garçon, morceau, cinéma
ch (like English 'sh')	chaussure
ge or gi (the g is soft)	géographie, gîte
gn (sounds like 'nyuh')	espagnol
h (silent)	hôtel, huit, thé
ill (sounds like 'y')	billet, bouteille
qu (sounds like 'k')	quel

r / rr	growled slightly in the back of your throat, e.g. *Robert, marron*
s or t	at the end of a word these are usually silent, e.g. *gris, petit, mais*
ail (at the end of a word)	travail
ain (at the end of a word)	demain
ais or ait (at the end of a word)	mais, fait
an or am; en or em	grand, chambre; sens, temps
im or in	impossible, international

1 Now try saying these well known French-speaking places with the correct accent.

Paris   Bordeaux   Marseille   Belgique   Avignon

🎧 The alphabet sounds

A	ah	B	beh	C	seh
D	deh	E	euh	F	eff
G	zheh	H	ash	I	ee
J	zhee	K	kah	L	ell
M	emm	N	enn	O	oh
P	peh	Q	koo*	R	err
S	ess	T	teh	U	oo*
V	veh	W	doobluh veh	X	eeks
Y	eegrek	Z	zed		

* *oo* pronounced with your lips pushed forward

Typing French accents and punctuation

One way to type letters with accents is to click on: Insert > symbol > then find the letter and accent you want.

Alternatively you can hold down the ALT key and type these numbers. Make sure that the Number Lock is on. It may be different for laptops.

131 = â	133 = à	135 = ç	130 = é	136 = ê	0156 = œ
138 = è	140 = î	147 = ô	150 = û	151 = ù	0128 = €

kerboodle!

Using a dictionary

French > English

- Make sure that you find the meaning that makes sense for the particular sentence you are translating. Many French words have more than one meaning, e.g. *le temps* = 'time' or 'weather'.
- If you are trying to work out the meaning of a verb, you will have to find the infinitive in the dictionary (ending in *-er, -re* or *-ir*) and then look at the verb ending to work out the person and tense of the verb, e.g. *mangez > manger* = 'to eat'.

English > French

- Make sure you know if the word you need is a noun (a person, place or thing), a verb (usually an action) or an adjective (describes a noun).
- Sometimes the word in English can be the same when written, even though you pronounce it differently.

Example of dictionary layout

Ignore the words in [ ]. They are there to show French speakers how to pronounce the English word.

light [laɪt] n. *lumière* **f.**

| English word | n. = noun | the French noun meaning 'light' | f. = feminine (you will need *la lumière* for 'the light' and *une lumière* for 'a light') |

light [laɪt] adj. *léger* **(not heavy);** *clair* **(colour)**

| adj. = adjective | the French adjectives for 'light' (two meanings) |

light [laɪt] vt. *allumer*

| vt. / vi. = verb | the French verb 'to light' (i.e. 'to light a candle') |

It is very important to understand that a dictionary will help you to find individual words, but you have to use your knowledge of how the French language works in order to put a sentence together. Very often the way a phrase is said is completely different from the English, e.g. *le chien de Paul* literally means 'the dog of Paul', but we would say 'Paul's dog'.

The most common mistake people make when using a dictionary is thinking that they can translate something literally word for word, without realising if the French they have looked up is a noun, verb or adjective. The result can be quite funny for an English speaker who knows French, but a French speaker won't understand anything.

See if you can work out what this student wanted to say, then try to produce the correct version.

Je boîte une pièce de théâtre football.

jouer + sport).
(infinitive of verb 'to play'); *au football (au* needed after
je peux ('I can' – irregular verb, present tense); *jouer*
Correct version: *Je peux jouer au football.*
football (football) – noun – this word is also correct.
théâtre
une pièce de théâtre ('play') – noun, e.g. a play at the
boîte ('can') – noun, e.g. a can of drink
Je ('I') – at least this word is correct!

Try to find the correct translations for these words:

1 a match (to light a candle)
2 a case (for clothes)
3 fair (as in fair hair)
4 move (as in move house)
5 fly (as in fly in a plane)
6 left (as in the past tense of leave)

Glossaire

A

à côté de   next to

à mon avis   in my opinion

à une époque   at one time

l'abricot (m)   apricot

accompagner   to accompany

acheter   to buy

l'activité (f) physique   physical activity

les actualités (f)   the news

l'ado (m / f)   adolescent / young person

l'agneau (m)   lamb

agresser   to attack / to assault

l'agriculteur / agricultrice   farmer

aider   to help

ailleurs   elsewhere

l'aire (f) de repos   stopping area (off the motorway, with basic facilities)

l'aire (f) de jeux   playground

l'alcool (m)   alcohol

alcoolisé(e)   alcoholic (drinks)

l'alimentation (f)   diet

aller   to go

aller à la pêche   to go fishing

alors   so

l'alpinisme (m)   mountaineering

l'alto (m)   viola

améliorer   to improve

s'amuser   to enjoy yourself / to have fun

ancien(ne)   former

l'anglais (m)   English

animé(e)   lively

l'année (f) sabbatique   gap year

l'anniversaire (m)   birthday

l'annonce (f)   advert

annuler   to cancel

août   August

l'appareil (m)   camera / machine

l'appartement (m)   apartment / flat

apprendre (appris)   to learn

l'apprentissage (m)   apprenticeship

après   after (that)

l'arbre (m)   tree

l'argent (m)   money

l'argent (m) de poche   pocket money

l'armoire (f)   wardrobe

l'arrêt (m) (d'autobus)   bus stop

arrêter   to stop

l'arrondissement (m)   administrative district of Paris

assez   quite

assis(e)   sitting down / seated

assister à   to be present at / to take part in

l'association (f) caritative   charity / charitable organisation

l'athlétisme (m)   athletics

l'Atlantique (m)   the Atlantic

attendre (attendu)   to wait

atterrir (atterri)   to land

attirer   to attract

au bout de   at the end of

l'auberge (f) de jeunesse   youth hostel

augmenter   to increase

l'automne (m)   autumn

l'autoroute (f)   motorway

l'avenir (m)   the future

l' averse (f)   (rain) shower

en avion   by aeroplane

l'avis (m)   opinion

l'avocat / avocate   lawyer

avoir   to have

avoir … ans   to be … years old

avoir chaud   to be hot

avoir envie de   to want to / to feel like

avoir faim   to be hungry

avoir froid   to be cold

avoir mal à la tête   to have a headache

avoir mal au cœur   to feel sick

avoir peur   to be afraid

avoir raison   to be right

avoir soif   to be thirsty

avoir tort   to be wrong

avril   April

B

les bagages (m)   luggage

se baigner   to bathe / to swim

baisser   to lower

la bande dessinée   comic book / cartoon strip

la banlieue   suburb

barbant(e)   boring

le basket   basketball

les baskets (f)   trainers

le bateau   ship / boat

en bateau   by boat

la batterie   drums

bavarder   to chat

le beau-père   stepfather (also means father-in-law)

beaucoup (de)   a lot (of)

la belle-mère   stepmother (also means mother-in-law)

le / la bénévole   volunteer

bien équipé(e)   well equipped / with good facilities

bien payé   well paid

bien s'amuser   to have a good time

bienvenue   welcome

la biologie   biology

biologique   organic

blanc(he)   white

bleu(e)   blue

le bloggeur   blogger

boire (bu)   to drink

la boisson   drink

la boîte   box / tin

la boîte aux lettres électronique   (email) inbox

la boîte de nuit   night club

bon anniversaire!   happy birthday!

le bord de la mer   seaside

la botte   boot

la bouche   mouth

le / la boucher / bouchère   butcher

la boucherie   butcher's

bouger   to move

le / la boulanger / boulangère   baker

la boulangerie (f)   baker's (bread)

le boulot   work (informal)

la boum   party

la bouteille   bottle

la boutique   shop

le bras   arm

briller   to shine

bronzer   to sunbathe / to get a tan

se brosser les dents   to brush one's teeth

le brouillard   fog

la brousse   bush / bushes

le bruit   noise

brûler   to burn

bruyant(e)   noisy

le bureau   office / study

en bus   by bus

le but   goal

C

la cabane   shed / hut

cacher   to hide

le cadeau   present

le cahier   notebook

la caisse   cash register / till

le / la caissier / caissière   cashier

le calcul (m)   sums / arithmetic

calme   quiet / placid

le camion   lorry

la campagne   countryside

le camping   campsite

le canapé   sofa

le candidat   candidate

la canne à sucre   sugar cane

la cantine   dining hall

la capuche   hood

car   because / as

en car   by coach

le car de ramassage   school bus

le carrefour   crossroads

le casque   helmet

casse-pieds   infuriating / a pain

la cave   cellar

le CDI (centre de documentation et d'information)   library

le centre   centre

le centre commercial   shopping centre

le centre culturel   cultural centre

le centre de recyclage   recycling centre

le centre sportif   sports centre

le centre-ville   town centre

le cerveau   brain

la chaîne   channel (TV)

la chaleur   warmth, heat

la chambre   bedroom

le chameau   camel

le champ   field

le champignon   mushroom

le changement climatique   climate change

la chanson   song

chanter   to sing

le / la chanteur / chanteuse   singer

le chapeau   hat

la charcuterie   pork butcher's / delicatessen

le chat   cat

chaud   hot

les chaussettes (f)   socks

les chaussures (f)   shoes

la chemise   shirt

le chemisier   blouse

cher(-ère)   dear / expensive

chercher   to look for

les cheveux (m)   hair

chic   smart

le chien   dog

la chimie   chemistry

chimique   chemical

chinois(e)   Chinese

le choix   choice

le chômage   unemployment

choquant(e)   shocking

le ciel   sky

le cimetière   cemetery

le cinéma   cinema

la circulation   traffic

la cité   housing estate

le citron   lemon

le clavier   keyboard

le / la client(e)   customer

le climat   climate

la climatisation   air conditioning

le cœur   heart

collecter (de l'argent)   to collect / raise (money)

le/la collègue   colleague

combien (de)   how much / how many

la comédie   comedy

comme d'habitude   as usual

comment   how

le / la commerçant(e)   shopkeeper

la commode   chest of drawers

compréhensif(-ve)   tolerant / understanding

le comprimé   tablet

compris(e)   included

le / la comptable   accountant

compter   to count

le concombre   cucumber

le concubinage   living together (without being married)

conduire (conduit)   to drive

la confiance   confidence

la confiance en soi   self-confidence

se confier à   to confide in

la connaissance   knowledge / consciousness

consacrer   to devote (time)

le conseil   council / advice

la console de jeu   games console

la consommation   consumption

consommer   to consume

construire (construit)   to build

le contrôle   test

la correspondance   change (on train journey)

la côte   coast / rib

la côtelette   chop / cutlet

la Côte d'Ivoire   the Ivory Coast

le coton   cotton

en coton   (made of) cotton

se coucher   to go to bed

la cour de récréation   playground

le cours   lesson

le coût   cost

la couture   high fashion

couvert   overcast

le crayon   pencil

créole   creole

la crêpe   pancake

la crevette   prawn

la **crise cardiaque** heart attack

la **croisière** cruise (holiday)

en **cuir** (made of) leather

la **cuisine** kitchen / cooking / cuisine (national)

le / la **cuisinier / cuisinière** cook / chef

cultiver to grow

D

dans in

le / la **danseur / danseuse** dancer

le **déboisement** deforestation

au **début** at the beginning

décembre December

la **décharge publique** rubbish dump

les **déchets** (m) rubbish / waste

décider to decide

décoller to take off (plane)

décontracté(e) relaxed

découvrir (découvert) to discover

défavorisé(e) disadvantaged

le **défilé (de mode)** fashion show

le **degré** degree

dehors outside

le **deltaplane** hang-gliding

déménager to move house

et **demi(e)** half past

le **demi-frère** half brother

le / la **demi-pensionnaire** day boarder (someone who has lunch at school)

démodé(e) out of date

les **dents** (f) teeth

dépenser to spend (money)

se **déplacer** to get around

déprimé(e) depressed

derrière behind

désespéré(e) desperate

le **dessin** art

le **dessin animé** cartoon (film)

se **détendre (détendu)** to relax / calm down

la **détente** relaxation / chilling out

détruire (détruit) to destroy

deux fois par mois twice a month

la **deuxième rue** the second street

devant in front of

le **déversement** dumping

les **devoirs** (m) homework

le **dictionnaire (bilingue)** (bilingual) dictionary

difficile (à croire) difficult (to believe)

dimanche Sunday

le / la **directeur / directrice** headteacher

diriger to direct / to manage

discipliné(e) disciplined / punished

disparaître (disparu) to disappear

se **disputer** to argue

divorcé(e) divorced

donner sur to look out over

le **dortoir** dormitory

le **dos** back

se **doucher** to have a shower

doué(e) gifted / clever

la **douleur** pain

doux mild

se **droguer** to take drugs

les **drogues douces** (f) soft drugs

les **drogues dures** (f) hard drugs

le **droit** law

à **droite** on / to the right

durer to last

E

l' **eau** (f) water

l' **éboueur** (m) dustman

les **échecs** (m) chess

échouer à to fail

l' **éclair** (m) lightning

l' **éclaircie** (f) sunny spell

l' **écran tactile** (m) touch screen

l' **effet** (m) **de serre** the greenhouse effect

l' **égalité** (f) equality

l' **église** (f) church

l' **électricien(ne)** electrician

l' **élève** (m / f) pupil

l' **emballage** (m) packaging

l' **embouteillage** (m) traffic jam

émettre (émis) to emit

l' **émission** (f) **de télévision** TV programme

empêcher to prevent / to get in the way of / to stop

l' **emplacement** (m) place / site

l' **emploi** (m) emloyment

l' **employé(e)** (m / f) employee

emprunter to borrow

en avoir marre de to be fed up of

en bonne forme in good shape

en ce moment at the moment

en ligne online

en version originale in the original language (films)

l' **endroit** (m) place

l' **ennui** (m) worry / problem / boredom

s' **ennuyer** to get bored / to be bored

l' **enquête** (f) enquiry / investigation

enregistrer to record

enrichissant(e) rewarding

enseigner to teach

ensemble together

ensoleillé sunny

ensuite then

s' **entendre (avec quelqu'un) (entendu)** to get on (with someone)

entouré(e) surrounded

s' **entraîner** to train

entre between

entre ... et ... between ... and ...

l' **entreprise** (f) business / firm

l' **entreprise** (f) **de logiciels** software business

l' **entretien** (m) interview

l' **environnement** (m) the environment

envoyer to send

épicé(e) spicy

l' **épicerie** (f) grocery shop

l' **épouse** (f) wife (spouse)

épouser to marry (someone)

l' **époux** (m) husband (spouse)

l' **EPS** (f) PE

l' **équilibre** (m) balance

l' **équipe** (f) team

l' **équitation** (f) horse riding

l' **escalade** (f) rock climbing

l' **espace** (m) **vert** park

l' **espagnol** (m) Spanish

l' **espoir** (m) hope

l' **essence** (f) petrol

l' **est** (m) east

et   and

l'étage (m)   floor

l'étagère (f)   shelf

l'été (m)   summer

éteindre (éteint)   to switch off / turn off

l'étranger / l'étrangère (m / f)   stranger (also, foreigner)

à l'étranger (m)   abroad

étranger(-ère)   foreign

être accro   to have a habit (addiction)

être hors d'haleine   to be out of breath

étroit(e)   tight / narrow

éviter   to avoid

excessif(-ve)   excessive

expliquer   to explain

exprimer   to express

F

se fâcher   to get cross

faire (fait)   to do / to make

faire beau   good weather

faire mauvais   bad weather

faire de la planche à voile   to go windsurfing

faire de la voile   to go sailing

faire des économies (f)   to save up

faire des randonnées   to go hiking

faire du jardinage   to do the gardening

faire du lèche-vitrine   to go window shopping

faire la cuisine   to cook

faire la grasse matinée   to have a lie in

faire la lessive   to do the washing

faire la vaisselle   to do the washing up

faire le ménage   to clean

faire les courses   to do the shopping

faire les magasins   to go shopping

faire une cure   to take a course of treatment

il fait beau   the weather's nice

il fait chaud   it's hot

il fait froid   it's cold

il fait mauvais   the weather's bad

le / la fana   fan / enthusiast

fatigué(e)   tired

le fauteuil   armchair

le fauteuil roulant   wheelchair

la femme   woman / wife

la femme au foyer   housewife

la femme de ménage   cleaning lady

la fenêtre   window

la fête   party / celebration

la fête de l'Aïd el Kebir   Id Ul Fitr festival

fêter   to celebrate

le feu   fire

feuilleter   to flick through

le feuilleton   soap (TV series)

les feux (m)   traffic lights

les feux rouges (m)   red lights (traffic lights)

février   February

les fiançailles (f)   engagement (to be married)

fier / fière   proud

la flûte   flute

le foie   liver

fondre   to melt

la fontaine   fountain

la forêt   forest

la forêt tropicale   rainforest

la formation professionnelle   professional training

le foulard   scarf

le français   French

frapper   to hit

le froid   cold

le fromage   cheese

la frontière   border (between countries)

fumer   to smoke

le fumeur   smoker

G

gagner   to win / to earn

garder   to look after

garder la forme   to keep in shape

la gare   railway station

la gare routière   coach or bus station

à gauche   on / to the left

les gaz (m) d'échappement   exhaust fumes

geler   to freeze

gênant(e)   inconvenient / annoying

gêné(e)   embarrassed

gêner   to be a nuisance

en général   generally

le genou   knee

le genre   type

la géographie   geography

le gigot d'agneau   leg of lamb

le gîte   self-catering accommodation

la glace   ice

la gomme   eraser

la gorge   throat

le goût   taste

goûter   to taste

le grain de café   coffee bean

la graisse   fat

grand(e)   large

la grand-mère   grandmother

le grand-père   grandfather

gratuit(e)   free (no cost)

gratuitement   free

le grenier   attic

la grippe   flu

gris(e)   grey

gros(se)   fat

la guerre   war

la guitare   guitar

le gymnase   gym

H

l'habillement (m)   clothes

s'habiller   to get dressed

l'habitant (m)   inhabitant

d'habitude   usually

l'habitude (f)   habit

la haie   hedge

les halles (f)   food hall

les haricots (m) verts   green beans

l'herbe (f)   grass

à l'heure   on time

heures   o'clock / hours

l'heure (f) d'affluence   rush hour

historique   historical

l'hiver (m)   winter

le / la HLM block of high-rise council flats
l'homme (m) au foyer house husband
l'hôtel (m) de ville town hall
l'hôtesse (f) de l'air air stewardess
humide humid

I

il y a there is / there are / ago (time)
il y a des nuages it's cloudy
il y a du brouillard it's foggy
il y a du soleil it's sunny
il y a du vent it's windy
il y avait there was / were
l'île (f) island
l'immeuble (m) building / block of flats
l'immigré(e) (m / f) immigrant
l'incivilité (f) rude behaviour
l'infirmier (m) / infirmière (f) nurse
l'informatique (f) information technology / ICT
l'ingénieur (m) engineer
injuste unfair
l'inondation (f) flood
(s')inquiéter to worry
l'instruction (f) civique citizenship
l'instruction (f) religieuse RE
interdit(e) forbidden
l'interprète (m / f) interpreter
islamique Islamic

J

j'en ai marre! I'm fed up!
jaloux(-se) jealous / possessive
jamais never
la jambe leg
janvier January
le jardin garden
le jardin public park / public garden
le jardin zoologique zoo
le / la jardinier / jardinière (paysagiste) (landscape) gardener
jaune yellow
le jean jeans

jeter to throw (away)
le jeu (les jeux) game / game show
le jeu vidéo computer game
jeudi Thursday
jouer to play
le jour de l'an New Year's Day
le jour férié public holiday
juif(-ve) Jewish
juillet July
juin June
la jupe skirt

L

le laboratoire laboratory
en laine (made of) wool
la langue vivante modern language
large loose-fitting / broad
se laver to have a wash
le lecteur DVD DVD player
le lecteur mp3 mp3 player
le légume vegetable
se lever to get up
la licence degree
le lieu place
la ligne line / route
lire (lu) to read
le lit bed
les lits (m) superposés bunk beds
le livre book
les loisirs (m) leisure activities
louer to rent / to hire
la lumière light
lundi Monday
lutter to struggle
le lycée high school (for students aged 16–18)

M

le magasin shop
mai May
maigre thin
le maillot de bain swimming costume
la main hand
la mairie town hall
mais but
la maison house
le mal de mer seasickness

la maladie illness
malgré in spite of
manger équilibré to eat a well-balanced diet
la manifestation (public) demonstration
le mannequin fashion model
le manque lack
manquer to miss / to be lacking
le maquillage make-up
se maquiller to put make-up on
le marché market
mardi Tuesday
le mari husband
le mariage marriage / wedding
se marier to get married
le Maroc Morocco
marquer un but to score a goal
marron brown
mars March
les maths / mathématiques (f) maths
de mauvaise humeur in a bad mood
de mauvaises notes (f) bad marks
le / la mécanicien(ne) mechanic
méchant(e) nasty / naughty
la Méditerranée the Mediterranean
la méduse jellyfish
mentir (menti) to lie
la mer sea
mercredi Wednesday
la mère mother
le métier job / profession
le métro the underground (in Paris)
en métro on the underground
la météo weather forecast
mettre (mis) to put (on)
se mettre en colère to get angry
mettre la table to lay the table
midi midday
mignon(ne) cute
le milieu rural rural environment
mince slim
minuit midnight
la mode fashion
moins le quart quarter to

mondial(e)   global

le moniteur   sports trainer

monoparental(e)   single-parent

la montagne   mountain(s)

montrer   to show

se moquer de   to make fun of

la moquette   carpet

mort(e)   dead

le moteur de recherche   search engine

mouillé   wet

le moyen de transport   means of transport

multinational(e)   multinational (company)

la municipalité   local council

la musculation   weight training

le / la musicien(ne)   musician

le / la musulman(e)   Muslim

N

nager   to swim

la naissance   birth

naître (né)   to be born

la natation   swimming

neiger   to snow

nettoyer   to clean

le nez   nose

le niveau   level

Noël (m)   Christmas

noir(e)   black

la noix   nut

le nord   north

normalement   usually / normally

la nourriture   food

nouveau (nouvelle)   new

le Nouvel An   New Year

novembre   November

le nuage   cloud

nuageux   cloudy

O

l'obésité   obesity

obligatoire   compusory

s'occuper de   to be busy with / to look after

octobre   October

l'œil (m) / les yeux   eye / eyes

l'œuf   egg

l'offre (f) d'emploi   job advert / job offer

offrir (offert)   to give (e.g. a present)

l'ombre (f)   shade

l'orage (m)   thunderstorm

orageux   stormy

l'ordinateur (m)   computer

l'ordinateur portable (m)   laptop

les ordures (f)   rubbish

l'oreille (f)   ear

l'organisation caritative (f)   charity / charitable organisation

ou   or

où   where

oublier   to forget

l'ouest (m)   west

l'ouvrier (m) / ouvrière (f)   worker

P

le pantalon   trousers

Pâques (f)   Easter

le paquet   packet

par   by

par terre   on the ground

le parc à vélos   bicycle park

le parc d'attractions   theme park

le passage à niveau   level crossing

le passager / la passagère   passenger

passer   to spend (time)

se passer de   to do without

passer l'aspirateur   to do the vacuuming

passer un examen   to take an exam

passif(-ve)   passive

la pâte (à pain)   (bread) dough

les pâtes (f)   pasta

la patinoire   ice skating rink

la pâtisserie   baker's (pastries, cakes)

le / la patron / patronne   boss/ manager

la pause-déjeuner   lunch hour

pauvre   poor

la pauvreté   poverty

le pays étranger   foreign country

le pays voisin   neighbouring country

le paysage   landscape / scenery

la pêche   fishing

la peinture   painting

la pelouse   lawn

pendant   during

pénible   annoying / a nuisance

les percussions (f)   percussion instruments

le père   father

perfectionner   to improve

permettre (permis)   to allow

petit(e)   small

le petit ami   boyfriend

la petite amie   girlfriend

la petite annonce   small advert / classified advert

le pétrole   oil

un peu de   a bit of

peut-être   perhaps

la photocopieuse   photocopying machine

la physique   physics

la pièce   room

à pied   on foot

le pied   foot

la piscine   swimming pool

la piste cyclable   cycle track

pittoresque   picturesque

le placard   cupboard

la plage   beach

plaire (plu)   to please

le plaisir   pleasure / enjoyment

la planète   planet

plein(e) de vie   lively

pleurer   to cry

pleuvoir (plu)   to rain

la pluie   rain

le / la plombier / plombière   plumber

la plongée sous-marine   diving

la plupart de   most of

pluvieux(-se)   rainy

le poisson rouge   goldfish

pollué   polluted

la pompe   pump

la pom-pom girl   cheerleader

la porte   door

poser sa candidature   to apply

le poste   job / post

la poubelle   (dust)bin

le poumon   lung

pourquoi   why

pourtant   however

pousser   to grow

le premier / deuxième étage   first / second floor

la première rue   the first street

prendre (pris)   to take

prendre une douche   to have a shower

prêter   to lend

prévenir (prévenu)   to prevent / to inform / to warn

le printemps   spring

la prise électrique   electric socket

le prix   price

le problème   problem

produire (produit)   to produce

le / la professeur   teacher

le / la programmeur / programmeuse   programmer

promener le chien   to walk the dog

la promotion   promotion / special offer

propre   clean

protéger   to protect

le pull à capuche   hooded top

punir (puni)   to punish

Q

quand   when

quand même   all the same

et quart   quarter past

le quartier   area of a town

que   that / what

qu'est-ce que   what

qu'est-ce que c'est?   what is it?

quel(le)   which / what

quelquefois   sometimes

qui   who

quoi   what

R

le racisme   racism

raciste   racist

ramasser   to collect / to pick up

la randonnée   hike (on foot) / ride (bike or horseback)

ranger   to tidy / to put away

ranger sa chambre   to tidy one's bedroom

se rappeler   to remember

rarement   rarely

rater   to fail

recevoir (reçu)   to receive

recyclable   recyclable

le réchauffement de la planète   global warming

la récréation   break (in school day)

redécouvrir   to rediscover

le redoublement   repeating a school year

redoubler   to repeat a school year

la réduction   reduction

réduire (réduit)   to reduce

le régime   diet

la règle   rule / ruler

le règlement   rules

rejeter   to discharge / to pour

remarquer   to notice

remplacer   to replace

rencontrer   to meet

rendre (rendu)   to give back

renouveler   to renew / to update

rénover   to renovate

les renseignements (m)   information

répondre   to reply

respirer   to breathe

le retard   delay

retenir (retenu)   to keep

la retenue   detention

se réunir (réuni)   to meet up

la réunion   meeting

réussir (réussi)   to pass (an exam) / to succeed

le rêve   dream

se réveiller   to wake up

réveillonner   to celebrate on Christmas Eve or New Year's Eve

le rez-de-chaussée   ground floor

le rhum   rum

le rhume   cold

rigolo(-te)   fun / funny

rire   to laugh

le risque   risk

la robe   dress

le robinet   tap

le roman   novel

le rond-point   roundabout

rose   pink

rouge   red

la route   road

S

le sable   sand

le sac   bag

la Saint-Sylvestre   the festival on 31st December

la Saint-Valentin   Valentine's Day

sale   dirty

salé(e)   salty

la salle à manger   dining room

la salle d'attente   waiting room

la salle d'informatique   ICT room

la salle de bains   bathroom

la salle de séjour   living room / sitting room

la salle des profs   staff room

le salon   living room / sitting room

samedi   Saturday

sans domicile fixe   homeless

sans plomb   unleaded

le / la sans-abri   homeless person

sauf   except

le saumon   salmon

sauver   to save

les sciences (f)   science

scolaire   school / to do with school

le / la SDF (sans domicile fixe)   homeless person

sec (sèche)   dry

le sèche-cheveux   hair-dryer

le / la secrétaire   secretary

le séjour   stay (in a place)

le sel   salt

le sens de l'humour   sense of humour

se sentir (senti)   to feel

septembre   September

la série   series

le / la serveur / serveuse   waiter / waitress

le short   shorts

le sida   AIDS

le siècle   century

le sirop   (cough) syrup

le site   site (internet)

le skate   skateboarding

la société   company / business
le soir   (in) the evening
le salaire   salary
les soldes (m)   the sales
le soleil   sun
le sommeil   sleep
sonner   to ring (phone, bell)
le souci   worry / problem
souffrir (souffert)   to suffer
souhaiter   to wish
souriant(e)   cheerful
sous   under
le sous-sol   basement
les sous-titres (m)   subtitles
souvent   often
spacieux(-euse)   spacious
le sport d'hiver   winter sport
le stade   stadium
la station balnéaire   seaside resort
la station de ski   ski resort
la station de taxi   taxi rank
la station thermale   spa resort
stressant(e)   stressful
le stylo   pen
les sucreries (f)   sweets
le sud   south
suivant(e)   following
sur   on
le sweat   sweatshirt

T

le tabac   tobacco
le tabagisme   addiction to smoking
le tableau blanc interactif
   interactive whiteboard
la tâche   task
la taille   size
tardif(-ve)   late
le / la technicien(ne)   technician
la technologie   D and T
tel(le)   such
télécharger   to download
le (téléphone) portable   mobile (phone)
la température   temperature
la tempête   storm
le temps   weather
de temps en temps   from time to time
à temps partiel   part-time
le terrain de camping   campsite
la Terre   (the) Earth

le terroir   local area
la tête   head
le texto   text (message)
en TGV (train à grande vitesse)
   by high-speed train
le thé à la menthe   mint tea
le théâtre   theatre
le Tiers-Monde   the developing world
les toilettes (f)   toilet
le tonnerre   thunder
le / la touriste   tourist
tous les jours   every day
la Toussaint   All Saints Day
tout droit   straight on
en train   by train
le traitement de texte   word processing
le trajet   journey / trip
en tram   by tram
les transports (m) en commun   public transport
le travail   work
le travail bénévole   voluntary work
travailleur(-se)   hardworking
la traversée   crossing (e.g. the Channel)
tremper   to soak
très   very
la troisième   French equivalent of year 10
trop de monde   too many people
le trottoir   pavement
le trouble alimentaire   eating disorder
la trousse   pencil case

U

une bonne ambiance   a good atmosphere
une fois par semaine   once a week
l'usine (f)   factory
utiliser   to use

V

la vague   wave (water)
varié(e)   varied
la vedette   star / celebrity (male or female)
végétarien(ne)   vegetarian
en veille   on stand-by
à vélo   by bike
le / la vendeur / vendeuse   sales assistant
vendre (vendu)   to sell
vendredi   Friday
le vent   wind
le ventre   stomach
vert(e)   green

les vêtements (m)   clothes
le / la vétérinaire   vet
le veuf   widower
la veuve   widow
la viande   meat
la victime   victim
vider la poubelle   to empty the bin
la vie   life
vieux (vieille)   old
la ville   town / city
violet(-te)   purple
le violon   violin
la visite guidée   guided tour
vivre (vécu)   to live
vivre en concubinage   to live together
   (without being married)
la voile   sailing
le / la voisin(e)   neighbour
en voiture   by car
le vol   flight
voler   to fly / to steal
le volet   shutter
le vomissement   vomiting
le voyage scolaire   school trip
la vue   view

Z

la zone piétonne   pedestrian zone

Acknowledgements

Illustrations:
Kathy Baxendale pp22, 57 (2a); Russ Cook p154; Mark Draisey pp14, 16 (1a), 20, 26, 38, 71, 117 (reporter), 120, 121, 130 (2a), 131, 137, 146, 157; Mark Duffin pp66, 85; Robin Edmonds: p46; Stephen Elford pp18, 24; Tony Forbes pp17, 36, 68, 100, 101 (2b), 113, 117 (3a 1–5), 135 (2b), 136, 151, 154 Dylan Gibson p96 (2b); Celia Hart pp 10, 11, 12, 16 (2), 19, 21, 25, 27, 28, 34, 35, 39, 59, 63, 67, 75, 79, 81, 83, 95, 96 (1a), 101 (4), 105, 107, 109, 130 (1a), 133, 135 (4), 139, 149, 152; Abel Ippolito pp42, 44, 56, 97, 143; Martin Sanders pp94, 106

The authors and publisher would like to thank the following for permission to reproduce materials:

Photographs courtesy of:
p15 (and banner) © Dominique LUZY – Fotolia.com; p21 © pressmaster – Fotolia.com; p22 © Sipa Press / Rex Features; p32 © iStockphoto.com / ruffraido; p24 © palangsi. Image from BigStockPhoto.com; p33 © Daniel Montiel – Fotolia.com; p34 © Fotosmurf01. Image from BigStockPhoto.com, © Hongqi Zhang / 123rf.com; p40 © Studio1One. Image from BigStockPhoto.com; p41 © David Hoffman Photo Library / Alamy; p43 © Médecins Sans Frontières; p54 © Images of France / Alamy, © Alain Jocard / Stringer / Getty Images; p55 (and banner) © iStockphoto.com / track5; p58 © iStockphoto.com / jhorrocks, © Paul Prescott. Image from BigStockPhoto.com, © iStockphoto.com / NathanMarx; p60 © iStockphoto.com / BirdofPrey; p62 © Pavel Losevsky – Fotolia.com; p63 © iStockphoto.com / shironosov; p64 © ginaellen. Image from BigStockPhoto.com; p67 © Steve mc. Image from BigStockPhoto.com; p69 © keeweeboy. Image from BigStockPhoto.com; p75 © Ben Goode / 123rf.com, © iStockphoto. com / elkor, © Nbina – Fotolia.com; p78 © iStockphoto.com / davidhills, © davinci. Image from BigStockPhoto.com; p80 © Durand Patrick/Corbis Sygma, © Uolir – Fotolia.com, © iStockphoto.com / Anyka; p82 © Christophe Testi / 123rf.com; p92 © iStockphoto.com / gelyngfjell, © Andrew Fox / Alamy; p93 (and banner) © Sébastien Closs – Fotolia.com; p98 © Oliver Grey; p102 © Roman Pieruzek – Fotolia. com, © p.lange. Image from BigStockPhoto.com; p104 © Stephen Finn – Fotolia.com, © Piotr Sikora – Fotolia.com; p105 © Tupungato. Image from BigStockPhoto.com, © Nicsolo – Fotolia.com; p106 © Peer Frings – Fotolia.com; p112 © iStockphoto.com / BremecR, © iStockphoto. com / ChrisMR; p114 © iStockphoto.com / Nnehring; p115 © Jonny McCullagh – Fotolia.com; p116 © iStockphoto.com / Nnehring; p118 © iStockphoto.com / jacus, © vhamrick. Image from BigStockPhoto. com; p119 © geogphotos / Alamy; p120 © Martina Berg – Fotolia. com, © iStockphoto.com / kreci, © Ilgiz Khabibullin – Fotolia.com; p121 © Joe Gough – Fotolia.com, © iStockphoto.com / dougallg; p128 © Stockfolio® / Alamy, © maredana. Image from BigStockPhoto.com, © iStockphoto.com / NoDerog; p129 (and banner) © iStockphoto. com / monkeybusinessimages; p131 © Marc Dietrich – Fotolia.com; p134 © Sally and Richard Greenhill / Alamy, © Directphoto.org / Alamy; p138 © Mark Burnett / Alamy; p140 © Image Source – World Portraits / Alamy; p141 © Christopher Howey – Fotolia.com, © Natalia Bratslavsky – Fotolia.com; p147 © iStockphoto.com / track5; p150 © AVAVA – Fotolia.com, © Michael Tweed / Alamy, © iStockphoto.com / ebstock; p152 © ginaellen. Image from BigStockPhoto.com, © Jaimie Duplass – Fotolia.com; p155 © Greenshoots Communications / Alamy, © iStockphoto.com / photoalex; p164 © ImageState / Alamy, © lisafx. Image from BigStockPhoto.com